M

The Scent of Dried Roses

'*The Scent of Dried Roses* touches a nerve no other English memoir has found; it does so in a way that seems not only affecting, but somehow important' Sebastian Faulks

'This is a moving, insightful, important book. It works as a personal story, as an analysis of the unknowable horrors of suicide and as a history of a changing Britain' William Hague

'In its slow and careful way, it unfolds a certain topography of melancholia, and the map Lott makes of his troubles mixes the intricate streets he has walked all his life with some pretty intricate places in his own mind and heart. We are left with a resounding lament for a small England . . . The book's recreation of a suburban world, its flashing-back and forward in real time, its compilation of whispers and roars and half-remembered truths, its reliance on the intimacies of interior monologue, are bound to make some people think of it as fiction' Andrew O'Hagan

'A moving, valuable account of a particular English family and their idea of England, as well as a sensitive record of the experience of a particular madness . . . He tells the story of his family during the golden age of pre- and post-war certainty, and the subsequent quick changes of post-Suez England . . . a very readable family history'
Tamsin Dean, *Sunday Telegraph*

'[A] wonderful book . . . essential reading for anyone concerned with depression and happiness' Dorothy Rowe

'His triumph is to take tragedy as his subject, and by exploring it, create a new myth of tentative hope. The reader is harrowed, intrigued and finally consoled' Michèle Roberts, *The Times*

'Lott sorts through the sepia-tinged photographs of his ancestry in search of the flaw in his family that leads him to depression and his mother to suicide . . . distinguished by its observation, its honesty and its ambition' Matthew de Abaitua, *Harpers & Queen*

'The Doc Martens and Sta-Prests, the dance-halls and favourite bands are all carefully recorded. The strange low-spirited optimism of the immediate postwar years, all rubble and rationing, nationalization and utility furniture, little of which Lott can have experienced himself, is carefully sketched in . . . These took some writing, and Lott can write' Frank Kermode, *London Review of Books*

'Breathtakingly powerful' Christina Hardyment, *Independent*

ABOUT THE AUTHOR

Tim Lott was born in 1956 in Southall, west London, the son of a Notting Hill greengrocer. In 1976, he took a job on the pop magazine *Sounds*, and in 1980, he set up the first glossy colour pop magazine, *Flexipop!* He left the venture in 1983 to attend the London School of Economics and after graduating accepted the editorship of the listings magazine *City Limits*. He resigned after only two weeks, and a period of acute depressive illness followed, during which his parents nursed him back to health. Shortly afterwards his mother, Jean, committed suicide. *The Scent of Dried Roses* grew from an *Esquire* article on Jean's depression and suicide, and its publication in 1996 met with universal acclaim.

Lott's novels include *White City Blue*, winner of the 1999 Whitbread First Novel award; *Rumours of a Hurricane* (2002); *The Love Secrets of Don Juan* (2003); *The Seymour Tapes* (2005) and *Fearless* (2007), a children's book.

Born in Yorkshire, Blake Morrison is a novelist, poet and critic, best known for two highly acclaimed memoirs, *And When Did You Last See Your Father?* and *Things My Mother Never Told Me*. He writes regularly for the *Guardian*, teaches Creative Writing at Goldsmiths College, and lives in south London with his family.

TIM LOTT

The Scent of Dried Roses

With an Introduction by Blake Morrison

PENGUIN BOOKS

PENGUIN CLASSICS

Published by the Penguin Group
Penguin Books Ltd, 80 Strand, London WC2R ORL, England
Penguin Group (USA), Inc., 375 Hudson Street, New York, New York 10014, USA
Penguin Group (Canada), 90 Eglinton Avenue East, Suite 700, Toronto, Ontario, Canada M4P 2Y3
(a division of Pearson Penguin Canada Inc.)
Penguin Ireland, 25 St Stephen's Green, Dublin 2, Ireland
(a division of Penguin Books Ltd)
Penguin Group (Australia), 250 Camberwell Road, Camberwell, Victoria 3124, Australia
(a division of Pearson Australia Group Pty Ltd)
Penguin Books India Pvt Ltd, 11 Community Centre, Panchsheel Park,
New Delhi – 110 017, India
Penguin Group (NZ), 67 Apollo Drive, Rosedale, North Shore 0632, New Zealand
(a division of Pearson New Zealand Ltd)
Penguin Books (South Africa) (Pty) Ltd, 24 Sturdee Avenue, Rosebank, Johannesburg 2196, South Africa

Penguin Books Ltd, Registered Offices: 80 Strand, London WC2R ORL, England

www.penguin.com

First published by Viking 1996
Published in Penguin Books 1997
Published with an introduction in Penguin Classics 2009
003

Copyright © Tim Lott, 1996
Introduction copyright © Blake Morrison, 2009

The moral right of the author and introducer has been asserted

Printed in Great Britain by Clays Ltd, St Ives plc

A CIP catalogue record for this book is available from the British Library

978-0-141-19148-5

www.greenpenguin.co.uk

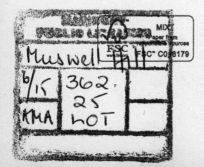

Penguin Books is committed to a sustainable
future for our business, our readers and our planet.
This book is made from Forest Stewardship
Council™ certified paper.

Introduction

In his short, classic memoir of depression, *Darkness Visible*, the American novelist William Styron describes his annoyance at those who see suicide as a mark of shame and weakness. 'The pain of severe depression is quite unimaginable to those who have not suffered it,' he writes, 'and it kills in many instances because its anguish can no longer be borne. The prevention of many suicides will continue to be hindered until there is a general awareness of the nature of this pain.' Part of the power of Tim Lott's book lies in its inside knowledge of anguish and pain. His mother killed herself because of them and a few months before her he came close to doing the same. His book is a double study, a search to understand his mother (whom he took for granted when alive, as sons often do), and a diagnosis of himself. 'Memoir' isn't the right label, any more than it is for Styron's book. Constructed like a novel or quest myth, *The Scent of Dried Roses* blends biography and autobiography, with topography, social history and psychology added to the mix.

The first chapter unfolds with chilling clarity. The 'I' of the son is present for the opening sentences, then disappears, allowing the all-seeing eye of an impersonal narrator to take over. Lott's parents become Jack and Jean, figures in a suburban landscape, going about their daily business, though the day in question will end like no other. There are hints of the impending tragedy: the neighbours who think Jean doesn't look well; the phone call she makes to cry off work; her sense of the house being 'empty', though every object in it is described in loving detail. But even when Jean resolves to 'get the job done', we can't be sure what kind of job she means. It's through Jack that we discover the worst:

Jack got home about five o'clock. The house was nice and tidy as usual, with all the breakfast things cleared away. He shouted for Jean. There was no answer. Deciding that she was probably in the garden, he walked through the kitchen and into the small patch of green at the back. It ran slightly wild, the garden. It was deserted. There was an old shed at the end, full of junk, but there was nothing there either.

He came back into the house, puzzled. It seemed so still. Suddenly he moved, fast, running up the cramped stairs. He did not know why he was running. Jack rushed into the bedroom. Jean's wig was on straight and nicely coiffed. Her feet – size four, petite like the rest of her – were maybe six inches from the floor. The blue necklace of rope held her tight.

Such writing might seem cold-blooded. The death of a parent is traumatic in any circumstances and when it comes as abruptly and violently as this a torrent of emotion is the expected response. But the mask of third-person objectivity is essential: 'picking over the fine details of the act', Lott is able to record an event he didn't witness and can hardly bear to contemplate. His prose doesn't emotionally manipulate the reader. It annotates commonplace actions and domestic objects. Facts, facts, facts are its brief. But the facts are heartbreaking enough.

Having reconstructed the crime scene, Lott sets about solving the mystery: what brought his mother to this impasse? His role is detective but also chief suspect, since he accuses himself of murdering her. This isn't just grief talking or a rhetorical flourish. Nor is it guilt that he has somehow infected Jean with his own manic depression. The offence is to have missed his cue when, on the night before she kills herself, his mother owns up to her despair. As an expert on antidepressants, he tells her that the drugs she has been prescribed will cure her but might take a couple more weeks to kick in; to which she replies 'I don't know if I can last that long.' An alarm goes off in his head but isn't loud enough for him to panic. Surely his mother — middle-aged, practical-minded, purposeful and caring — will be all right.

As the story unwinds, and takes us back to Jean's adolescence and early married life, it slowly emerges that she has been far from all right for years. Not that she *seems* unhappy. She has a husband who loves her, three sons she's devoted to, good friends, a part-time job as a dinner lady, hobbies (gardening, painting and tennis) and a home of her own. But there's the alopecia she develops when pregnant with Tim, a difficult thing for a woman as proud of her appearance as Jean is to live with (and another reason for her son to feel guilty). There's a tendency to hide and repress uncomfortable truths such as her brother's fragile mental health. There's a competitiveness that, as a housewife, she can't express. And in the last months of her life, there's a collapse of self-esteem. Simple tasks such as parking the car or playing cards are suddenly beyond her. She is, she complains, 'no good' at any-thing. 'It is time to get out of your life,' she tells her husband in her suicide note, 'I am holding you back.'

The same note leaves another clue to her breakdown: 'I hate Southall, I can see only decay. I feel alone.' Southall is an outer London suburb and her sons feel the same about it as she does: that it's a dump, a lower-middle-class subtopia, a place to leave as soon as you can. Tim left it years before but when he's drawn back after his mother's death, revisiting his childhood haunts and seeing the changes there have been, he can feel the damage it did them both. It's not just the environment — the concreted-over front gardens, the double-glazed aluminium windows, the dog shit on the pavement — it's the whole cramped idiom that goes with it, the stoic clichés people fall back on in order to cope: *These things are sent to try us, Might as well look on the bright side, What can you do?* London suburbs have no monopoly on deadly dullness. Nothing, like something, can happen anywhere: 'It's not the place's fault,' Larkin said. But Lott has no doubt that Southall *is* partly to blame for making Jean feel worthless. Against the denuded present, he gives tantalising flashes of an England (not Britain) to which his mother wanted to belong, not a bullying, racist and imperialist nation but 'innocent, decent, quaint, a bit pompous, fond of a lark' – and long since dead. With a brilliant, almost Orwellian command of social and historical nuance, Lott conveys what the country looked and felt like, from 1930 to 1988. *England Made Me* was the title of one of Graham Greene's novels. Lott's book could have been titled *England Unmade Me* because of the way it connects his mother's depression with the nation at large.

Gradually, too, it connects her story with his. For several chapters he takes centre stage, leaving her in the wings. The hare-lip he was born with, his teenage bolshiness, the experiments with cannabis and LSD, his girlfriends, his precocious business success in the Thatcher years, his time as a mature student at the London School of Economics, the job he miraculously got but immediately gave up as editor of the listings magazine *City Limits* – all this serves as a prelude to the depression which leaves him standing on a rooftop ready to throw himself off. Once again, as with Jean, the private and public come together. 'It is not only me who seems to be falling apart but, eerily, the world outside,' he writes, as the 'confused, self-hating' national psyche reaches a nadir in the autumn of 1987. The Hungerford massacre, the October hurricane, the Enniskillen bomb, the stock market crash and the Kings Cross fire: to Lott, *in extremis*, it 'all seems to knit together in a great cross-stitch of decay and chaos that merges with the darkness inside my head'.

To his surprise, and in defiance of Sixties prejudices he has inherited from *One Flew Over the Cuckoo's Nest* and R. D. Laing, Lott finds that four years of depression are cleared up within three weeks: all it takes is a visit to a psychiatrist and the right medication. A convert to antidepressants, he's certain that his mother will be redeemed too – which makes her suicide all the harder for him to accept. But his book doesn't end bleakly. There are green shoots through the tarmac, fresh pastures for Jack, the experience of parenthood for Tim. However sad its story, this is a hopeful and cathartic book, presenting depression as an illness like any other, potentially curable and not a matter for stigma or shame.

The 1990s saw a surge in memoirs, not by the great and good, but by youngish men and women looking back on their childhoods and/or their struggles with loss, trauma and addiction. Mary Karr's *The Liar's Club*, Nick Hornby's *Fever Pitch*, Andrea Ashworth's *Once in a House on Fire*, Elizabeth Wurzel's *Prozac Nation*, Kathryn Harrison's *The Kiss* and Linda Grant's *Remind Me Who I am Again* are examples, along with personal accounts of mental illness such as Styron's *Darkness Visible*, Andrew Solomon's *The Noonday Demon* and Kay Redfield Jamison's *An Unquiet Mind*. Tim Lott's book is similarly intimate and confessional. It's compelling because authentic: we trust the teller as well as his tale. But the devices of imaginative literature are employed, too (plot, characterisation and dialogue), giving the book its place in an older tradition of madness, one that runs from *Medea* and *King Lear* to John Clare's poems, *Equus* and *The Bell Jar*.

Above all, perhaps, *The Scent of Dried Roses* is a celebration of storytelling. 'We cannot live without stories,' Lott writes, envying the simplicity of the narrative that sustained his father, the one that gave him stability and direction. His mother lived by the same narrative and died when she stopped believing in it; losing the plot, she lost her reason for going on; her illness is 'the illness of those who do not know where they fit, who lose faith in the myths they have so painstakingly created for themselves'. Lott, by contrast, has no sustaining narrative at the outset, 'only scatterings of impressions that light up the landscape like flares, then disappear again'. Yet by the end he finds his way and the story is there – as told by a grieving son in order to appease his pain and guilt, but articulated for the benefit of us all.

Blake Morrison, 2009

For my father

'Harry hates people who seem to know. They would keep us blind to the fact that there is nothing to know. We are each of us filled with a perfect blackness' – John Updike, *Rabbit is Rich*

Thanks to Sarina for her patience, to David Godwin for his faith, and to Dorothy Rowe for her wisdom.

Also to Jeff and James for their love and support, and to everyone who appears in this book who has given me their stories. To those whose stories – whose pasts – I have shared, then stolen, I can only say that I have tried my best to handle them with care, and always with affection.

Chapter One

The time that I dream of, that I imagine, that I reconstruct more than any other, is a Monday early in March 1988. Oddly, I have never troubled to check the exact date, yet in every other detail I try to be meticulous.

That day I remember as being neutral, without any sense of imminence. Perhaps there was a slight wind that made the rowan tree on the tiny front lawn of my parents' house falter. When my father, Jack, woke at around eight, Jean, my mother, was already awake. She had been sleeping badly of late and had been prescribed what she told Jack were sleeping pills.

Jack slept naked, but Jean wore a nightie. It would have been a pastel shade – Jean tended away from strong colours. Muted tones edged the lives of her and her friends. They lived in pale houses between magnolia walls with faint watercolours. They wore clothes that were slightly flounced, or slightly frilled, or inscribed with floral prints; clothes that were cream, or cucumber, or scrubbed lemon. They did not wear black, or abstract, or self-confident, shouting blue, but colours that were either apologies, or absences, or blustery smiles at unselfconscious jokes.

Jean also wore a headscarf in bed, knotted tight in gypsy style, the way girls – women really, but they were all *girls* then – had been taught during the war. It kept their long hair safe from the machinery that was punching out igniters, capstans, locking mechanisms, firing bolts, grenades and light arms to fight the German enemy.

Jean's hair was long, thick and chestnut in those days – a waterfall tumbling back from the crown. There is a black-and-white picture of her when she was sixteen years old, in 1947, straight out of *Photoplay*: the sultry glance cast just to the left of the photographer's shoulder; the full, dark lips and arched, confident eyebrows; and above all the thick hair, falling casually on to those thrown-back shoulders (one turned towards the camera). She was lovely, a catch, a perfect skirt. Or so Jack had thought when he first saw her, in the Empire Snooker Hall, Ealing, in 1951. He was there with Ronnie Van Den Bergh, like most nights when he wasn't dancing or at the movies. Jean wore a tight sweater – after Jane Russell in *The Outlaw* or Lana Turner in *They Won't Forget* – that made her stand up, stand out, proud, perfect, the ultimate wife-to-be (for all women, then, were wives-to-be). Those breasts, that nipped-in, tidy waist, the pertness, the promise of those careful, poised eyebrows.

But her hair, her beautiful hair. Now it was gone, had been gone for years. Jean was quite bald, and even her eyebrows, once dark seagulls, were now only painted skin. She felt the shape of her head with one hand, not to touch the baldness, but because she was dizzy. She thought she would fall if she stood. Jack was beside her, sitting up. He had long since stopped noticing the headscarf. Jean was . . . *Jean*, the woman he had loved without pause, or doubt, for nearly forty years. Strange, when he thought about it, since she went bald he had never seen her without the scarf, or without her wig. He had never seen her without hair.

At first it had been a few strands, nothing much to worry about. When they were married, it was still there, all the bulk and confidence of it. It spread across the pillow shapeless as a pool. Then it began to feel thin, somehow, and shampoo didn't work, not the Vosene or the yellow stuff – Thorium X paint – the doctor gave her, or the heat treatments, or the vinegar and brown paper her mother, Grace, said never failed. Then slowly, oddly, there were tiny patches, a brittleness. This was 1953. She was already married.

Two years later, when she was pregnant for a second time, the problem was diagnosed. It was alopecia, the doctors said, and she

2

was given tablets to cure it. She was slightly concerned that they might damage the unborn baby, but one thing she did know was that doctors were clever and good and could be trusted. But the tablets didn't work. Worse, the baby was born sick and nearly died. So slowly, as if in punishment, she moulted. By the early 1960s she had lost all her hair. No one could ever find out; and not even Jack could see.

And now these sleeping tablets weren't working, just like those other pills more than thirty years before. She made an effort to stand up. It was quiet. Sometimes, even this early in the morning, you could hear Indian music from the family next door. The room – white Melamine, brown hessian cylinder lampshade, plain modern dressing table, divan bed – reeled and she nearly fell.

Jack moved to help her, but she steadied herself. He was still a big handsome man, even at sixty-two. He looked like Robert Mitchum, in a certain light. He had even won a lookalike contest once, at the Torbay Chalet holiday camp in Devon.

Jean walked into the hall. To her right, on the wall, the only decoration was a small framed print of an apple, a pear, dried flowers. Her feet scratched the damson sisal carpet. They had bought it because it was cheap and would last, but now it was beginning to show signs of wear, the frayed fibres straying tiredly out from their once-perfect close weave. She stepped carefully into the tiny bathroom: green patterned tiles and a Marilyn Monroe printed mirror (a present from one of her three boys). The room was plain – no cover on the toilet, no knitted mat.

Jean performed her ablutions – as she called them – and stepped out after a couple of minutes. Jack, now in a blue towelling bathrobe, took her place inside. When he emerged fifteen minutes later, showered and shaved, Jean was dressed and preparing her wig expertly. It was made of real hair. She had once trained as a hairdresser, but had given it up and gone to work as a seamstress, at Berkertex, near the Palace Cinema in Southall.

Her clothes were immaculate, neat and pressed, in good, sensible taste. She wore slacks and a blouse. On her finger was her engagement ring, bought up in London, in Notting Hill Gate in 1952, for a month's wages: platinum with a single solitaire, £30.

3

She made up her face in front of the dressing table, from where she could look out on to the small garden that she loved: winter jasmine, cotoneaster, laburnum, eucalyptus, winter rose, camellia, lilac, thyme, forget-me-nots; a small rockery; an arch of honey-suckle; a bird-house. A robin came every year. Her make-up was plain, unfussy: a little foundation, a little mascara, lipstick. The mirror showed a woman who looked ten years younger than her fifty-seven years. Everyone said so.

Jean went downstairs to prepare Jack's breakfast, while Jack dressed. When he came down (past the landscapes that Jean had painted herself at evening classes, copied exactly from prints, calendars and magazines), toast, cornflakes and tea were on the table. The table and chairs were Ercol, dark wood with slightly splayed legs in the 1950s style. There was a serving hatch between the kitchen and living room, lopsided, since Jack had made it – he was such a bodger, everyone had laughed. On its ledge, a pair of egg coddlers with tiny birds and nature scenes depicted. In the corner, a small table Jean had made herself, covered with dun-coloured tiles. There was a hanging pot with ivy, a leaded miniature arboretum, framed prints of cathedral towns and hunting scenes. The kitchen had been too small when they first moved into the house, in 1958, but in the 1970s they had had an extension built, like everyone did then, and now it seemed almost spacious. Behind where Jack sat, there was a pine wall clock. Jack read his *Daily Express*, which he bought despite having voted Labour all his life, drank his tea and ate his toast and marmalade. Jean would eat once he had left.

After a while, Jack rose to go. He opened the door on to the street. Jean stood behind him, ready to say goodbye. When they had first moved to Southall, it had been a lovely place. The front gardens were neat and tidy, trees lined the streets and the kids played safely outside. There were trolley buses at the end of the road. The houses were then still new and mostly immaculate. They were all much the same, built in the 1930s, with bay windows, pebble-dash, hedges, fake Tudor beams, window seats, half-timbered, pitched roofs, two small bedrooms and a boxroom upstairs, french doors at the back.

4

Now, many of the front gardens had been concreted over to make room for second-hand Sierras or Novas. The original windows had almost entirely been replaced by aluminium or thermoplastic-framed double-glazing. Half a dozen or so houses in the street were stone-clad. Satellite dishes had multiplied. Many of the lawns were untended and the hedges raddled. Sometimes you had to step over dog mess on the pavement. Jean used to dream that one day they might be able to move to Greenford, the next strip of suburb in towards London, but that would cost maybe another £10,000 or £15,000 and she knew that they couldn't afford it. Still, money wasn't everything. Being happy was what mattered, wasn't it? Jean often finished her sentences with question marks.

They kissed, briefly, on the lips. *Goodbye, Jackie*, said Jean. *Goodbye, Jeannie*, said Jack. That was the closest they ever got to pet names. Except sometimes, because Jack's ears, for as long as she could remember, had been covered in thick white hair which he had to keep trimming back, she sometimes called him 'Furry Ears'. She watched him go down the path, get in his car and drive away, without looking back. His red Volkswagen Jetta was on its last legs. He drove in his usual haphazard fashion, only braking at the last moment, pulling out without indicating. She closed the door. It was quiet inside.

Jean had a job to do. For years, she had worked as a dinner lady at Beaconsfield Road School in Southall, helping to look after the children. They were mostly second- or third-generation Indians, Bangladeshis, Punjabis and Pakistanis. This was the only real job she had had since meeting Jack, apart from a brief spell on the production line at the big EMI factory in Hayes back in the 1970s. She wasn't even sure what she'd been making then, but she'd had to sign the Official Secrets Act, because it was something to do with bombs.

After Jack left, she went out shopping, just for a few bits and pieces for his dinner. She also drove a Jetta, slightly older, blue. She went to the Top Shops, so-called because you had to turn a corner and then go 300 yards up to the top of a hill. Once there had been a chemist's, a big Co-op, a butcher, two or three bakers, sweet shops, the Forbuoys newspaper shop and a toy shop. Now the Co-op had closed and half the rest were boarded up. There was an off-licence, of course, that also rented videos and a tobacconist that was also a greengrocer, selling vegetables she didn't even recognize.

Jean was careful when she came back from the shops. Only a few days before, she had had an accident which knocked the side of the car in. It was all her fault – so much was her fault. Now she parked, outside Charlie and Flo Rowden's house, two doors along at No. 35. Charlie was a cockney, with a face like a fresh wad of tobacco. He had moved here in the 1940s from Shoreditch.

Flo watched as Jean parked the car, about two or three feet from the kerb. *She don't look well, Charlie. And look at the way she's parked that car.* Charlie didn't speak, or go to the window.

Jean made sure that the house would be neat and tidy for when Jack came in. The sun was now out, catching a million motes of dust suspended in the room. Nothing was really clean in the end. She decided she had better ring Betty Buckingham, the secretary at the school.

Betty, she said, *I'm terribly sorry, but I shan't be able to come in today. Or the rest of the week.* Betty was surprised that Jean didn't give a reason, but she was sure that there must be a good one. Jean had never let them down before. She sounded fine, so perhaps it was Jack who was ill.

Irene Downhill, Jean's best friend since adolescence, also worked as a dinner lady there and was surprised when she turned up at Beaconsfield Road to find that Jean wasn't there. She'd seen her the previous night and Jean hadn't said anything then about him being ill. She'd seemed absolutely OK, laughing and joking. She had given Irene a big hug at the end of the evening and – this was unusual – a kiss, then driven home. *Irene*, she had said, *you've been a good friend to me.* Then off she'd gone, in that banger, the ten-year-old Jetta, with the golf clubs and the tartan rug in the back.

Jean sat down at the living-room table to write. She was good at writing. Unlike Jack, who had a half-legible scrawl at the best of times, Jean's handwriting was neat, precise, compact. She never

6

found that words came easy, but they came somehow. It was always her who wrote the little poems and messages to the family at Christmases and birthdays.

To her side, the hardwood shelves that Jack had fitted himself. A GEC Sonata record player, bought in the 1970s. The boys had laughed at Jack for still buying British, but Jack believed in England. Above the record player, there were the family photographs next to the Reader's Digest Condensed Classics. There was Jeff in his home in New Orleans, handsome, serious, with something of the look of Dustin Hoffman. In his mid-thirties and still no children, divorced and now married again. Timmy, his blond hair now thinning slightly, his face in a slight grimace – he always hated to smile into the camera, said his mouth was too small – still unmarried. And James, the youngest, always larking about, pulling faces for the camera – now he had left home too, to live up in London.

Jean checked the carriage clock on the mantelpiece. The house was so empty. Next to the photographs there were trophies: golf, tennis, badminton, bridge. They all seemed to be for runners-up. The Lotts were famous for losing gracefully.

She finished the letter and folded it neatly. After checking that the house was still tidy, she decided to get the job done. She went upstairs.

It was a nothing day for Jack. He worked part-time for Age Concern. He didn't think of Jean. She did what she did. After the dinner job, she would probably go and see her sister-in-law, Olive, or chubby little Rene from round the corner who had lost her husband a few years back. Or she would practise golf at the club in Perivale, although she wouldn't join because she lacked confidence that she knew how to score properly – Jean found arithmetic difficult.

Jack got home at about five o'clock. The house was nice and tidy as usual, with all the breakfast things cleared away. He shouted for Jean. There was no answer. Deciding that she was probably in the garden, he walked through the kitchen and into the small patch of green at the back. It ran slightly wild, the garden. It was deserted. There was an old shed at the end, full of junk, but there was nothing there either.

He came back into the house, puzzled. It seemed so still. Suddenly he moved, fast, running up the cramped stairs. He did not know why he was running. Jack rushed into the bedroom. Jean's wig was on straight and nicely coiffed. Her feet – size four, petite like the rest of her – were maybe six inches from the floor. The blue necklace of rope held her tight. Her eyes were closed. She looked unconcerned. There was a letter on the bed, with *Jackie* written on it. A stool had been kicked away.

Jack ran downstairs. He was a practical man. He had to cut her down – although he knew she was dead and that it wouldn't serve any purpose. There was a line around her neck, the blood pointlessly rushing to protect the delicate skin in the purple of a bruise. There was a line of blood.

He searched the kitchen drawer, but couldn't find the scissors. He decided to make do with a bread knife. Upstairs again, he sawed through the tension of the rope. It took only a second. She fell into his arms lightly, as if they were dancing. He laid her on the perfectly made-up bed. Then he went downstairs and called 999.

The ringing tone no longer suggested a bell, merely a series of impulses. Jack's voice held steady as the line was picked up.

Hello. There's been an accident. My wife is dead, I think.

I see, sir. The address? Spell it please. 31 Rutland . . . As in the county? Thank you, sir. We'll be with you as soon as we can.

OK. Thank you.

He hung up, gently, as the line went dead. He decided to go upstairs again, dreaming now. He sat on the bed and held Jean's hand, rocking gently back and forward, trying to find balance. The bed was firm, to guard against backache. She was cold, of course.

The letter was addressed to Jackie. The handwriting was neat and tidy, 'Jackie' in a different colour ink to the rest of it. There was a doodle at the top and the paper was folded into four. Jack opened it and began to read, tears now dissolving everything slightly. The letter was logical and clear, but it made no sense, no sense.

Jack decided to go back downstairs. He let go of Jean's hand, giving it the tiniest squeeze. Goodbye, Jeannie. He walked slowly down the stairs, the note still in his hand.

He sat in the living-room armchair, which was a gold-brown velveteen. Now there was blue light at the net curtains, flashing on to the walls. A knock at the door. There were two young men, policemen. There were men in white who went upstairs, without a word, without even asking.

One of the policemen, the older one, spoke.

Sit down, sir.

Jack had not returned to the chair and was wandering around without very much purpose.

I think you could use a drink.

The policeman poured a full glass of something or other and Jack took a deep swig, almost choking. He sat, listening to the noises upstairs, footsteps and something that sounded like furniture being moved. He felt a little groggy now. He tried to stand, to get to the phone to call his sons, but couldn't remember their numbers. It was strange, because he'd known them all off by heart, for years.

Of course, they would be in the 'Addresses' book. Jack rose to his feet, went to the hall and picked up the vinyl-bound volume. He thumbed through the pages, but found it hard to keep the book still. In the end, he couldn't do it. The policeman gently eased the book from his big, collapsing hand. Jack gave him the names and he quickly found the numbers. The policeman began to dial the first one carefully.

Jack sat down again. His jaw worked, but he wasn't sure whether or not words were coming out. Certainly the police-man didn't respond, but then he was busy speaking on the phone now. Yet Jack felt it only proper that he be told what had happened, exactly, and why.

Chapter Two

I could have answered my father's questions, although, of course, he hadn't put them to me yet, and although they were the wrong questions. As the policeman replaced the receiver at my father's house, I knew why. I listened to the tone for a few seconds, then put the phone down at my end.

It was an open and shut case. The motive was there, and the method and the witnesses. There were fingerprints. Suicide took the blame because it is bound to in these circumstances. But to ask why – that is, why suicide? – was a red herring. Actually it was murder, as plain and bright as the moon. It was a knife in the heart, an uppercut in the delicate pit of the belly. It was fatal bruising to the softest parts. Internal bleeding finished the job. So the correct question was, who, or what, was the murderer? I had my suspicions. First, it was an inside job, someone with access. Also, it was the job of an expert who was clever and ruthless. And, as with a Mafia hit, the killer had been someone she had trusted completely. There was only one person who fitted that particular profile.

I realized that I was still staring at the telephone, as if I expected it to ring again to inform me that there had been a mistake. Plainly, this was absurd. I sighed, though not completely spontaneously. I felt instead this was something that was called for. I felt I needed to act in a grown-up fashion, although I was unsure what that involved.

I supposed that I would have to confess. In mitigation, I would be able to say only that, although I had known what I was doing, it had to be done. There were more important things in life than the survival of mothers, and it was her or me. I had to move first. Anyone would have done the same under the circumstances.

My father would, I knew, say that I was being too hard on myself, that I was suffering a guilt reaction, as described in the counselling and self-help books. But in fact it was as true to say that I was being easy on myself, because I killed Jean not just once but twice.

The first time had been about six months previously. I had been in a strange mood, I confess. Rocking on the edge of Notting Hill Gate westbound tube platform, feeling the rush of wind from the approaching train, now, I thought to myself. No, now!

Was it before or after that that I balanced on the edge of the roof of my stucco terrace in Portobello Road, five floors up, at three in the morning? I was waiting for courage to invade me like grace, but, as at the station platform, it never came.

It was soon afterwards, I am sure, that I drove into the countryside with a pair of handcuffs and a length of rubber tubing so that I could pump carbon monoxide into the car, cuff myself to the wheel and throw away the key. It was certainly around that time that I went to see Jack and Jean, to deliver the news, in quiet, measured tones, that their second son had lost his reason. As I drove down the Western Avenue – one slip of the wheel and bang, the matter would be taken care of – I suddenly seemed to know that what I had to say would destroy Jean. It didn't matter. Shame, consideration for others, had become vague memories. Survival was all that counted, not that there was much hope of that.

The second time I murdered Jean had been the night before her death. On that occasion, though, it was less overt, more a crime of omission. My brother James and I had gone to visit, as we often did, not out of duty but because we liked to. We were all good friends. Jean had made dinner, a curry or a continental stew of some sort. She had been taking evening classes in cookery and had transformed her once-rudimentary technique.

Previously it had been white fish in white sauce, toad in the hole, kidneys in batter, roast hearts or an egg and ham flan that always made me retch slightly. Now she was modern and cosmopolitan. There was beef carbonade, chicken paprika, fish mornay with Duchesse potatoes, sweet and sour pork. Apple strudel, banana bread and flan Normande had begun to replace chocolate pudding with chocolate sauce, Eccles cakes, spotted dick and semolina pudding. She would watch the Galloping Gourmet and note down recipes. She sometimes had wine, a Liebfraumilch – Blue Nun on special occasions – a red Lambrusco or a Piat d'Or; Mateus Rosé and Black Tower were out of fashion now. Jean herself drank mainly sherry, but rarely more than a small liqueur glass. *It'll get me all tipsy*, she would say, knowing perfectly well that it wouldn't. I had never seen Jean drunk in my life.

And so it had been last night. It was an ordinary evening in every respect. We laughed, exchanged scraps of news, made fun of each other, maybe played a few hands of cards – nomination whist or pontoon perhaps. Such simple things seemed good to me since I had finally recovered from the madness that had sent me driving home that day along the Western Avenue, plotting my own extinction and praying for sanctuary. Just to be OK, to be fallow, was enough, for the time being.

Things weren't entirely sorted out, it was true. I was still unemployed and unattached, and spent more time than I ought by myself in bed, staring at the sandstone of All Saints' Church in Clydesdale Road through the french windows of my bedroom. I was inclined to be morose and fatalistic, and certainly appeared to have lost the sharpness, ruthlessness and drive that propelled me through the early 1980s, through business success, academic success, personal failure and finally breakdown. But the idea that I might commit suicide had disappeared. It now seemed simply ridiculous.

Against my better judgement, and at the urging of my parents, I had taken a variety of antidepressant drugs. I'd had absolutely no hope that they would work, but they did, and decisively. I rediscovered what it was to laugh. I knew what it was to feel emotions other than rage, grief, hollowness and regret, although things – for the time being at least – seemed rather softened at the edges, and damp and insubstantial underneath.

So Jean's apparently balanced demeanour – which, as I say, was normal for her – was predictable. She had never been an obviously neurotic or a nervous woman anyway, although she thought of herself as sensitive. I had apparently recovered from a terrible crisis. She had dealt with it, got on with it, coped, as she always prided herself on doing. Now her life continued, and it was a good life, on the whole. Her family was close and she wanted for nothing in particular. She seemed to have good friends – many of whom envied her – and a full, active social life.

At the end of the meal James – or Jack, as he had rechristened himself, taking our father's newly fashionable name in his constant attempt at reinvention and escape from Southall – left early. He was going back to the Notting Hill flat he had shared with me ever since I walked out on Becka for the last time and she had left, after smacking me in the face with an open palm and hurling a heavy glass ashtray at my head. The mark on the wall was still there.

I offered to drive Jean to the house of her old friend and workmate Irene Downhill. Her son was a car mechanic and had been repairing the dent in Jean's Volkswagen. The accident had happened when she lost concentration one day the previous week and pulled out into the path of a motorcyclist. Jean was upset, but the rider was only slightly hurt. It was the second such accident in the last few months. Jean had begun to fret that age was making her lose her coordination, but Jack had told her not to be silly, that such things happened and were simply part of life.

We left Rutland Road at about eight o'clock. It had been dark for several hours. We drove through the centre of Southall, past sari shops and sweet centres. After five or so minutes in almost total silence we approached Irene's house in 'Old' Southall. This was the smartest part, near Southall Park, where Olive and Rene occasionally played bowls on the municipal green. There were cottages with carriage lamps, detached houses called Rosewood, Cranleigh and Bona Estada. There were Vauxhall Carltons, an Audi 80 1.8, a Mitsubishi Gallant Sappho. Modest attempts at topiary surmounted wooden fences painted with creosote. Jean could not have afforded to live here, although she would have liked to. It was so English, and Jean, like Jack, loved England, or at least the ordinary, suburban England held suspended in her imagination.

Irene had married someone towards the top outside edge of our class, Bob, who was a computer whiz. Lower middle class almost, rather than upper working, a character from *Butterflies* rather than *Terry and June*. He was a nice man, except that he hated the 'coloureds' or the 'brownies' and would bang on about them for what seemed like hours.

Jean seemed to be tensing herself as we negotiated the long part of the T that led to Irene's road. When she spoke, it was very quietly, but steadily, without any obvious tremor in her dainty, over-polite voice. She had worked her way down slightly in her seat, so that her head barely rose above the back.

I've been to St Bernard's, you know.

What?

I've been to St Bernard's. They've given me tablets.

I stopped the car, shocked. St Bernard's Hospital was the nut-house in Hanwell, the bin. What on earth was my mother doing going there? I found myself inspecting Jean closely, something I rarely, if ever, did. Yellow light from the streetlamp made parchment of her face. She was still a pretty woman, even I could see that, though marks of wear were becoming more insistent now, as she neared the end of her fifties. It occurred to me that there was something stretched about her, as if some force inside was forever demanding, and being denied, expression.

Why?

I don't know. I just haven't been feeling right. A bit down, I suppose.

I tried to think. Was she depressed? Not very seriously, that was for sure. I had been acutely depressed very recently. You couldn't be bothered to get out of bed. You could barely be bothered to wipe yourself after the toilet. You spoke drivel, if you could manage to talk at all. You constantly threatened suicide. That was depression, not this neat, composed, defensively smiling person sitting beside me.

Jean raised her face to mine. She was a good deal shorter than me, even when we were both sitting, and the tension within her seemed to draw her down further, giving the impression that she had shrunk.

Do you think I've been a good mother?

I was surprised at the question and let this show in my face. I shook my head slightly, with an incredulity that came as a spontaneous reaction.

You've been the best mother anyone could ever hope for. You're a wonderful mother. Truly. I don't know what I would have done without you.

I was gushing, perhaps nervous, but I meant it. She had been a good mother, almost ridiculously so, or so I felt. She didn't move or respond. I felt a pang of love, which vulnerability often elicits from me, like the sight of a misspelt word on a shopping list. I reached over to hug her and to reassure her. Oddly for her, she didn't hug back. She was stiff and somehow limp at the same time.

I don't.

What?

I don't think I've been a good mother.

Why on earth not?

Oh, I don't know.

Her eyes were wary. She seemed to fear saying too much, as if she had been instructed not to reveal her secrets too easily.

Come on, Mum. Tell me.

Oh, well, you haven't been very happy, have you?

That's got nothing to do with you. For Christ's sake, it's not your fault.

I said this without irritation. Jean looked unconvinced. She sat absolutely still as she talked, her voice seeming to become fainter having been challenged.

Then there's Jeff. He got divorced from Helma.

Helma was Jeff's German–American wife for seven years. I had liked her a great deal. The new one, Maria, was from Honduras. Jean had yet to meet her.

Yes, but now he's married again.

Hmm.

15

The silence gathered charge. I didn't quite know what to say and found myself feeling vaguely embarrassed. Jean had never really shown me her problems before.

What does Dad say?

Oh, I haven't told him.

I pondered this. For some reason, it did not occur to me what an astonishing thing this was. Jean told Jack everything, or so she had always claimed. Why was she confessing this glaring, heart-breaking fact to me rather than to him?

Mum, I think you're perhaps unwell. I think you are ill.

She was silent. I had decided that she was probably suffering from mild depression, which, presumably, was why she had been referred to St Bernard's in the first place. Dr Garg, the GP from Allenby Road, would have made the referral. She would have been prescribed antidepressant tablets, some of the new generation that took over from the tranquillizers of the 1970s: imipramine, a tricyclic, most probably. I was a bit of an expert on them nowadays. They had worked well for me and I was inclined to evangelize. When I spoke again, it was with that edge of pomposity my voice often took on when I wished to assert my educational superiority over my parents.

Look, it's an illness, like TB or something. It's entirely curable. You know that it is. Look at what happened to me. Look what I was like three months ago – a gibbering wreck, a blob. Now I'm fine. And you're in much better shape than I was.

Are you? Fine?

Jean didn't sound very convinced.

Of course I am. Absolutely OK. Really.

It was true, more or less, although I was still a little punchy from being strung out for so long. I often counted up how much of my life I had wasted through what I considered to be 'my illness', for all that time undiagnosed. It worked out at about four solid years and was time I still grieved for.

How long have you been taking the tablets for?

I tried to look her in the eyes, but she dropped her gaze and gave a simple shrug.

I took the first ones today. I can't sleep.

16

It won't work yet. Losing sleep, it's a classic symptom of clinical depression. They take a couple of weeks to work. You just have to wait. You'll soon feel better, I promise you. I swear to God.

She looked at me, again not quite in the eyes.

I don't know if I can last that long.

Something in me, a faint monitor, merely flickered where it should have glowed red. But my instincts betrayed me, gave only a slight start, because Jean was so obviously OK, so ordinarily behaved, so active, so perfectly dressed. *I don't know if I can last that long.* What on earth could that mean? Only one thing. This I knew, with hindsight, but at that moment it simply wasn't conceivable. Not after all that had happened to me. It was too ridiculous, too melodramatic by far. The gods, I knew, weren't crazy or psychotic. They were simply indifferent, or, more probably, absent.

I hugged Jean again.

You're going to be all right, I promise. I love you. You're a wonderful mother. Just take the tablets. Please. Take the tablets.

Jean nodded. She didn't speak again. So I suppose 'I don't know if I can last that long' are her last words to me. That and 'goodbye', just an ordinary, generic 'goodbye'. I drove the next 100 yards to Irene's house and dropped her off, with a wave. *Goodbye*, said Jean. A small alarm kept sounding – not loud enough. I decided to call Jack the next day, when he came home from work, to let him know that mum was taking antidepressants, but also reassure him that she would be OK in a week or two.

I stopped waiting for the telephone to ring again and sat down in a chair that I had bought in the market. It was falling to bits already. I checked myself to make sure that I was thinking straight. I felt surprised by my lack of surprise. Because on one level I had known, or at least suspected just such a thing. So the question – of guilt, of responsibility – was the first thing on my mind after the policeman called, but it faded, almost instantaneously, blotted out by a larger and more frightening thought. It was, perhaps characteristically, a thought for myself.

It's all going to happen again.

It was unbelievable. After four years in the darkness. Outside, such an ordinary day. There were pigeons on the balcony. The blankness that falls when something so large occurs had invaded already. I lit a cigarette.

I shall go mad again.

How could it be otherwise? I juggled my box of matches. The flat was quiet for once. Portobello Road, although you could see it from the window, was too far away for the market noises to penetrate. Upstairs they were out at work, so the whine of their television was shut off. *A cigarette, all I care about is cigarettes.* That was what I had written in my note. What – four months ago? *I loved you all so deeply when I had a heart to love with, when I possessed a soul. Now all I care about is cigarettes.* Jumping had seemed best to me, quick, decisive. Or carbon monoxide poisoning, if you had the patience. But hanging?

I decided to go and face Jack. I had heard him howling in the background when the policeman telephoned – my father, whom I had never seen cry, except at sentimental films.

My eyes still dry, I moved out into the narrowness and claustrophobia of the corridor. The flat had been a cheaply executed 1970s conversion, undertaken laterally so that four houses were linked together on each floor by winding passages. The light bulbs frequently went unreplaced as they burnt out, so you staggered along, feeling the walls with your fingertips.

The lift was out of order, so I walked down. On the landing, I met James, heading up. His eyes were round and his hair stuck out at odd angles, as if it had been cut badly. I nodded. On the stairs we held each other, waltzing slightly back and forward, then we separated. The shock was still keeping the tears frosted and buried. A sense of urgency passed between us, as if Jean could be revived if only we were capable of moving fast enough.

Do you want a lift home?

No. I've got to get something from the flat. I'll see you there.

Yes.

We parted. James was white. I headed down to my car, an

18

almost new Peugeot 205, and I set off for home. Nothing seemed very different.

The drive along the Western Avenue was neutral, suspended. I passed the bingo hall at Savoy Circus, then the Deco landmarks of Hanger Lane station and the Hoover Factory, relics of the 1930s. I passed the more typically modern cheap, sponsored, plastic shop signs of Greenford and the old Granada cinema, now a Tesco's. The people were badly dressed, predominantly white, with complexions like pumice stone. There were cladding and pebble-dash, porches and school playing-fields.

Outside my parents' house, there was an ambulance and a police car. The sense of suspension, of absence, increased. As I walked up the front path I felt, as only once or twice before in my life, the gulf between what life was and what I had imagined it to be.

My father answered the door. He was babbling and drunk. I had never seen him lacking self-possession before and it concentrated my love. We held each other and then I realized, with a shock of relief, that I was going to be OK. I felt a strength between my shoulders that seemed to tell me I would hold together.

Everything blurred into two or three scenes, out of focus, at least in my memory. Jack was telling me that she was still beautiful, she still looked beautiful, and that he loved her. *Oh, I loved my Jeannie*, he said again and again, sometimes staring at me as if he were making a surprise announcement that needed my acknowledgement to make it true. *I loved my Jeannie.* He rocked back and forth at the dining-room table. Sometimes he would modify his recital to *Why, Jeannie, why?* His head rested on his crossed arms. James, who had arrived minutes after me, sat several feet away. I gazed silently at ornaments and furniture, picking over fine details of the act, like a husband betrayed by his wife.

The ambulancemen began bringing my mother's body down the stairs. I didn't look. I hid at the back of the house while the thudding footsteps carried away Jean.

The wider family began to arrive. Some of them we hardly saw at all nowadays. I had a sense of a hidden, denied bond suddenly exposed and reasserted. These were people I thought I had nothing in common with, people from Barratt-like homes on Green Belt estates whom I had patronized, not always secretly. Now I saw that I was them, and that all the stucco terraces in Notting Hill and all the university degrees in the world formed into a moat could not deny that connection. And as we hugged each other, I was glad of it, for once. To know who I was, for a rare moment, was a comfort instead of an embarrassment.

I volunteered to make the phone calls to relatives and close friends. I didn't mind. In fact it was quite satisfying in a way, because it was something to do that was real and necessary. What I feared, what we all feared, was the exhaustion of these rituals. What would the gods demand of us then? Perhaps they weren't indifferent after all.

Chapter Three

In fact, our family don't believe in gods – even though sometimes I find myself being careful with my thoughts, as if I suspect they are being monitored. It's just a word I use to indicate vicissitude or circumstance. My earliest lesson in circumstance was from my father.

It's unfair, I would complain, as children do.

Get used to it, Jack would respond with a shrug in his voice. For Jack, the essential characteristics of life were first boredom, then injustice. *Get used to it.* So the gods I invoke don't act purposefully, because they are non-existent. Still, 'gods' is a better word than 'luck', because whatever I know to the contrary, there is always this feeling that someone else is determining events, while nevertheless holding me to account.

As the days and years passed between me and my mother's death, I came to understand that the gods truly were indifferent, whatever my imagination had once told me. Yet I remained confused about where the line stood between their blind power and my culpability. However, this much I knew: I wasn't the sole culprit. It was more in the nature of a joint enterprise, I would say, as in *The Mousetrap.* There were as many different fingerprints at the scene as on the butt of a gun in a gumshoe thriller. The threads that bound up the life that ended with that abrupt, confessional act were as numerous and interconnected as the fibres of the hanging rope.

The past was everywhere in that simple bedroom, invisible

and inescapable like the air, the backsliding force that drafts out the present. Parts of that history, as if elements of air, could be teased apart. There was the force of heredity, knitting with childhood experience. There was adult drama, sparking with the larger inner history of the old, odd, transformed country within which Jean was a tiny connection.

Psyche, if that's what you want to call it, was also there as a shadow on the wall – the workings of the subconscious, the operations of the will, the convulsions of mental illness, the mysteries of biochemistry and clinical depression. And the gods, too, were there right enough, shadows behind shadows, blank and disinterested, dishing out varieties of fortune – variously disguised, of course. And finally, I was there, a photograph on the sideboard, doing my part to tighten the knot.

All these things I wished to consider, to take into account and hold responsible, but above them all Jean was there, Jean herself, the constellation of powers that makes up a single personality. It was Jean who wrote the note, Jean who sought out the rope, Jean, finally, who kicked away the stool. But who was Jean?

When I first asked that question of myself, I was taken aback by the reflex answer, which was that I had only the vaguest idea. She was simply Mum, a lovable, bright cartoon who cooked us meals, was pleasant, loving, available. Despite having borne me in her belly, having suckled me and raised me, having shared a house with me for twenty years, there were probably a score of people whom I knew far better. She was insubstantial to me as a personality, although not as a person. Her presence was dense despite being intangible, bound to me by love, respect and a genuine affection that went well beyond what was biologically necessary. I liked and admired Jean as well as loved her. Yet, I began to realize, I had no more idea of what made her tick than I knew what made the universe expand or a leaf tumble from a tree. Jean was not so much a person as a soft and muddy idea whose purpose was to comfort me.

If I was to find out what made her commit suicide – how metallic, how abrupt and tactless that phrase still feels – I needed to get to know her, if only in retrospect. I had to examine the

22

traces of her life, the products and waste products, like a forensic scientist, inferring, deducing, blind-guessing. At the same time, I knew that I needed to find out about myself, a greater mystery to me perhaps than even Jean was. After all, I too had been where Jean had stood, on the precipice, waiting to die by my own choice, if choice it was. We had been forged in the same foundry, out of our blood, and our class, and our England. To understand Jean's death, I needed to understand my own death wish and the way it fed back into the shape of my own life.

I wanted to do what was, perhaps, impossible: to try to see Jean with eyes scrubbed of worship, or caricature, or simple hope; to look at her straight, and through her see myself in a less distorted way. I wanted to understand her life, the world she was born into and the way that shaped the person she became. I also needed other kinds of knowledge, to get an understanding of what many doctors imagined as a largely physical illness, and what many psychologists imagined, quite differently, as a crisis of the self, of meaning and faith. The inquest said that Jean took her own life as a result of clinical depression, as if it were like a heart attack or a brain haemorrhage. But this was no explanation. I needed to learn the secret language of suicide. I needed to get inside Jean's head, and through it inside my own. Or perhaps it would turn out to be the other way round.

I am sitting at my desk, in the room where I write. The window overlooks the Westway Flyover and there is an unceasing low hum of traffic. The Portobello Road is twenty yards away.

Mine is an expensive house, a few hundred yards north of my old flat, but much of the area is poor, despite being fashionable. Crack-heads, yardies, droolers, screamers and totters, child-whackers and curry-pukers parade the streets outside. I live here because it is as far away from England as possible, as far from Terry and June and Wendy Craig as it's possible to be. This is where misfits congregate, by choice or injunction. James has christened it the Bronx, but it is a place peculiar to modern England rather than America. There are fifty nationalities and languages and as many income brackets, backed up on to each other's doorstep.

My heart is beating faster than usual and my fists are clenched. There is a folded piece of paper in front of me, torn from what might have been a school exercise book. It is ruled in blue, with a one-inch left-hand margin marked in red. *Jackie* is written on the front. I stare at this scrap of paper, reluctant to touch it. Then, in a quick motion, I unfold it. Immediately, my eyes flood. They overflow.

In the top right-hand corner, in blue ink, there are two doodles, both in the shape of an L, or right angle. One has the vertical strut extended to three times the length of the other. The first word, *Jackie*, is written in blue ink and is followed by a comma. Then a new line starts, in black ink. The writing is slightly more untidy than Jean's usual hand.

Now I am sobbing, in deep, sharp jags. I move the paper to one side so that my tears do not stain it and take short, struggling breaths. It is only the second time I have read this note. The first, I was numb with shock. Now time has shrugged off my protection. I can manage only one sentence at a time without breaking off for a few moments to try to collect myself. I cannot stop moaning out loud. But I force myself to read it all the way through.

Jackie,
Please forgive me for this terrible thing I am doing, but at least it is one <u>brave</u> thing I am doing.

I cannot keep up this pretence. We have had so many happy year's and I can see the strain this is having on you, in the end you will grow to hate me. So it is time for me to get out of your life. You have so much to give such a bright mind and I am holding you back.

This will be so bad for everybody but I hate Southall, I can see only decay, I feel alone.

I have loved you alway's and this is something you will have to be strong enough to get through, but you will, and then you can start life with somebody who will take you on to better times. Please forgive me. I love you forever.

Tell my dear friends they have been great pleasure in my life.
My darling son's. I love you.
Forgive me. Forgive me.
Jeannie

Then there are two diagonal crosses – kisses.

I squeeze my eyelids together and rub them with the heel of my palm. The misplaced apostrophes are crushing, somehow. I swallow, and swallow again. I feel a fathomless sadness and repeat the same phrase again and again in my head. Poor Jean. Poor, poor Jean.

From time to time, over the next few weeks, I take out the note and read, when I feel strong. At first it tends to affect me for several days, but now it is unpredictable. Sometimes I can shake it off, sometimes it scratches and vexes me in the middle of the night. But I need to read it, again and again, because I want to understand, and I have to start somewhere.

This will be so bad for everybody but I hate Southall, I can see only decay, I feel alone.

I am driving towards Southall, to try to reimagine the place I grew up in, that I left twenty years ago. The place that Jean could no longer stand to live in. I turn the phrase from her note over and over in my mind.

I arrive through Greenford, the first stop off the Western Avenue on the way to Southall. I drive past the anonymous shops. There is an ugly 1950s church, Our Lady of the Visitation, just before Cardinal Wiseman High School. My school, Greenford County Grammar, would play them at football. To the right, the Golf Links estate, white high-rise blocks, where I would go to visit friends from my school who were not lucky enough to be owner-occupiers, Ds and Es rather than C2s. Here, the skinheads would gather to brood and swagger, but racial attacks were largely unheard of, or perhaps simply unreported, at least until Gurdip Singh Chaggar was murdered outside the Dominion Cinema in 1976. After that there were the National Front march in 1979, when Blair Peach died at the hands of the

Special Patrol Group, and then the Southall Riots in 1981. Both were largely orchestrated by outsiders.

Skinheads were not dangerous then anyway, or so it seemed to me. They just liked dressing up differently: boneheads, suedies, peanuts. They didn't even take drugs like we did, we who styled ourselves, laughably, the *heads*, or the *hairies*. They were better than the straights anyway, the kids with water-slicked five-shilling haircuts who made A grades and were never rude to their parents.

On each side of the road, stone-cladding, pebble-dash and red-tiled roofs. Satellite dishes collect junk from the heavens. There is an empty playground with a skeletal rocket ship, its brightly coloured paint invaded by rust. On the opposite side, West Middlesex Golf Club. On the days it is open to the public, Jack, James and I play a round if the sun is shining. Dad is reliable and consistent, James flamboyant and reckless, me wholly inadequate and unpredictable. It is a surprisingly working-class game now. There are lager cans in the litter bins and builders who smoke Marlboro Lights as they mishit the ball.

I brake to avoid golfers who are suddenly dragging trolleys across the road from one part of the course to another. One man gesticulates angrily at me, then passes out of sight. I speed up again. I am approaching the border with Southall. Past the Pig and Whistle – 'West London's Premier Public House' – past what were once known as stockbrokers' Tudor houses, although there are no stockbrokers here and there never were. Instead there are software buyers, computer programmers, local shop-keepers, skilled workers, financial services salesmen, bank employees.

These houses, like most in Southall, look worn and dispirited. It is hard to believe they were built as part of a great common dream of England, one that emerged around the time Jack and Jean were born. They *are* England, more than any palace or flag or uniform, with their dull, decent reflection in every city and town.

Until the First World War, such suburbs – where they existed at all – had been fenced off for the middle and upper-middle classes. The working classes would have been in rented accommodation in the inner cities, like Jean's family, crammed into a flat in Shepherd's Bush, or Jack's parents in the two-bedroom flat in Lambeth they shared with another family. The new houses – with their front and back gardens, their inside toilets – sprouted, like Southall, around the arterial roads and tube lines that pushed out from central London. The estates of ridge-tiled semis and terraces with their round stair windows, porches, creosoted gates and privet hedges must have seemed part of an almost mythic vision, a prospect of privacy, independence, peace and quiet. This was the most visible sign of the then much-vaunted new Jerusalem. People, it is said, believed in such things at that time.

I turn right into the Uxbridge Road, with Brunel's Iron Bridge to my left and, beyond that, St Bernard's Hospital, where my mother was referred. It was once less delicately known as Hanwell Asylum for the Insane Poor, one of the first great nineteenth-century mental-health projects. It has been largely converted into a new housing estate now, with typically cramped windows and belligerent red brick, although the hospital survives, facelifted and remarketed as a 'community resource'. Acute depressives still languish here in locked wards, waiting for the slack nurse who will leave the medicine cabinet unlocked.

I drive past the used-car showrooms, a line of semis with garages, then Southall Park, where my Uncle Alan – Jean's brother – worked as a park-keeper, until they found him asleep in his barrow and gave him the sack. Men with turbans are playing cards on the benches. There are drunks beetling pointlessly along the paths.

To my right, the youth club I spent night after night during the dead zone – between thirteen and fifteen years old, between childhood and the pub. I try to imagine myself loping through the door, surprised now that I was tough enough then not to be unnerved, for it was mainly a skinhead haunt. There were feather-cut girls French-kissing overgrown boys in Doc Martens steel-capped boots and thin clip-on braces, hoiking up two-tone Sta-Prest to expose the regulation white socks. But I had a bruiser's face, scarred and coarse, and I had been known to punch. It was just enough of a reputation to make them wary, but not enough to challenge them. They danced with short, stubby movements to Laurel Aitken, the Skatalites, Prince Buster, *Trojan Chartbusters Volume 3*. In my hipster Wranglers, black Converse All-Stars and maroon tie-dyed three-button grandad vest, I tried to sneak Neil Young with Crazy Horse, or the Fugs or Iggy Pop and the Stooges on to the busted-up record player. It was always swiftly removed, with an amplified squawk.

The youth club shrinks in the rear-view mirror. Now I move past the entrance to Southall Horse Market, a Victorian relic which actually still does trade horses once a week. On Saturdays it was a general market. I bought my first record there, an ex-jukebox copy of Lee Dorsey's 'Working in a Coal Mine'.

Into Southall proper, past the abortively ugly police station, from which one of the drafted-in SPG officers battered to death Blair Peach in the riots. The signs read Curried Halal Meats, the Queens Style Carpet Centre, the Shahi Nan Kebab, Fine Fabrics: Specialists in Sarees and Dhuptas, the White Hart Pub – now Shadows Night Club, Karaoke Most Evenings, West London's Fun Club. Past the White Hart and the town hall, boarded up and crumbling: These Premises Controlled By Security Officers. There are mock Doric columns, bathetic, supporting the roof to the entrance. Beyond and to the right, the plaster melted wedding cake of Southall Mosque. To the left, Mohammed Jewellers. Diagonally opposite, the astonishing folly of what was once the Southall Palace Cinema, its two giant Golden Dragons still intact and scowling down at the street scene. Now it has been broken up into small market units selling cloth, gewgaws and pencils.

I hate Southall, I can see only decay, I feel alone.

The odd thing is, Jean and Jack were the only ones in the family who, so we thought, didn't hate Southall. Jeff, James and I loathed the place, like a bad cell within ourselves which we feared would infect the other, healthy ones. Jeff left at the age of eighteen to go abroad and never came back. James, when asked where he came from, would always say Ealing, the London borough we were a small part of. At the age of sixteen, returning from a holiday with his girlfriend in Denmark, he cried on the bus back from Heathrow to our house as it progressed through the dead, littered streets of Hayes and Harlington to the tired, spiced air of Southall, of suburban England. I got out as quickly as I could, at the age of nineteen.

At the time, Southall had the largest concentration of Asian immigrants in the country, at first largely Sikhs from the Punjab, but later Muslims and Hindus from East Africa, Bangladesh and Pakistan. But we didn't bolt because we disliked Asians. The fact that they were there at least gave the place some identity, some interest, some special status. To be honest, we didn't go out of our way to court them either. They were an insular community, as were we, I suppose, and you had little chance of kissing the often beautiful girls. We were just indifferent; each community kept itself to itself.

No, we bolted because Southall was a dump, because it was nowhere, like most of subtopian England. We hated it for the reasons we imagined our parents liked it – because it was predictable, safe, conservative and limited in scale and possibility. We hated it because we could see that it didn't know what it was, or where it belonged, or what it was for.

But Jean stayed, tending her isolated front garden, as the other gardens in the street were paved over for car-parking space, as Sikh traditional styles – saris, turbans, salwar and kameez, dhuptas and guths – became more familiar sights than Aran sweaters or M & S belted raincoats. She would nod and say hello, always be polite and friendly, chat over the fence to Mr and Mrs Mukherjee at No. 29. Perhaps she was secretly prejudiced, although she never said anything.

I drive through the entrance to Southall Park, past Villiers High School, once Southall Grammar. An aircraft roars overhead on the flight path to Heathrow, five miles west. As a child, I would lie in bed listening, scared that they were carrying A-bombs.

In the car park there is a man with a can of super-strength lager. I used to come to this park all the time, along the primula path, to the tennis courts, or the Scout jamborees, or the Summer

Holiday Shows, dull magicians and pompous brass bands. It was horribly boring. The primulas are still lovely.

There is a train whistle in the background, still an oddly pre-war sound. The little building which used to take the fees for our Sunday games of park tennis is boarded up and marked Keep Away. There is graffiti, as predictable in its presence as the man with the can: El Krew; Sanj; T. Nungs (the Tooti Nungs, Asian gang rivals of the Holy Smokes). Under the awning of the building, unpunctuated except for unnecessary speech marks, a sign which reads 'Do Not Stand Under Here Private'. There is what looks like verdigris on the roof.

By the municipal bowling green, still in reasonable condition, a pit bull off the leash and a scatter of Asian boys, once passive and polite, lauded by the *Daily Express*. Now they walk the pimp walk, the cockney strut, the Lambeth Walk, shoulders back, with a fuck-you swing. And the older men, turbaned and bearded, gossiping over broken park benches. They look wise and disappointed with life.

I leave the park. There are gypsy flower sellers working the porches and driveways. For some reason the sight of them annoys me. I walk down a small tunnel that traces the railway line. The graffiti now reads *Chelsea* and *Clash*. Through the tunnel there is a light industrial estate to the left, clean, ugly, then, incongruously, to the right, a dray horse in a field. Framed behind the field, a real factory, towering 100 feet high and issuing steam and unidentifiable mechanical grunts and swoons. Pastoral, urban, modern, postmodern, Victorian, an undifferentiated mess.

There is no sign on the factory. It pumps and boils anonymously. What does it make? The path is hedged about by wild flowers I cannot identify. There is a yellow sign set in concrete with an H and two numbers. I do not know what this is for. The leaves on trees I cannot name are filthy.

The path ends at Norwood Green, Old Southall. A lorry marked 'Expandite' thunders past. The neat houses are decked out with a jumble of modest details of dreamed life – a caravan or boat in the front yard, a cartwheel on the wall, carriage lamps at the entrances, We Love Jesus stickers. It is nice, quiet, unself-consciously ersatz.

I walk on past the fir trees and privet hedges, and after five minutes burst through to the far end of Southall's main drag, marked by another police station, with an old-fashioned blue lamp. At the Golden Chip, I order cod and chips and cover it with a crust of salt and vinegar. The woman who serves is white, in late middle age, with a blue rinse. The food tastes good. Looming above me to my left, the vast, abandoned Southall Gasworks, the scene of endless car chases filmed for *The Sweeney* or *The Professionals*.

This is Norwood Road. There is a St John Ambulance Brigade in the clearly Victorian Norwood Sisterhood Hall, whatever that is, or once was – perhaps a suffragette meeting house. It faces the symbol of a different, changed England: the Southall Black Sisters Women Only Advice Campaigning Resource Centre.

There are gnomes in rockeries, a gents' hairdresser with Michael Portillo-type hairstyles, slightly blown, twenty years out of date. Further along, the Halal Fast Food Takeaway Tandoori and Sweet Centre, the window illuminated with a light that almost seems to come from within the eerily coloured confections. A poster: Vibha Bhangra Princess at Le Palais, Hammersmith, where Jean and Jack once did the jive and the jitterbug. Le Christmas, says another poster, hip-hop, bhangra, swing beat, rave, live PA, Wrecking Force, ragga, jungle.

The lollipop man who ushers me across the road is a Sikh. In the newsagent's, a reproduction print is for sale, a river scene in Wharfedale. It looks like one of my mother's paintings. At the back of the newsagent's, a post office and a Giro queue.

It is entirely Asian now. I eavesdrop on the conversations. They talk of children, money, illnesses, marriage. Everything is the same at this level, the art of the necessary. On the corner, in front of the sari shops, drunks, also Asian, swaying in the slight wind.

There is a church opposite the sari shop. It is broken down, the gravestones worn or shattered. I now wish we had buried Jean, instead of cremating her in the light-industrial style. But we are a practical family, by habit. Here among the graves, I read the inscriptions. The drunks in front of the sari shop eye me amusedly, as if I am mad.

So Mote It Be, says one stone, and *Until the Resurrection Morn. Heaviness May Endure for a Night But Joy Cometh in the Morning.* There is graffiti on the church walls, but not the gravestones.

In front of the church is a war memorial, with fresh flowers and poppy wreaths. They are dedicated to the fallen, from the St John Ambulance Brigade, the British Legion, the Scouts, the Red Cross Society, the Royal Ancient Order of Buffaloes, Southall Working Men's Club. A separate, unidentified, tribute to the those who died at San Carlos Bay. I wonder who these representatives of England's grief are. I wonder if it is grief that is being represented.

Back in the graveyard I become entranced by the stones. *His Life a Beautiful Memory, His Absence a Silent Grief; She Gave of Her Best; Think of Me As Withdrawn into the Dimness, Remembering Where I Wait, and So Where I Wait, Come Gently On.*

Most of the carved messages have one thing in common, the conviction that the occupants are just absent, or waiting, or asleep, or have entered into rest. I carry on walking, thinking of Philip Larkin's 'What will survive of us is love' and how he was wrong. What survives of us is denial.

And the Night Shall Be Filled with Music and the Cares That Infest the Day, Shall Fold Their Tents, Like the Arabs, And As Silently Steal Away. 1937.

The church is Pentecostal. What does that mean? I know nothing more about the creed of the Pentecostals than I do about the Hindu Temple opposite, yet I feel it is knowledge I am expected to have. Who are the Royal Order of Buffaloes? Was St John the same as John the Baptist? Who was Cardinal Wiseman? We are many, our name is legion, the British Legion. Those who died in San Carlos Bay, which England did they die for? Was it Jean's?

I walk across the railway bridge, past Southall Manor House, the only genuine Tudor building in the borough. There is a sign for Beaconsfield Road School, where Jean worked. I turn the other way, walk towards the railway bridge and cross it. I used to stand here and watch the trains for no fathomable reason. On the other side is Bridge Road, and Southall Community Centre, astonishingly, just as I remember it as a child. It is reassuring, and a little unsettling at the same time, like a once-treasured toy found unexpectedly in the attic. The building is completely incongruous, stranded between the railway line, an urban clearway and a patchwork of dull factories.

Jack was unpaid chairman here for a decade. I would come when it was empty and he had paperwork to do, and I would wander on to the gilded stage and pretend I was famous. We would play badminton here together in the high-roofed halls. Jean and Jack always pronounced it 'badmington'. Later, Jean came here for yoga evening classes. In cream and gilt, it is not architecturally remarkable – it is one of the lesser creations of Alexander Marshall Mackenzie, the architect who designed the Waldorf Hotel and Australia House, both in the Aldwych – yet in the context of Southall, it is a palace.

It was originally a recreation centre built for workers at Otto Monsted's Margarine Factory, just before the First World War, when Bridge Road was still called Margarine Road. Monsted was a philanthropic businessman, a species now more or less extinct. Monsted's Maypole Institute, as it was then known, was run by the factory workers for their own benefit.

Inside it is still almost perfectly as I recall: classical influence, in the Beaux-Arts style, with Doric columns, both solid and in fresco; vast plush, braided curtains; polished maple parquet floor; high windows allowing milky light into the rooms; the lush stage, as large as that of many West End theatres, with a gilded crest above. On that stage the factory workers would assemble their own orchestra and a male voice choir which would perform for audiences of up to 1,000. Singers, musicians and comedians from the workforce would all appear here. There was once a reading room, with a library of 1,000 volumes. There are still oil paintings and gilt mirrors. Not grand exactly, it is more like a location from a scratched print of a Powell and Pressburger movie; more like the Morris Oxford and the Ford Zephyr were shrunken, likeable versions of the real thing.

Somewhere in this hall, although I suppose it is, strictly speaking, French in style, I feel a resonance of the England Jean perhaps imagined she wanted to belong to – warm, slightly eccentric, innocent, quiet, decent, quaint, a bit pompous, fond of a lark. It is probably the same obscure, half-inherited feeling I get watching *A Matter of Life and Death*, *Colonel Blimp*, *The Ladykillers* or *Arsenic and Old Lace*. It is the sense of an impossible, gentle, romantic, imagined England, an alternative to the pompous, conceited, bullying, Imperial England hymned still by the politicians and nostalgists, or the irredeemably guilty, racist, rapacious England imagined by the marchers, the shouters and the air-punchers. Anyway, it is an England that has gone now, even as an idea, a dream. There is nothing we have thought of to put in its place. There is, in fact, no place to put it; the cohering forces themselves have collapsed. The centre could not hold, had gone even as I was born. But for Jean, it must have once meant something.

Forgive me, forgive me.

It isn't a question of forgiveness. There is nothing to forgive. I admire what Jean did – I know the courage it takes to murder yourself – although I wish desperately that she hadn't done it, although she was crazy to do it. No, if there is a question, it remains eternally Jack's. *Why, my Jeannie, why?* And why had I wanted the same thing?

For Jean and me, when we plotted our own murders, our lives were good, better than most. We had friends, health, enough money, plenty of love. So what drove us both to madness? Was it hidden and interior, some sickness of the brain? No – it was larger external powers, the flooding force of a disintegrating England, of mobility, dislocation, crumbling identity, separation, unbelonging, advancing relentlessly, too slow and massive to see or resist. No, no again. It was our individual characters, weak, inflexible and unresolved. It was *our fault*. No.

I don't know. Causes are more like vapour than facts. Facts are rarely hard, but soft as loam. Yet I like to make guesses, I like to

34

tell stories. I can do that. To start to make answers, to have a framework in which to think, a line has to be drawn somewhere, and that line must be somewhere in the past. It is my frame, my lens. Where else is there to look?

It is arbitrary to a degree, I suppose, because causes go back – and in a sense, forward – for ever. You can blame a car crash on the invention of the motor car. You can blame Henry Ford for imagining a future with motor cars in it. Yet for Jean, and therefore for me, I have decided that the past begins on 27 January 1926. This is the day Jack was born, into an England quite as strange to me as China, an England before the flood.

Chapter Four

'There is something distinctive and recognizable in English civilization . . . it is continuous, it stretches into the future and the past, there is something that persists as in a living creature. What can the England of 1940 have in common with the England of 1840? But then, what have you in common with the child of five whose photograph your mother keeps on the mantelpiece? Nothing, except that you happen to be the same person. Above all, it is your civilization, it is you . . . Good or evil, it is yours, you belong to it, and this side of the grave you will never get away from the marks that it has given you'
– George Orwell, *England Your England*

I have thirty photographs in front of me of people I have never really thought of as human, as actual. They are my relatives, my most recent ancestors, momentarily trapped in the 1920s. I have sorted all my family snaps, several hundred of them, into separate decades up to the present day. Taken all together, given the speed of a camera shutter, they probably add up to maybe a few seconds of exposed life. It is as if a sudden flashlight has been held up to illuminate my past and is then tantalizingly switched off, leaving only an engram, a faint memory trace.

People in other countries formally worship these memories, but I have simply boxed them up and put them in a drawer and forgotten them until now. In parched black and white, in sepia and ochre, these ghosts run with my blood. I am soaked in, constructed of, their residues. But in my mind, they have always been no more than music-hall curiosities.

The tones in those photographs, mostly taken on Verichrome film on Box Brownies, can never be seen now. The colour of modern England, the England that dates from the mid-1950s, from when I was born, is different, primary-coloured, vulgar, brash, its inhabitants displaying their lobster skins as badges of new affluence, as trophies from the sun. These old prints, aged by the air, seem to speak of an elegance and gravity in their subjects, and an eerie magic. Looking at them – at that England – is oddly heartbreaking, like seeing a photograph of the face of a soon-to-be abandoned child, hopeful, before his mother has fled and stolen everything precious from inside him. Some of them are professionally posed, which adds to the sense of seriousness and gravitas. Also, most of the subjects are dead, and this rarefies the photographs, because you are touching ghosts.

The elegance and magic are an illusion. The people who stood in front of the camera were certainly as florid, loud and rough at the edges as anything caught fifty years later, by more recent relatives, at the Torbay Chalet holiday camp, for instance, toasting the camera with advocaat snowballs topped by fake, carcinogenic cherries and saucered glasses of Asti Spumante. And yet in another way these images suggest an England that breathed a different air, something that stains the photographs with more than just chemicals.

Here is the shop where my father was born, 100 yards from the great towers of the Crystal Palace, that incredible, glittering monument to the self-confidence of Victorian England. The shop sign says: *Wells and Lott, Fruiterers and Greengrocers*. The typography is that of a fairground roundabout – florid, stocky, confident, Edwardian. There are five people standing in the forecourt of the shop, which is decorated with wicker baskets and hemp sacks of podded peas and chestnuts. There are boxes of melons, potatoes, cabbages. Brown paper bags hang from the doorframe.

On the left, Charlie and Floss Wells are smiling dutifully for the camera. Charlie is wearing a short kipper tie, a black waistcoat and a white shirt. A watchchain traces the contours of his ribcage. He has the shadow of a moustache that suggests an office or town hall clerk. Charlie and Floss are serving a customer, a woman who could be anything between twenty-five and fifty. She is taking a pound of apples.

To the right of the photograph is Cissy – Cecilia Starr – my paternal grandmother. Her hair is tied in two buns, one on each side of her head – 'earphones', as Jack christened the style. Her husband, Art, will be devastated when, a few years after this picture, she impulsively cuts off all her hair. She wears a pinstriped blouse and high-waisted skirt. Her look is flat and neutral, her character – which is soft, kind and rather lazy – is hidden. She is averagely attractive, with a thin mouth, a sharp nose and a round, pleasant face.

To the right of her is Art, Arthur Walter Frank. He looks cocky – according to some, the origin of his closest named tribe, *cockney* – and handsome, pleased with himself. There is a trace of my father there somewhere, but I cannot pinpoint it. He is known as a tough, unsentimental man, not particularly fond of women or children, who nevertheless dotes on his wife and, it is said, spoils her terribly. Like his partner Charlie, Art is dressed like a clerk, in a white Eton collar, but his tie is as thin as his smile. The uniform is revealing. Even then, we were respectable, preparing ourselves for the shunt to home-owning, blue-collar suburbia. Art and Cissy did not fight, drink or gamble. Art did not swear in the company of women and never struck his wife, or anyone else. These vices were imagined to be more or less confined to the class below them, the working class of the Victorian imagination, roughnecks in gin palaces, slum cockneys, costers, totters and barrow boys, the feckless, undeserving poor. Jack's family even had a private vehicle, a Wolseley van, and later, a Citroën Tourer. The van was used itself as a shop, on day runs to the smarter parts of south London – Croydon and Dulwich.

It would be easy to pigeonhole Cissy and Art, Charlie and Floss, as members of the lower middle class, the usual fate of such families when anyone bothered to chronicle them, right up until the present day. But this would be incorrect, sloppy. They were, in fact, a distinct, vast and emerging presence in England that remains largely, strangely unnoted, perhaps because they appeared as no more than a mongrel, a penumbra of other classes. And yet they were, as today, real enough, the upper, or well-off, working class, something quite discrete. It is not a trivial distinction, for England then as now was as tribal in its way as modern Bosnia, Rwanda or Northern Ireland. The tribes, though, were more subtle, more finely graded and easy to confuse. Class *was*

English life. Who you were was infinitely more important than what you did.

Unlike the lower middle class, they did not aspire to ape their betters. They disdained the hypocrisy, the airs and graces of the bank teller. They were self-confident, suspicious of education and 'improvement'. When Rita Cole, Cissy's gifted niece, was admitted to the local grammar in the 1930s, the other children in the street simply stopped talking to her. Such airs and graces were hated and sanctions were used against them. The peculiarly English phrase 'too clever by half' was hurled at her as a stinging rebuke, as was 'getting above yourself'. To want to join the middle classes was an abandonment of pride and identity. For in this England there was an absolute suspicion of all that was not familiar, plain, straightforward or common sense. Having witnessed Rita's fate, Jack, when offered a coveted grammar school place, turned it down, to the indifference of his – Tory-voting – father.

My ancestors were sceptical and secular, which once again fenced them off from the social layer above them. They did not bother with church except for births, weddings and funerals, preferring the cinema, cycling or cards – nap and pontoon. They were suspicious, often resentful of authority, the authority that was everywhere, whispering *don't do that* or *behave, behave*. But that authority was feared or at the very least grudgingly respected. Even Old Tom, the park-keeper at the local rec. opposite the house in Essex Grove, was never known to be defied, or even much cheeked, by local kids. A uniform of any kind meant the prospect of retribution.

The habit of deference maybe stemmed more from an awareness of raw power weighing down on them than from any sense of inferiority. Doctors and teachers, and of course the king, were naturally regarded with respect. But policemen, army officers, civil servants, lawyers and pettifogging tax officials were simply to be tolerated, representatives of an unwelcome law of nature. My family were not so distant relatives of the lawless, violent, occasionally heroic slum cockneys and had not lost the habit of cocking a snook.

At the same time, they were cautious and apprehensive of that true, lumpen working class, who were liable to be violent, bolshie, loud and stupid, and were just one degree away in the dense, complex social layering that divided up England then as it does now. Yet their characters overlapped, in their instinctiveness, irony, informality, warmth and honesty. This was a counterpoint to, a cancelling of, what they scorned as the stiffness, arrogance, frigidity, hypocrisy and pretence of their 'betters'.

As I stare at them, and they stare back, I know suddenly that they are in me, the stuff of their bones in my mine. But what world do they inhabit in their imaginations? Is there any connection there, in this pre-war, half-lit world, between them and me? Can anything so remote possibly have anything to do with Jean's death, with my nervous breakdown? No, is my first answer. Then, clearly, the thought comes: *perhaps*. That air, that climate, which shapes their clay, which makes their thoughts, will also shape and limit Jack's. And Jack's world will be identical to Jean's, for the English world was all connected up then, and it is a world that possesses him, and her, rather than the other way around. It is a world that I would one day struggle pathologically to escape from, to redefine, just as my mother would cling to it like precious, drenched jetsam.

I stare at my grandfather, trying to make him out through the pall of seventy years. Art looks well-to-do, but he was brought up on the barrows, in the markets. He went from the stalls to a cart pulled by two horses, one called Bill and the other, with some irony, Lightning. Then he bought the Wolseley. He is still only one, maybe two steps from being a coster. Here is the first great dividing line between him and me. He knows who he is. An Englishman, and a native Londoner before the idea became themed, diluted, mocked and bastardized. He is also very clearly a man, a patriarch in the Victorian sense, and a worker, working class. These things define him, just as they hem him in. He is also poor, extremely poor by my standards, but not by those of his time. He lives in a two-bedroom flat above the shop, with his three boys, Ken, Jack and Arthur. He shares the flat with Floss and Charlie and their two children.

The choice of the shop as backdrop for the portrait is apt. This world is one entirely driven and measured by work, for there is little in the way of welfare and the price of failure is shame and destitution, or worse, charity. Cissy, although known as something of a slacker, was back working in the shop the day after my father was born. At busy times, after the family left the flat in 1936, Art slept on the floor of the shop rather than wasting time by going home.

Art worked from Tuesday to Saturday in the shop, then on Mondays used the shop van for furniture deliveries. There were no problems regarding the purpose, the use of time, as there will be for my relatively spoilt generation. It was there to ensure the only ambition possible, that of survival, through diligence and graft.

I notice that the three women in the photograph – Floss, Cissy and the customer – each have precisely the same expression. Coy, noncommittal, bland, it is entirely sexless, for in this England, sex remains subterranean and furtive, couched about with ignorance and shame. There are in fact 75,000 prostitutes in London, but that is a world that does not stretch to this part of Lambeth, where people would not even kiss or embrace in public.

I sort through the rest of the photographs. They can, I see, be divided into three categories: professional portraits, printed on to postcards, inscribed on the back with a gap for the address and stamp; group photographs, of family, clubs, associations; and snapshots, of holidays and picnics, and occasionally the streets of Crystal Palace.

I inspect the postcards first. Here is Art, standing in front of his van in leather knee boots, jodhpurs, a flat cap and a cravat. Here he is again, this time in the uniform of the Royal Horse Artillery, holding a riding crop in one hand and his daughter, Vera, in the other. She will die a few years later. In this world, death is still an insistent and hectoring visitor, still devoid of the taboo that now labours to deny it. Cissy sits next to him, holding Jack's older brother, Ken, who is maybe a year old. She looks fresh and pretty, and slightly apprehensive of her happiness, as if she senses some fragility in it.

Here is Hetty, one of my grandmother's five sisters, looking beautiful and shy in a black belted jacket and a wide-brimmed hat decorated with white feathers. The photograph is inscribed, in luscious copperplate, *Yours Sincerely, Hetty*. Further down the pile, another posed shot of her, her face now turned chisel-tough, posed in a blinding snowstorm, staged by a studio photographer. The bitter lines of her mouth suggest that her sons, unborn in the first photograph, have by now been swallowed up by larger forces, George, the RAF pilot shot down over France, and Arthur taken by epileptic seizures.

It is as if Hetty has been paid back for her extraordinary good luck in marriage. George and Arthur were the sons of a Swiss 'noble' (the title was purchased) and Lloyd's underwriter, the Count Emil de Villemieur, whom Hetty had skivvied for, then run off with. Such dalliances were not unusual – *droit de seigneur* for anyone who employed domestics was established practice. It was rumoured that Cissy herself was the daughter of the dentist who Granny Starr skivvied for. But to marry the help was virtually unheard of.

Here is Hetty again with her daughter, the survivor, Ladybird, or Bud as she is known. And one more snap, all of my grandmother's sisters together with their mother, Granny Starr: Edie, Rose, Daisy, Cissy, Nellie and Hetty. The choice of their names was strictly defined by their social place, as was every other aspect.

Class was merely one of the many invisible borders that divided up England then, a time over-simplified as a single, seamless unity. Cissy and Art, apart from their social standing, were metropolitan, Londoners, English and powerfully prejudiced. They looked askance at, and down upon, country yokels, clog-wearing Northerners, the crafty Welsh, the thick Irish and the mean Scots. Art would have had no doubt about who was the feebler sex, and foreigners didn't even count as proper people, except possibly Yanks, who were nevertheless flashy and big-headed. The rest were slimy wops, greasy dagos, funny coons, poofy frogs, rapacious Ikeys, humourless squareheads. When Bill Cole, Cissy's brother-in-law – nicknamed Tony because of his Mediterranean darkness – was branded a dago while a farrier in the army, he threatened to put a pitchfork through his accuser. When the insult was not retracted, Tony threw a knife at him and narrowly missed killing him. *Nobody calls me a black bastard*, said Tony, proudly. It was the ultimate insult, to be supposed to be not white, not English.

I pick up the last three postcard portraits, the only ones of this period from Jean's side of the family. The first two show her older brothers, Alan and Norman, at about a year old, one perched on what appears to be a cheap mahogany table, the other balanced on a velvet cushion. Norman as an adult will turn to drink after his wife abandons him and his three daughters, and Alan will become a chronic mental patient. It is strange to see them here, innocent of the future and yet perhaps with the future stored up in them, as an oak tree is inside an acorn. And last of all, barely recognizable, here is Jean, also innocent of her fate, again on a cushion, this time embroidered with flowers. She too is maybe a year old. Her face is as round as a football and her hair sticks up like a rooster's comb. Try as I might, I cannot imagine her as my mother. She is just an anonymous, rather overweight baby.

I turn to the next batch of snapshots. These are group shots and the groups are large, thirty or so people, for this is an England that is collective, communal, extended. The loss of place, the vacuum that is around us now like murderous, invisible fall-out, is beyond their imagination. On top of the pile is a picture of the house in Essex Grove, half a mile from the shop, which Cissy and Art rent in the mid-1930s. They will share the house with Daisy, my grandmother's sister, and her husband, the knife-throwing Tony, who is a bus driver. Ken, Jack's oldest brother, shares a room with his wife-to-be, Irene. This is unusual, unconventional, and Cissy does not approve, but she puts up with it.

Ken works in the Hey Presto! dry-cleaners on Anerley Hill, half a mile away. Almost immediately opposite lives Vic Cole (no relation to Tony), who is married to Cecilia's other sister, Edie. Rose, another sister, who is wild, a little touched, lives a few streets away in one direction. Granny Starr, who has a job cleaning toilets at the Crystal Palace, lives a few streets away in the other, in Berridge Road. Everything is interlinked, communal, close-weaved.

There are three group shots, each of them of the St Margaret Wheelers, the cycling club that Art ran from Essex Grove. Cycling, hiking and rambling are booming at the time, partly a manifestation of the 'fresh air and exercise' cult imported from Germany, partly of the bottomless English love of countryside. Cissy and Art, with Jack sitting on a petrol can, would follow the cyclists down to Brighton, ready to pick up anyone who got the 'bonkers', or cramp.

The cycle club, along with the shop, is the hub of Art and Cissy's social world. At weekends the place is like a club – Art even installs a cigarette machine when they move to Essex Grove. There are many forms of amusement, even in this work-haunted England: cinema, radio, eurhythmics (pre-war aerobics), dirt-track racing, wrestling, football, pigeon-fancying – the list is long and varied. There are also cheap books, for England, even working-class England, is by far the most literate country in the world. But the only bought book in the Essex Grove house is James T. Farrell's *Studs Lonigan*, a racy thriller that Ken hides in his drawer and Jack furtively speed-reads while he is out at work.

Most of the people in the photograph are local and would have been known to Art and Cissy quite separately from their involvement with the cycling club. It is, in fact, unusual to see anyone in Gipsy Hill or Essex Grove whose name you do not know. The people in this England are not anonymous; they have names and histories.

The faces in the photograph look tanned and healthy, and strangely modern since the hairstyles – long fringe, swept back or with side parting, short at back and sides – were rediscovered in the 1980s. One of the men, inexplicably, even appears to be wearing a baseball cap.

The final batch of photographs comprises snapshots, mostly taken on trips to Margate or Brighton, or picnics at Runnymede or Windsor, but occasionally in the streets of Crystal Palace. Here is Jack in a heavy steel pram on a bright day. My father, when he appears in this first batch, squints at me through infant though recognizable eyes, pursing the mouth that would one day recite its single sad question. By the thickness of his mother's coat, I suppose it must be cold. The street behind, which is wide and unmarked by white lines, is entirely empty of traffic, moving or stationary, except for one solitary black Wolseley. The car cult, which, like television, will tear apart these insular yet interleaved lives, is again beyond imagination.

The seaside snaps are somehow the most evocative, because the sand and the sea feel buried deep in the English unconscious, the romance of starfish and rock-pools, red crabs the size of tea plates and cubes of ice-cream. Here are Arthur, Ladybird and George, in one-piece bathing singlets that cover their chests. Here are Arthur, Jack and Ken, paddling in the surf and digging in the sand. With their scratchy, soaked cotton shorts – there are no artificial fibres – they are wearing ties and white shirts. Formality is inescapable, even here. In the background of the photos are stolid boarding houses and low-rise hotels. Even if they could have afforded it, Cissy and Art would not have felt comfortable in the hotels. The buildings are organic, gentle, slightly pompous, not geometric, or brutal, or dynamic. The language is one of security and provincial snobbery, of tea-cakes and chequered Battenberg and fish paste sandwiches.

In another photograph, this time of a picnic, Art and Cissy are in full Sunday dress, Art dark-suited and flat-capped, Cissy with fake pearls and a soft brimless hat. Here are Arthur and Jack, with handkerchiefs around their heads. They will be eating pies, pickles, Cheddar cheese, bleached white bread. They will not argue or shout too loud, even on this day off. Everything here is muffled, kept back. It is Japanese in its restraint.

It occurs to me that almost every modern, ordinary English family must have photographs in their drawers of such familiar strangers, drenched in dead light. These photographs are a link between me and these other, faceless families, people I have always imagined as quite separate, nothing much to do with me. But perhaps we remain connected after all, if only by a lost, half-forgotten past.

As I spread all the photographs from the 1920s randomly in

front of me, it occurs to me that the black-and-white world they show is more true to life than you might expect, because England in the 1920s tended towards the monochrome itself. There is little in the way of coloured cloth or paint. The women's make-up, if it is there at all, is pale and natural. The newspapers have no colour printing, the cinema has no colour movies. The sky is usually dun or grey, and there are frequent fogs, 'London Particulars', though more rarely here in Norwood – the 'Fresh Air Suburb', as the marketing men of the 1930s dubbed it. There are no lurid posters or psychologically colour-coded product packaging. Advertising is simple and informative rather than surrealistic and lurid.

The monochrome wash goes beyond the visual, inside and under the skin. Values in this place are without grey tone, are well defined and stark. Right is right and wrong is wrong and the difference is simple enough, and inscribed in the law. Criminals can be hanged and are often flogged, for relatively minor property offences, but there is little crime, largely because there is very little to steal. Women guilty of under-age sex or adultery are sometimes put in asylums and prisons. Men who beat their wives and children are thought to be within their rights. There is none of the modern sense that what is clearly wrongdoing needs treatment rather than punishment – no counsellors, or helplines, or group therapy centres. You get on with it. You cope. If you break the rules, you face the punishment and you don't bleat. It is this world, sanitized of course, that a rigid, regretful part of England even now aches for – that certainty.

But if this world, or at least the myth of this world that Jack and, five years later, Jean were born into, was in some ways, to some eyes, enviable, it was also dull, cold, spartan and entirely hedged about by necessity. As Jack emerged into the London air, screaming blue murder, his family could have little doubt about what his future would bring. He would go to school until fourteen, changing into long trousers at the age of eleven. Then he would go to work, probably for the family. Having secured a job, which would be manual and at best semi-skilled, he would be considered a man. He would get married in his mid-twenties and

46

have children, who would then have children in their mid-twenties. If they were lucky, they would live in a house with a garden. And that was it, that was life. Everything was mapped out in advance. There was no burden of choice or rage at limits, because that was a waste of time. The cake was baked and cut.

Jack's childhood was unremarkable in almost every respect. After a brief period living in the flat above the greengrocer's shop, Art and Cissy moved into a rented house half a mile away in Essex Grove. The business was doing well and the Lotts, by the standards of the time, were growing prosperous. They even had a telephone. But if the trappings were upwardly mobile, the psychological place they inhabited remained fixed, with its private, particular language and customs. They ate dinner, not lunch, at midday, and tea, not supper, in the evening. If it was a special occasion, they had serviettes, not napkins. They listened to the wireless on a settee, not a sofa, in the lounge, not the living room. They used a toilet instead of a lavatory. The hats, when they wore hats, were flat, or small bowlers cocked to one side (parodying the larger bowlers of the professionals), trilbys or Homburgs. Each clearly advertised their origins, their immutable place.

There was a parlour, a 'best room', that was almost never used. The front step was attacked with soap and bristle every day. Cleanliness was the totem of respectability. Neighbours — and the opinions of neighbours mattered — checked laundry and curtains for signs of slippage. They smoked Woodbines, or Players, not De Reszke or Du Maurier. Cissy kept the end on a hatpin so she could take it in to the last gasp — the best bit, she always said. Their language itself proclaimed their identity. Cockney — rhyming rather than the rarer backslang of Covent Garden market — although diluted and half-ironic already, was still threaded unselfconsciously through their language, and was still private to some extent, separate and secret to the other layers of England.

The patterns of Jack's life as a boy were much the same as any of the well-off working class. While Cissy worked in the shop, he was brought up much of the time by his Aunty Rose, who visited from Colby Road, 100 yards away. In the morning, he would lie in bed and listen to the cows come down from the field to the

Express Dairy three doors along. Urban England even smelt different then, of horses, dung and soot, rather than petrol and dog shit.

Jack loved Rose, although she was a rough diamond by any measure, a hobbledehoy. Tall and thin, with red hair and only one tooth, she would pick up men in the pub and let them take her in the backs of cars for the price of a drink. She drank, smoked and swore. She had three husbands: Ted, a no-good who beat her; One-Legged Jim, who left her; and Alf, who gave her triplets.

At the age of five Jack went to Woodland Road School in Cawnpore Street, where he did well, but was teased because he was gnome-like and fat. At the age of nine, when the family moved to Essex Grove, he transferred to Rockmount School, where he was teased again, by Nobby Reeves, who had a hole in his nose where he had been shot by a peashooter. Nobby would swing him around by the legs and once swung him against an iron lamppost. Jack finally turned and attacked him, absolutely bloody creased him (no child would say *fucking* then, not even in their head). The bullying stopped.

The routines of school were punctuated by the routines of family and English life. The three-times-daily food was plain stodge. They ate for sustenance rather than for pleasure, or theatre, or sensuality: boiled hams or fish, Cornish pasties, mince and onion pies, roast meats and fry-ups, bubble and squeak, bread with dripping. The vegetables – potatoes, sprouts, cabbage, peas – were heavily boiled. The puddings and cakes were dense, a kind of ballast – rock cakes, scones, semolina pudding, bread pudding, suet pudding, treacle tart, spotted dick, jam roly-poly, stewed rhubarb or gooseberries, custard, cake with salad cream on it.

There was a fair amount of ceremonial life which would, decades later, be whittled away by shopping and home improvement. There were the now forgotten, abolished or largely ignored public celebrations of Empire Day, Commonwealth Day, May Day, the National Day of Prayer, St George's Day and Armistice Day.

Jack would actually dance around a maypole. Rural England penetrated deep into metropolitan life, with English country dancing, hornpipes and reels taught in all the schools. He went to Sunday school and sang hymns and folk-songs – 'Jerusalem' and 'The Ash Grove' were his favourites – and attended Cubs and Scouts at the 37th Croydon in Coopers Yard, behind the High Street, pledging loyalty to King, country and Empire, and occasionally going camping with the troop.

What mostly engaged Jack's attention, though, were the first ripples of the electronic common culture that was beginning to establish itself, operating from two poles, one of them domestic, the other largely – and uniquely in this England – foreign. The BBC had begun broadcasting in 1922 and by the 1930s nearly every household had a crystal set or wireless. The programmes were staid, educational, cosy, but it was an amazing thing to hear sounds collected from the air emerging from a rosewood box. Jack would fall asleep listening to *In Town Tonight* or Arthur Askey or the plummy, reassuring tones of the newsreaders.

But it was the cinema that thrilled Jack's – and every other child's – imagination more than anything else – the first great hustle by another culture into the isolated life of England which, up until this point, had remained a unique, peculiar and yet essentially European place. Great cinemas were being built around him: the Electra, the Albany, the Rialto, the 4,000-seat Davies Cinema in Croydon. He watched cowboy movies, monster movies and war movies endlessly. You could stay in the cinema all day without paying extra, and they would bring you a cup of tea and cakes while you watched, and sucked it all in.

I move to the next batch of photographs, the 1930s. In the larger world, there is the Great Depression, the Spanish Civil War, the rise of Stalin and Hitler. But the faces in these photographs are untroubled, and there is a certain truth in this, at least for anyone who had work. Then, as now, the newspapers would talk about the 'nation' being shocked, or saddened, or outraged, or angry, but such a nation is largely fiction. Cissy and Art, and Grace and Billy – my mother's parents, who begin to emerge tentatively from the photographic negatives now – are insular and uninterested in the larger world, except as a sideshow, as light entertainment or drama. They do not march, or write letters, or join political parties, or carry placards. King George, who dies in 1936 and is genuinely mourned nationally, had summed it up: *I don't like abroad. I've been there.* Survival, and the family, are the only imperatives. What strange, irrational foreigners are doing is of only anecdotal interest in Lambeth.

In these photographs, there are still only a few traces of my mother, my father dominating the family history still. Here he is once more in poses that are concentrating into cliché: lost in a group of grinning Boy Scouts, nervous on a donkey at Margate, attending to a kettle outside a tent. He is developing, like an emerging Polaroid, into the man I still recognize today, the narrowed, puffy eyes, the slight arrogance which I have inherited and inflated, the confident good looks, which I have not. Three photographs stand out.

In one, Jack and his brother Arthur are standing in an alleyway. Jack holds the bat and Arthur, the ball. They wear threadbare V-neck pullovers, knee socks, shorts, sandals. The background is a brick wall and a gritted, unfinished street. It is not the content of the photograph that is unusual but the texture, the emptiness of the light, the particular grain – the atmosphere. It is washed out, closed in, somehow delicate. For some reason it reminds me of a still from Max Reinhardt's *A Midsummer Night's Dream*. They are a mixture of Puck and the silvery street urchins photographed by Bert Hardy for *Picture Post*, lost boys. The colour of the picture, a china tea stain, the colour of that world is touched with something like innocence, and is entirely gone now. I cannot explain its poignancy, yet it provokes a definite, rich sadness in me, like many of these pictures.

In the second, Jack is standing as one of a group of four. He is at the back, with Arthur next to him and two young girls in front. They are seven or eight years old. They stand in an open field and a chestnut tree spreads in the far background. Arthur and Jack are in uniform, the Boys' Brigade. They wear simple pillbox hats. Arthur blows a toy trumpet with a Union Jack attached to its stem. There is no wind to move the flag. In front of them, the two little girls are in white dresses and also pillbox hats. They too have Union Jacks, which they hold as if told to do so firmly by a grown-up. One of the girls is clutching a white handkerchief and looks shy. The other seems annoyed, and one imagines her knuckles white around the flag stick that she so fiercely clutches. Arthur is grinning full-bloodedly, trumpet to mouth, while Jack is smiling faintly, his hooded eyes almost disappearing under the squint of the light. It seems that he feels ridiculous.

The third photograph is simply funny. It was clearly taken at the end of the decade, for Jack is now an adolescent. He is standing in a half-lit field, and the shadow of the photographer, a woman by the silhouette, is etched on his midriff. What is funny about the photograph is that Jack is ludicrously fat and is stuffed into a three-piece suit that does not fit. It is presumably his first suit and it is something he is very obviously unaccustomed to. His fists are clenched, perhaps in embarrassment, and his face is buried in a roll of jowl and cheek; he is grinning desperately. It is around this time that Jack is christened Fatty Lott at school and the appellation, though cruel, fits. The buttons on the suit are clearly defying natural laws in order to stay in place, suggesting that the cloth will burst off in all directions at any moment, leaving my father naked among the leaves.

And this is the end of it for Jack, for my father, in these pre-war years; this is all I can make of him. A fat, ordinary kid with a tough father, a tolerant, rather lazy mother and a family rough as worsted at the edges. His childhood is unremarkable for the era, entirely typical, which to me is why it is interesting. However, in childhood Jack will witness two events which interrupt the accustomed banality, one of them poetic and national, one entirely personal, both of them disastrous.

Chapter Five

But where is Jean, my mother? Her ghost is still cautious, hidden, rarely captured by light. There are only two photographs of her and they seem simply echoes of the earlier snap, of her unfamiliar and perched on a cushion.

Here she is on a rocky beach at Southend, in white, poking at the ground with a stick. She is staring into the distance, with clenched eyes. There is something in her whole self – perhaps this is my imagination only – that suggests determination. Is it the set of the mouth?

In the second photograph she is older, maybe four or five. Now I begin to see her, but only very slightly. The odd thing is, she looks scared, nervous, in a setting that is clearly meant to be comic. It is the back yard of her parents' house in Southall, a few streets away from Rutland Road. She is sitting astride the lid of a metal dustbin, wearing a coarse woollen pullover. Her legs are bare and her socks have ridden down to her ankles. Her hair has grown now, and is indeed beautiful, stuffed with ringlets, shining. In the background, the tiny house where she grew up. It strikes me that in none of the three photographs that exist of her before the war is she smiling.

The only other snared moment from Jean's side of the family is a picture of Billy, my maternal grandfather, sitting in an anonymous field smoking a cigarette, wearing a three-piece suit and tie. He is a small, compact man, with hair brilliantined into place, which gives his face a severe, angular look. His cheekbones punch out from space between ear and mouth, and a cigarette projects from his lips as proud as a Churchill cigar. He too is unsmiling, and there is strength and a sort of anger in his face. His shoes are flashy, white. There are no photographs of his wife, Grace, or Jean's brothers, Alan and Norman.

But I know more about Jean and her brothers, and Billy and Grace, much more than the photographs can yield. I know that the world she inhabited was, in most of its fundamentals, a mirror of Jack's: the same class, the same private language, the same cluster of attitudes, the same narrow clutch of possibilities. Of course, Jean was born a girl and this confined her in a number of unique ways, but mainly they grew up absorbing the same certainties.

Jean was born on 17 January 1931 in a small rented flat in Shepherd's Bush, west London. Billy Haynes had been a baker at the Lyons factory in Battersea ever since the end of the First World War. Then he was on the Russian front with the White Army, sent to crush the upstart Bolsheviks. Had he seen men die, perhaps killed one across the snow with his Lee Enfield? He never once talked about it. This blanket of silence, the suspicion of thoughts and feelings openly expressed, linked England, at all levels, like no other trait. Everything had to be guessed at, inferred. As if in self-defence, sadness was never aired, was walled up. *Just get on with it.* Life was life. Say what you like, it won't change anything.

Billy walked to Battersea every day, leaving Grace, his large, plain wife, to look after the three children. One generation back, Billy's family were agricultural labourers, while Grace's paternal grandfather's profession is described on her parents' wedding certificate as 'artist', and the maternal grandfather has the given name of Jacob. At the time of the wedding in 1897, they lived in Forest Gate, at the centre of the Jewish settlement in the East End.

Rockley Road in Shepherd's Bush was dirty and poor, though still respectable, but after Jean was born the flat became cramped. Like thousands of inner-city families in the 1930s, Grace and Billy began to hope that they might move out to the new suburbs that were rising on the clay at the city's edges. A massive house-building process was under way, sucking the population into the inner-outer suburbs much as the railways created so many provincial towns in the previous century.

Grace, who, it was accepted, ran the household, had begun to feel this pull, away from the grime and insecurity of inner London to a different dream, of gardens and trees and inside bathrooms. It would mean getting a mortgage, but they would have true independence for the first time. She mentioned it to Billy, who was normally compliant, passing over the pay packet dutifully, unopened, at the end of each week. But, always deeply conservative, he was against it, thinking it too big a step.

Then, as chance would have it, it turned out that Billy's manager at the bakery, Harry Hecken, was earning a little cash on the side by acting as an agent for a Wimpey site manager in Southall, where a new and quite archetypal development was sprouting at the edges of the Western Avenue on one side and the Great West Road on the other. The houses were small, arranged in terraces, brand new and bright as a pin. Harry introduced Billy to the site manager, in the hope of picking up his £5 commission.

The site manager could see that Billy was nervous and wavering. He offered him six months in the house free, to give him time to earn the deposit for the mortgage company, and said that for fifty shillings he would put in a path at the back and build a shed. Even Billy was tempted, though it would mean two ten-mile cycle rides a day, to and from work. But to be a house-owner, a man of property, now that was something, that was substance. What with Grace *gung ho*, and the three kids running wild in the small flat, Billy made his decision. *Harry, I want it.* Harry was pleased that Billy, a good worker, a straight arrow, was doing the modern thing, quite apart from the commission. In the end he split the fiver with Billy anyway.

When they moved into the house in 1934, the street was still being built around them and was full of gravel and cement mixers and shouting workmen. This was a different world from the Bush, though. It was clean and there was fresh air, with roses and rowan trees in the front gardens.

There were two rooms downstairs. The parlour at the front, Grace decided, despite the lack of space, would be used only for best, on Sundays, for visitors. The back room, which had an open fire and french doors out to the coal cellar and scrubby garden, would be where the family lived. From here there was a door through to the tiny kitchen and scullery, with its deep sink, water heater and wooden draining board.

Upstairs, Grace and Billy took the largest room at the back, which overlooked the garden and was next to the small inside toilet, which they would learn to call a loo when being polite, just as they would adjust to call a pudding *sweet* or pronounce garage (*garridge*) as *garaadg*. Alan and Norman took the larger of the front rooms, overlooking the still uncoiling Rosecroft Road, and Jean had the box room, no more than six foot by six foot but with the unaccustomed promise of privacy.

Over the next few years the house began to take on the modest trappings of the entirely new class to which Billy and Grace now belonged, the suburban, home-owning working class. It was not prosperous – there were still children in the street who had no shoes – but it was undoubtedly progress.

Grace and Billy set to work to make their mark and show they were in the ascendant. The floors were decked in a dun-coloured mosaic lino, with a scrap of maroon carpet in the back room and a stair runner laid by one of the neighbours who worked as a fitter at Harrods. The front room, as Grace intended, was pristine, a sort of shrine, with a hard, scrubbed clean *settee*, and a glass case full of souvenirs from Margate and cheap ornaments – nickel silver spoons, crystal glasses from broken-up sets, a bottle of sherry, a few books, Zane Grey or Edgar Wallace. There was even an upright piano which Jean would half-heartedly take lessons on, only to give up after two or three years. It was always cold in this room, with a prissy, formal air.

In the hallway was a hatstand, a mirror and a framed print of a gypsy woman pouring tea in her caravan. The hard lino led you into the warmth of the back room, where there was the closest Grace and Billy had to an heirloom, a Victorian *chaise-longue* in red velvet plush, the wood polished furiously into a thick sheen. There was a table, usually with knitting needles and balls of wool on it, and a large mahogany gramophone, the turntable of which Billy would sometimes use for piping icing on to cakes. There were two brass candlesticks and a cheap oval mirror engraved with the image of a Victorian lady with a floral hat. There were plates with mottoes and sentimental rhymes about the sanctity of the family and the value of friendship. The ceiling was Camp coffee brown.

The kitchen smelled of stewed tea, and the taps had long rubber nipples on them to direct the flow of water from the Ascot heater. In the larder, custard powder, butter, cochineal made of crushed red beetles, flour, Bovril, cream crackers, evaporated milk, Libby's tinned peaches. Grace would wash clothes in the butler's sink and work them on an old scrubbing board. Even when washing machines came within their budget, she turned the idea down. They couldn't get Billy's white overalls clean enough, she said.

In the main bedroom upstairs, a large double bed, the bed Billy will one day die in, as I watch, a child, puzzled. *Timmy, I'm so scared.* There was a bolster under the pillow. Two paintings of Greek Muses, semi-nude, which disappeared when Alan and Norman reached puberty. An airing cupboard full of towels and fresh clothes, a candlewick bedspread, tasselled around the edges. There were doilies made out of heavy wool, a dressing table with three mirrors and a silver-backed brush with matching hand-mirror. It was a feminine room, soft with feather pillows and the smell of clean shirts, decorated with flowers, and cream print floral curtains. The wallpaper was pale green and blue flowers confined within horizontal parallels.

The boys' room was sparse, two beds and a few cheap toys – Airfix models and Dinky cars, jigsaws – while Jean's had hardly room for anything except the bed and a tiny dressing table. There was eau-de-Nil wallpaper, small soft squares that contained geometric patterns, containing, in turn, floral designs.

The doorframes were cream, with opalescent lights above all the doors.

After a year or two in the new house, Billy decided that the cycle rides every day were too much. There was a job for a baker at the Lyons factory in Southall and he took the job for a slight increase in wages. He and Grace were happy, although they didn't think about it in those terms; you didn't ask whether or not you were content. Everything was about continuity, nothing more. All other spoken or thought life was waste product, indulgence.

Initially the children seemed to be doing well, all attending Lady Margaret Infants and Junior School, but then there was some trouble with Alan. He seemed a little slow and uncertain, unable to keep up. Some of the teachers thought he would do better at a special school and reluctantly, slightly ashamed, Billy and Grace agreed that he should be moved to Talbot Road School in Southall, where, they were told, his needs would be better catered for. It turned out that the school was full of the mentally handicapped, with Down's Syndrome children and autistics. It seemed a bit extreme to put Alan there, just for being slow, but Billy and Grace decided that the authorities knew best.

Jean was a good, well-behaved if slightly spoilt girl who rarely gave trouble. She adored her older brothers, particularly Norman, who was already showing some of the waywardness that would fully flower after the war on the disreputable edges of the Soho underworld. Norman was tough and had a reputation as a scrapper. It made Jean feel safe and a little proud.

For Jean the 1930s were spent much as for Jack, the beat, beat, beat of automatic life: school; a week's holidays at the seaside once a year – Southend instead of Margate; playing in the street; listening to the wireless; going to the cinema; reading. Jean might have read *Girls' Own Paper* rather than *Champion* or *Hornet*, might have seen *Gone With the Wind* instead of gun movies with Tom Mix or Edward G., might have spent a hot evening dressing up in front of the mirror rather than kicking a football over the rec. But the messages were the same: always behave; work hard; know your place; keep your nose clean. Things might be tough, but they would turn out all right in the end.

I stare once more at the three photographs of Jean, hard, as if I can penetrate them somehow by force of will. There is no trace of any aberration, any twist or wrinkle in Jean's childhood that might have curdled her inside, that might have tended her towards buried rage or desperate self-hatred, to be carried through life like a loaded gun in the bottom drawer. No one can remember that she had anything other than a happy childhood with a loving, rather conventional family. Memory is treacherous, a myth-maker and liar, but it is all there is left of Jean, the only light with which to probe. There was no clue in her behaviour – no truancy, uncontrollable rages, over-compliancy, physical eruptions – to what was still out of sight in an identical house, in an identical street, 250 yards and half a century away, an ambulance trembling outside.

But there was one vital component in her make-up, in the ways open to her to make sense of the world – not individual so much as general, at least generally female – that did vary essentially from my father's. For a girl from Jean's class in the 1930s there was only one destiny: she would be a housewife and mother.

To be a woman was to be married, to be married was to have children. Then you would give them your all, and their happiness would be the emblem of your success. Sacrifice and devotion were not just possibilities chosen from some vague, unprinted menu. It was the role cast by every source of knowing that there was. Each romantic film the cinema threw out made for proof of a woman's proper destiny. The selfish, the clever, the ambitious, those that deviated, were left alone, or died remorseful, or gave up their careers and got married gratefully. This same pattern appeared in comics, in books, in radio serials, in advertising and *Good Housekeeping* magazine, in every kind of popular storyline. The crippled, orphaned, martyred ballet dancer of *Bunty* or *Mandy* was finally, joyfully redeemed. The heroine of every Mills and Boon romantic novel suffered terribly for love, to be rewarded finally with a kiss and an offer of marriage and motherhood.

Just as the male was there to go out and vanquish, to slay dragons, the female was required to cast herself into the flames if necessary, to save the only thing, absolutely the only thing, that really mattered: the family – the man and the children. Imagination, public imagination, was curtailed, whalebone-corseted.

Jean could distinguish fantasy from reality, inasmuch as anyone can. She was no fool, but smart and knowing, in her way. She did not swallow the movies and comics like a computer uncomplainingly swallows its software. However, perhaps it was not what was put into the films and books but what was left out that counted. It was that absence that set horizons to the imagination. If you were going to dream of a different future for yourself, you would have to be a person with remarkable self-confidence and determination.

Jean possessed determination, but she lacked, like many women of her generation, a strong sense of self. That was the way life was arranged, always had been, to keep things the same. And this is something to bear in mind, maybe the first indisputable, unavoidable clue – since it is clues I suppose I am looking for – the first thread in the hanging rope.

Like Jack's, Jean's childhood ended, practically speaking, in September 1939, when war broke out. It had been an undistinguished time, as unremarkable as Jack's. In fact, it was even more unremarkable, because, as I have said, real drama touched Jack's early life on two occasions.

If the Crystal Palace could cast shadows, it would have settled, on a late summer afternoon, over the Wells and Lott greengrocer's shop in Gipsy Hill. All through Jack's childhood, it was a presence as firm and indestructible as all the other, still more transparent structures that bounded the space within him.

The palace was a building of awesome proportions. Made entirely of glass and iron, it was capable of enveloping more than six St Paul's Cathedrals, although the walls were only eight inches thick. Although lopsided now, due to a fire in 1866 which destroyed the north transept, it was the incredible conceit of an age that considered itself immutable, without end and blessed by God.

It was first erected in Hyde Park for the Great Exhibition of 1851 at the behest of the Prince Consort, Albert, who gave the commission to the Duke of Devonshire's gardener, Joseph Paxton. The great hall was to show examples of British design and manufacture, together with exhibits from all over the world, and would be a symbol, according to Prince Albert, of peace and love between individuals and nations.

Paxton conceived of an amazing structure that would dazzle a world up until now enclosed in opaque, heavy brick and plaster, stucco, tiling and cement. His building would enclose tremendous volume with negligible mass. As a design, it was derided – 'a cucumber frame between two chimneys', according to John Ruskin – but from the moment of its erection, the palace dazzled everyone who saw it. It was described as the eighth wonder of the world. When Queen Victoria arrived to open it, so proud was the singing of the national anthem that many in the 1,800-strong choir and orchestra were seen openly to cry.

The cliffs of glass that enclosed whole elm trees and fields where sparrows still flew wildly in the roofs, seemed an apparition. Four hundred tons of glass and cross-braced iron framing enclosed 100,000 exhibits. The glass had a magical, hallucinatory quality and seemed to change colour with the weather. Inside there was a fountain made of crystal twenty-seven feet high, together with boating lakes and mazes, all enclosed within the great naves, towers, arches and transepts. Eden itself, said one diarist. A place of wonder and mystery, said another. A fairyland, said Queen Victoria.

After the exhibition closed, the palace, which had attracted vast crowds – 6 million in all, the total population of England at the time – was moved to Upper Norwood, with views that spread across the metropolis in one direction and towards Brighton in the other. In its reincarnation, it was even more massive, impossible to take in at a glance, rising to six storeys in places and with the addition of two new barrel-vaulted transepts. It opened with a performance of the 'Hallelujah Chorus', accompanied by the immense Handel organ, around which the whole structure spread, 4,568 pipes stretching towards the smiling heavens. One of the greatest and most glorious days of our lives, said the Queen. New rail lines were laid in order to reach it and two huge water towers, each 100 feet taller than Nelson's Column, were built at each end of the nave to feed the largest fountain in the world, 250 feet high, and the great cascades below it.

The new palace was divided up into courts – Greek, Roman, Egyptian, Moorish, Medieval and so on. There were great sphinxes, a zoo, exotic plants, huge models of thirty-three dinosaurs. Magnificent firework displays took place every week, culminating in great flaming portraits and tableaux ninety feet high and 200 feet wide: the launching of Stephenson's Rocket, the Battle of Manila Bay, portraits of English heroes like the Duke of Wellington and Baden-Powell or 'exotics' – Cetewayo, King of the Zulus, and the Shah of Persia. Concerts took place regularly, and balloons flew over the palace with acrobats hanging from trapezes by their teeth. There were restaurants and cafés, and landscaped gardens. Visitors were sucked into its trapped emptiness from all over the world. It was intoxicating, impossible.

By the time Jack was born, the great palace was showing signs of wear. The Handel concerts had been replaced by brass bands, the fountains had mostly dried up. There was dog racing and football now, and boxing, dances, dog shows, dirt-track racing. The great firework displays continued, watched every week by the infant Jack from his bedroom window, but the company that ran the palace had gone bankrupt and the vast edifice was wreathed in a cloud of shabbiness evinced by peeling paint and dirty corners. Yet it remained an incredible thing, perhaps the greatest surviving symbol of English self-confidence.

On 30 November 1936 Jack had spent an ordinary, dull day at Rockmount School, shouting, kicking a ball about, hurling water bombs. Already overweight, he fended off bullies as best he could. He looked forward that night to going to the talkies with Rita Cole, his now ostracized cousin. They were both outsiders in their way, both smarter than they should have been. Jack went home to the house in Essex Grove and had some tea – sausage toad and leftover batter with jam for pudding. Still in long socks and shorts – the change into long trousers would come next year – he set off with Rita to the Albany Cinema in Anerley Hill. It was cold and windy, so he wore a rough wool sleeveless V-neck pullover under his coat. There was a double bill playing: *Public Hero Number One* (a B-grade rejoinder to Edward G.'s more famous film) and something else, cops and robbers, cowboys and Indians, or prisoners and warders.

It was about half-way through the first feature that the rumour began to spread around the cinema. There were noisy whispers that some of the audience tried to quell with a chorus of shushing. Jack listened closely, his attention wandering from the flickering gun battle. The whispers were inaudible but persistent, gathering strength, interfering with the story unfolding in celluloid frames.

After a while, the manager walked on to the stage, his shadow big against the screen. Behind him gangsters walked away from the carnage. He held up his hand and there was a hush as the announcement was made. The cinema had to be evacuated. There was, the manager said, molten glass falling from the sky. The hush took on the character of disbelief. Glass didn't burn, everyone knew that. Anyway it was the palace, the *screaming Alice*; nothing could happen to something so vast and solid. Orderly, subdued, Jack and Rita rose with the audience and pressed towards the exit doors.

Outside, the sky had flared into orange. Standing on the high ground of Sydenham Hill, the palace could clearly be seen glowing through liquefying windows. There were great clouds of smoke and burning fragments in the air. In the gutters, cascades of molten glass and iron. Jack watched people pick bits up and roll them into tiny balls for souvenirs. How did they not get burnt?

Jack knew he should get home, for Art and Cissy would be worried, but the spectacle was irresistible. He stood and stared. Whole panes of glass were flying through the air and crashing into the street. There were frightening sounds too, a terrible groaning and whining like some tremendous mythological Fury. Air was being forced through the bellows of the giant Handel organ in a final, impromptu fugue, pushing out sad, misshapen chords.

Birds were screeching, trying to escape from the aviaries within the palace. The doors were opened and the birds took flight, but the fumes from the smoke overcame them and they crashed insensible, dying, to the ground. Flames, sodium yellow rather than red now that the glass was on fire, were shooting 150 feet into the air, sending clouds of sparks over Gipsy Hill and Sydenham. Higher overhead, there came swarms of planes, rented by sightseers determined to see the greatest firework display ever. The glow from the palace was colossal, and was seen as far away as Dover and Brighton. In the middle of the Channel the pilot of an Imperial Airways plane flying eighty miles away could see the light.

The immense iron girders buckled and twisted grotesquely in the heat. Hundreds of thousands watched as the Crystal Palace turned to liquid and carbon, a great pyre. Jack and Rita reluctantly worked their way home through the crowded streets. Anerley Hill was packed with cars carrying tourists staring at the sky, climbing trees to get a better view. A few hundred yards way, Churchill, on his way from the Commons to Chartwell, watched in tears. *This is the end*, he said. There was a phenomenal crash as the central transept collapsed. Around him, like Churchill, many of the crowd were in tears. But Jack was just excited, thrilled by the largeness of the drama. He and Rita dawdled home, half turning back to listen to the crack of one and a half million square feet of glass disintegrating, and feeling, like the whole of England felt, something end.

The next day Jack got up early to look at the site. The palace had simply gone. Only the water towers still stood, teetering and filthy. At the north end, a few bronze statues gazed down on an ornamental fountain in which there were still goldfish, their scales turned completely black. Nobody died in the fire. Nobody tried to build it again. *The Crystal Palace is finished*, said Henry Buckland, the stricken manager. *There will never be another.*

A year or so after the fire, Jack began to notice a change in his mother, Cissy. She was spending less time in the shop now and seemed constantly tired. Her hair was falling out.

Art didn't like to tell Jack that Cissy was dying. It wasn't something he wanted to think about. Nobody seemed to know what was wrong with her. A 'wasting disease', said the doctors. Tuberculosis perhaps. One thought she might have damaged her insides while working in the shop, hefting sacks of potatoes while she carried Jack inside her.

Her deterioration was plain for anyone to see. The hair, now grown back from the bob that Art hated, framed a face that was increasingly pale and skeletal. Her breathing was fading, becoming strained. Nobody talked about it. Early in 1939, she was admitted to Elmers End Hospital. Jack went to visit her, but could hardly hear her voice sometimes. She told him that she loved him. Jack understood what was happening, although nobody told him.

In May 1939, Cissy died in Elmers End Hospital. Jack had known death before, when Cissy's father, known only as Red Rufus because of his enormous auburn beard, had lain at Granny Starr's house in Berridge Road in the upstairs room, pennies on his eyes. Jack was told to kiss the corpse but he refused, frightened.

This time, Cissy was laid out in the top room of the house in Essex Grove, on the snooker table, and family and friends came to pay respects. Cissy's remains, in the style of the time, were public, to be viewed, kissed or touched. Her favourite niece, Dusty, would stand by the casket, flip out Cissy's long hair and brush it until it shone. The brush had a pearled back, tinted green. Green was allowed now; while Cissy had been alive the colour, in any shade, was not permitted in the house, since she deemed it unlucky. Now her relationship with luck of any kind had played itself out.

Jack avoided the room with its bizarre new furniture. The idea of seeing his mother dead made him queasy. Art was beyond consolation and would not get out of bed. Jack, still only thirteen, understood he had to be strong, that there was no time for grieving. He had to be strong for his father, in his imagination so tough, who had snapped like something rigid but brittle gives way when a force is concentrated in just one place. Art still stayed in bed, although the business was beginning to suffer. Jack began sharing the bed with him at night, worried that his big, powerful father might be lonely. They held each other. His father wept.

On 1 June 1939, Florence Cecilia was buried in Elmers End cemetery. One word appeared on her gravestone: Peace. Aunty Rose moved into Essex Grove to try to help, but things were collapsing; that which moored them had been sheared. Art would just not get out of bed, day or night. Charlie Wells pleaded: the shop would not survive if Art did not come back. Already they had lost Cissy as a worker, and the pressure on Charlie and his wife was becoming impossible. But still Art stayed in bed, and the weeks became months. No doctors came, but the grief had deflated him, taken him beyond grief itself. He was, it was said, suffering from a nervous complaint. In those days, the word 'depression' was not much used. Charlie knew there was no way back and he sold the shop. Art just lay there, beyond help, as everything softly collapsed.

Chapter Six

I am staring at more pictures. This time they are anonymous, grotesque, rather than familiar and faintly reassuring. The pictures are from a book about madness. Here is a tall, semicircular brick construction that has latterly been converted to a linen cupboard. It was used at the Mapperley Hospital in Nottingham during the nineteenth century. Patients were confined within it, then drenched in freezing water in the hope of shocking them out of their melancholy. Here is an ingenious contraption which features a latticed pagoda in the centre of a gently curving bridge over a lake. It has been fixed with levers to collapse in the middle when stepped on and send the centre of the pagoda plunging into the lake below, taking the patient by surprise, again in the hope of scaring him out of his dolour. The date is 1826. Here is an innocent-looking machine which John Wesley used to electrically shock patients in the head in the eighteenth century. And here is an eighteenth-century psychiatric outpatient ward with grotesques pulling on giant magnets, invented by Mesmer in the hope that the magnetic force would rearrange the 'magnetic fluids' in the brain. And here, most horrifically, is a man, apparently terrified, being held by the head while another man – presumably a doctor – thrusts the point of a scalpel into his forehead. It is a seventeenth-century Dutch print of a quack treating mental illness. It is horrible, and I feel glad that these treatments for depression are confined to distant history.

I turn a few pages on. There is a photograph of a serene, patrician-looking man, with thin lips and slick, greased hair. The caption says, 'Egas Moniz'. A Portuguese neurosurgeon and diplomat, António Egas Moniz was shot the year of my grandfather's breakdown by one of his patients. I find this funny for some reason. In 1949, I read, having recovered from his gunshot wound, he was awarded the Nobel Prize for having developed a new method of curing severe depression: prefrontal lobotomy. This involved hacking out portions of the front part of the brain, or injecting alcohol into the cortex to kill off brain cells. I begin to see that this history is not so distant after all, and that it presses distinctly on to the fates of my family.

It just so happens that about the time my grandfather suffered his mental collapse a great wave of new 'scientific' ideas was sweeping away what had previously been characterized as primitive, semi-religious approaches to mental illness. Apart from lobotomy, already being practised by Egas Moniz and other doctors, there was electro-convulsive therapy, pioneered by Ugo Cerletti after experiments on pigs, which sent patients into fits so violent they often fractured bones. There were drug treatments, many of them addictive. Some of them, like insulin shock, were capable of putting the patient into a permanent coma, while others, like cardiazol injections, could give the patient an awful terror of impending death – which was not always misguided, as cardiazol could lead to thrombosis. There was psychoanalysis, pioneered by Freud and now becoming famous, which analysed dreams, mesmerized patients and which in some versions forbade masturbation. There was electric sleep, in which a charge of electricity to the head rendered the patient unconscious.

If Art had decided to visit a doctor who had 'modern' ideas, these represented the menu of ostensibly new but in character rather medieval, magical treatments that could have been tried out to solve the 'problem' of his intractable grief. But my grandfather, so far as I know, did not visit a doctor during his collapse. Quite apart from the expense, to do so would have been the final abandonment of his pride and strength, of what he was meant, by culture, to be: self-reliant, enduring, independent.

Had he overcome those barriers, he would as likely as not have simply been told to go to bed, or to take a warm bath and then 'pull his socks up'. Many doctors, like many laymen, were not sympathetic to what was perceived as weakness or self-pity. Yet if what Art was suffering from could be described as simple grief, his practically comatose state, and its duration, suggest something more.

'Nervous breakdown' is a vague, rather innocent-sounding phrase that suggests a physical failure of the 'nerves', the central nervous system. And in the 1930s that was, despite the vogue for psychoanalysis, how it was largely seen – as a physical complaint. People had 'bad nerves' or 'suffered nerves'. Art's (hypothetical) doctor, if sophisticated enough to be sceptical of the efficacy of baths and the hoisting of socks, may well have prescribed either drugs – amphetamines, barbiturates, both highly addictive – or a period in a mental hospital, for this was the most common form of treatment. And admittance to the hospital *was* the treatment. Patients were just left to lie there, in the hope that the depression would lift, as most depressions do, spontaneously, in six to nine months. The prospect of such a hospitalization would have terrified Art, since it conjured up – as it does now – images of drooling idiots, strait-jackets and padded cells. These images, in 1939, were as often as not perfectly accurate.

All these approaches, despite the avowed modernity, had deep roots. They were developments in many ways of ancient, equally blatant witch-doctoring. Depression – from the French *déprimer*, to push down – was not used as a medical term until the end of the nineteenth century, but the condition has been recognized throughout history. The treatments always came down to a few basic approaches. There was shock, what you might call the 'kicking the TV' approach. There was radical surgery. There were narcotics of one kind or other. And there were the 'talking cures', which predated Freud by about 5,000 years. Then there were other, in many ways less bizarre, treatments which had only relatively recently been abandoned by the time of Art's breakdown, such as blood-letting and hydrotherapy.

To read about the history of this particular strain of madness, depression, is to be struck by how little ideas and even cures changed from ancient times to the middle of the twentieth century. Even in its earliest manifestations, ancestors of organic and psychoanalytic treatments were clearly discernible. The ancient Egyptians, like the doctors of the 1930s, prescribed sleep as a cure. Under Imhotep, vizier to the Pharaoh's temple in 2900 BC, patients were washed and purified, then made to sleep overnight at the temple. Their dreams would be interpreted by priests, and those eruptions from the subconscious 'talked through'.

At the temples of Asclepius, the ancient Greek god of healing, snakes were supposed to lick the eyelids of patients sleeping there and induce healing dreams. Priests would interpret the dreams and this would lead to a resolution of conflicts. In *The Odyssey* Homer suggested narcotic treatments for melancholy, particularly the root nepenthes, believed to be borage.

Imhotep, Homer and the Greek temple doctors believed that melancholy, in ancient Greece recognized as one of the four kinds of madness, had mainly physical causes. The Hippocratic doctors believed it was due to an imbalance of humours, in this case an excess of black bile, stored in the spleen. The cure was purging or blood-letting, a method that would be used up until the end of the nineteenth century, as would the belief in the 'black juice'.

It was the Greek dramatists who identified despair and suicide as products not of some bodily malfunction but of inner conflicts between love, desire, revenge and duty – as well as defiance of the gods. Ever since this distinction was made, so far as I can tell, a dirty war has been going on over the real meaning of depression, with the battlefield divided between these two camps. On the one hand, there are mind 'doctors', who tend to concern themselves with medical treatments and the activities of the brain. Nowadays, we call them psychiatrists. On the other, there are mind 'experts', who, although not trained medically, attempt to treat psychological dysfunction. We now call them clinical psychologists or psychotherapists, or, if they are followers of Freud or Jung, psychoanalysts. Each view contains momentous, quite different implications. Each view claims a level of objectivity, but both are soaked with judgements and values.

The Romans, being Romans, followed the lead of the Greeks. They characterized melancholia as being '*larvatum plenum*', 'filled with phantoms'. This is, I know from experience, a frighteningly accurate description of the condition. In AD 14 the Roman writer Celsus suggested curing the malady by frightening the patient, or by stopping his heartbeat momentarily with drugs or by swinging the patient around in circles by his feet. This was the beginning of 'kicking the TV' cures.

The Cappadocian physician Aretaeus, in the second century AD, was the first to describe melancholy in a way that I can recognize:

> [Sufferers] flee to the desert from misanthropy . . . they are suspicious of poisoning, and turn superstitious . . . they contract a hatred of life. The patients are dull or stern, dejected or unreasonably torpid without any manifest cause. They become peevish, dispirited, sleepless, and start up from disturbed sleep. Unreasonable fear seizes them. They complain of life and desire to die.

As Christianity began to spread, the thinking on depression gradually took on religious and moral aspects. St Augustine and Thomas Aquinas stigmatized suicide as cowardly and an offence against God, for which there was no chance of repentance. This thinking informed the Church and law up to the 1960s in England. If Art had made an attempt on his life, he could have been put in prison for two years. In the ten years after the Second World War, nearly 6,000 people were prosecuted for attempting suicide.

In the Middle Ages, the Arabs attached leeches to the anus to cure persistent sadness. The Incas anticipated Egas Moniz by drilling holes in the skull to let out evil spirits. But by the sixteenth century, melancholia had begun to lose some of its bad reputation, and take on some of the glamour it would later hold for twentieth-century nihilists and rock stars. It was seen as a mark of depth and contemplation. The greatest of all tragic heroes, Hamlet, is in fact the first dramatic depiction of someone suffering from a depressive psychosis.

When I was suppurating in my bed, six months before my

mother's death, I became obsessed with Hamlet. In him I saw clearly a reflection of what I imagined to be my own struggle. For Hamlet is clearly undergoing a nervous breakdown. He is obsessive and misanthropic; he cannot sleep properly, or make up his mind about anything; he drifts in and out of reason; he wishes above all to die, but the fear of death prevents him; he feels in the grip of an immutable destiny which he knows will destroy him; he is full of disgust for himself and for everything else. Hamlet is tortured and elemental – someone who cuts through all the crap and just finds more crap. He is the patron saint for depressives, at least male depressives. Perhaps Sylvia Plath serves that role for women.

Intriguingly, Hamlet, along with a number of other 'Shakespeare' plays, was, according to some sources, written by Robert Burton, author of The Anatomy of Melancholy, the key seventeenth-century text on depression. Burton, himself crippled by melancholy, had the insight that his state of mind was a veiled hostility and resentment towards the world in general, a sort of self-hatred in disguise. Illuminatingly, in Old English, the word anger meant sorrow as much as rage.

Burton also recognized that emotional pain could be a product of past experience: 'A man,' he wrote, 'may be undone by an evil bringing up.' So here the idea of childhood trauma enters the picture, the power of the personal, distant past to act ruinously on the present. But all Burton had to offer as a remedy was talking to a friend, listening to soothing music or the consumption of a variety of exotic herbs – eglantine, sweet briar or, poetically, the scent of dried roses.

Later in the seventeenth century, the treatments, like society, became more Baroque. Jean-Baptiste Denis, physician to Louis XIV, drew out blood and replaced it with calves' blood for two days. This apparently worked. However, the results were unpredictable. One patient died after receiving lambs' blood. Transfusions of one kind or another to treat depression continued until the end of the nineteenth century.

At around the same time, more shock treatments were being developed. At the Salpêtrière asylum in Paris, jets of freezing water were shot up the anus, taking the sitter by surprise. Others were immersed under the sea for as long as possible.

These desperate, in themselves practically psychotic, attempts to cure persistent dolour continued. The French doctor Théophile Bonet bled a young girl thirty times to cure her depression. He was disappointed, but can hardly have been astonished, when she died as a result. In England, patients from Bedlam were sent to the Fens to contract malaria, what was known as 'fever shock'. This had predictable, if terminal, results. More successfully, in 1792 two cases of melancholy were cured by applications of electricity to the head by John Birch at St Thomas's Hospital in London.

The nineteenth century was a watershed for the treatment of mental illness, partly because the widespread establishment of asylums made the study of symptoms possible for the first time. Hanwell Asylum in Southall, where my mother was sent for consultation – known locally, to me as a child, as the bin – was established in 1831. Even then it was criticized for its prison-like atmosphere, gloomy corridors and warders dressed like gaolers. Hospitals such as Hanwell marked the wholesale introduction of padded cells and strait-jackets.

The brain doctors were entirely dominant through this materialist century, the age that christened the 'nervous breakdown' and saw suicide rates begin to push upwards at an alarming rate. Their typically materialist view was well put by the modern medical historian Dr W. L. Parry-Jones, when summarizing the conclusions of the eminent psychiatrist Dr Henry Maudsley's 1883 book *Body and Will*: '[Maudsley believed that] mind and all its products are a function of matter, an outcome of interacting and combined atomic forces, not essentially different in kind from the effervescence that follows a chemical combination or the explosion of a fulminate.' Melancholics, as they were still called, were not suffering from life problems or inner struggles. They were simply suffering from a disease, like TB or gout. You had a 'broken brain'. The prejudice with which the common public viewed the mentally ill, seeing sin, evil and failure there, was irrational; you might as well hate and shun someone because they suffer from persistent migraine.

This physical perspective was underlined by the discovery of the first proof of organic madness in syphilis early in the century. German psychiatrists went on to discover the physical basis of what Emil Kräplin divided into two kinds of madness, schizophrenia and manic depression. Schizophrenia, or dementia praecox, is the classic, full-blown barking madness, of Napoleonic delusions and God complexes. Manic depressive psychoses manifest themselves in alternating mania and depression, and most doctors have little doubt that they, like schizophrenia, are seated in brain malfunction.

But there were those even in that famously empirical age who thought that a physical glitch was not enough of an explanation for many kinds of melancholia. Sir Andrew Halliday, who campaigned for the reform of asylums in India, in 1828 asserted that serious mental illness was due to excessive use of mental powers, a by-product of Western civilization. The nineteenth-century writer and doctor Oliver Wendell Holmes asserted that mental illness was 'often the logic of an accurate mind overtaxed'.

Towards the end of the century, the sociologist Emile Durkheim similarly claimed that suicide was a result of changes in society, that depression – as it was then starting to be called – was a cultural product. He noted that the populations of Protestant countries were much more inclined towards suicide than their equivalents in those countries dominated by Catholicism. This he attributed to the spirit of free inquiry implicit in Protestantism. Depression was, as Halliday suggested, the result of thinking too much. He also noted that more 'civilized' countries, like Germany, had much higher suicide rates than less developed countries like Portugal or Spain. A sort of collective unhinging took place as societies became more complex and therefore more atomized and less integrated. Suicides kill themselves because their accustomed world has been destroyed or lost and they cannot make sense of what replaces it.

Suicide, for Durkheim, was all about a sense of place, of identity. For instance, he noted that for all the problems and responsibilities associated with a large family, it was demonstrably true that members of such families were far less inclined to suicide than the unmarried. What was more, suicide of the Western, self-hating variety was virtually unknown in traditional societies, which were intimately interconnected. It wasn't personal circumstance that set people on the path to self-destruction, it was the stress of adaptation and change. People who became wealthy too quickly were observably more likely to kill themselves than those who remained poor. Being stable and integrated was the great inoculation against despair. To lose your fixed point of reference, at whatever level, was to be in danger of losing your mind.

If I was looking for some intellectual justification for imagining that the collapse of both my mother and myself may have been partly rooted in a wider crisis in England, Durkheim was a touchstone. One phrase in particular struck chords, at least as regards my own breakdown: 'The lower classes have their horizons limited by those above them, and because of that their desires are more restrained. But those who have only empty space above them are almost inevitably lost in it.'

At the other end of the telescope – looking from mass to individual – was Sigmund Freud. Freud, although he accepted that some depressions could be organic, believed that in many cases there was a deeper, as yet unplumbed explanation.

Freud studied at the Salpêtrière in Paris under the neurologist Jean Martin Charcot, who followed on from the work of Franz Mesmer. It was Mesmer who had developed a method of hand passes and eye fixations to lull anxious patients into a trance. To help the process, the patient was connected to a covered tub filled with 'magnetic fluid' by cords and rods. The hint of voodoo around mesmerism was less obvious with Charcot, a brilliant neurologist, although there was still a certain end-of-the-pier value in his 'three stages of hypnosis' – lethargy, catalepsy and somnambulism – and he entertained audiences throughout Europe with demonstrations.

Freud was impressed by these demonstrations, which were crucial to his formulation of the idea of the unconscious mind, that in depressives – more likely to be described as 'neurotics' or 'hysterics' at that time – there was a mass of disassociated, unintegrated mental material that distorted the proper operations of the mind.

It was Freud who formulated the idea that within the unconscious mind there was a death instinct (Thanatos) which vied with the life instinct (libido, or Eros) for dominance. Thanatos was present from the beginning of life and worked continually to unbind connections, to destroy, to return what is living to a null but peaceful inorganic state. Eros, the pleasure principle, was continually seeking to unite, to renew, to preserve.

In Freud's model of the mind, there was a three-way split: ego, the sense of self, of very identity; superego, a sort of inner policeman that makes judgements on the self; and id, the vast hidden glacier of the subconscious and unconscious, a theatre in which secret conflicts and ancient desires and instincts compete. For the depressive, the superego turns savagely on the ego and becomes an avenger, punishing the perceived failings of the self. This is manifested in crippling guilt and self-hatred. In the worst cases, Thanatos, the instinct to death, infects the superego and drives the ego towards destruction, either of self or of others.

The source of this guilt – a sort of terrible, unacknowledged displaced anger, turned inward – was, for Freud, lodged in childhood experience. Here the immature perceptions of the child attempting to make sense of some trauma – perhaps physical or sexual abuse – become lodged as part of that individual's way of making sense of the world, a distorted lens through which the whole of experience and the world are interpreted.

In such cases, drug treatments, surgery, electric shock, would all be quite useless, argued Freud. The only way for a neurotic or hysteric to 'recover' – or at least cope with their anxiety and pain – was to confront buried memories of the trauma and somehow work them through, re-experience them, make fresh sense. Hypnosis, dream analysis and free association would give the psychoanalyst the clues to probe the unconscious. The catharsis of simply talking about these memories – under the guidance of the principles of psychoanalysis – would release trapped energies and help to integrate the personality once more.

Disturbingly from my point of view, in *Mourning and Melan-*

cholia (1915) Freud also pointed out that the bottomless rage and self-hatred of the melancholic is really a kind of displacement activity. The real subject of loathing, the real – in the case of suicide – murderee, is not the depressive at all but the 'lost object', the person or thing towards whom feelings of love can no longer be maintained. The sadism and hate which must be present in a suicide are directed against the depressive's own ego, because they do not find it acceptable to direct it against the real culprit.

As one of Freud's followers, Wilhelm Stekel, put it, 'No one kills themself who has never wanted to kill another, or at any rate, wish the death of another.' In other words, when Jean murdered herself, she was symbolically, as well as literally, punishing someone else, was giving vent to a bottomless rage towards someone else, which she could not bring herself to express properly. And since she could not kill that other person, or even express rage towards them, she raged at, and finally killed, herself.

From Art's perspective in 1939, all this theory would have sounded about as convincing as allowing temple snakes to lick his eyelids, but psychoanalysis, in the inter-war period, was enjoying increasing popularity. Taken up by the Bloomsbury Group, feeding the art of surrealist painters and appearing regularly by now in popular films and newspapers, Freud was as fashionable as Marx, at least among intellectuals. My grandfather would have viewed the ideas of both as middle-class tosh, a 'con' not worthy of his attention, and the prejudice would have been obliquely returned, for most psychoanalytic patients were from the middle classes. The working classes were not really considered sophisticated enough to suffer neuroses, rather in the way that in the 1950s black Africans were not thought sophisticated enough to suffer depression.

Psychoanalysis made its first big breakthrough after the First World War. In Britain there were 30,000 psychiatric casualties from the trenches, most of them suffering 'shell shock' or 'soldier's heart'. Psychotherapists were brought in, along with neurologists, to effect treatment. This was not a universally popular move, particularly among psychiatrists, who, priding themselves on being true doctors, viewed it as little more than foreign, pseudo-intellectual mumbo-jumbo. The view of one, that it was an 'insidious poison', was far from rare. The war between mind doctors and brain doctors reached a new pitch.

Victims of shell shock were told to 'look cheerful' (the behaviourist school of psychology, 'you are what you do', was the dominant psychiatric doctrine at this time), to take warm baths and to divert their minds as best they could. Some were hypnotized, and some fledgeling electrical treatments were offered. Drug treatments were also provided, with the terrifying shock of cardiazol or the numbing effects of paraldehyde, the sour smell of which dominated mental hospitals throughout the country. After the end of the war, sleep narcosis was developed as a treatment using Somnifane, which would put the patient to sleep for up to ten days. Permanent coma would sometimes result.

In 1923 it was noted that some depressed diabetics treated with insulin showed a marked improvement in mood. This was the beginning of a fifty-year reign for insulin shock treatment. By inducing hypoglycaemia – a condition of catastrophically low blood sugar levels – faintness, sweating and tremors would occur, frequently leading to mental confusion and coma. Drug treatments were gathering force now, with Benzedrine and purple hearts being prescribed, the first feel-good pills. They, like many others, made a swift appearance on the black market. Both cocaine and cannabis were used as treatments for depression, perhaps more informally than not – folk cures, you might call them.

It was in the 1920s and 1930s that ideas of depression began to divide sharply into the rival camps where they still remain. On the one hand, there was the psychodynamic explanation, which saw depression as a form of neurosis based on conflicts, and on the other, the psychiatric model, which saw depression as psychosis – that is, a mental illness, an integral part of the mental makeup located in the structure and mechanisms of the brain. Where these explanations didn't cancel each other out – for there were many in each camp who entirely denied the usefulness of those in the other camp – they suggested two quite distinct types of depression.

The first, and most severe variety, was so-called 'endogenous' depression. Endogenous means 'growing from within' and – for those who believe the theory – such depressions are set in train by biological changes in brain chemistry. There was not – at least in the mind of whoever was doing the diagnosis – sufficient reason to be found in external circumstance for the apparent level of distress. Such serious, organic depressions were character- ized by lack of pleasure, or any kind of sensation whatsoever. Thinking and activity would become retarded and often cease altogether, producing symptoms akin to, say, senility. There would be massive apathy and sometimes loss of ability to speak at all. Sleep patterns would be disturbed, memory would fade. Work, personal appearance and the needs of others would be entirely neglected. There would be loss of sexual drive, a sense of low self-esteem and guilt, and sometimes religious or other kinds of delusion. The endogenous depressive would feel abandoned by friends and family, and feel themselves to be a contemptible wretch, deserving no better than to die, justly punished for some real or imagined misdeed. The sufferer would pretty much go crazy.

In this description, this outline of the purest hell, I recognized clearly the condition I was to find myself in shortly before my mother's death. But there was – again, according to the main- stream definitions – another, frequently less serious form of depression, one that my grandfather probably suffered from.

Reactive depression, the second variety, as the name suggests, occurs as a response to some external event. In Art's case, this was clearly the death of Cissy. There is some kind of real rationality in this mind state, and it is far closer on the spectrum to genuine grief or unhappiness than organic depression.

In this state there is some variation in the level of depression – it will abate from time to time. The depressive will most likely still be able to think and talk perfectly adequately. The emotional pain is liable to be expressed physically – headaches, backaches and so on. Art, according to some family members, suffered acute shingles after Cissy's death.

As in organic depression, there is a loss of self-esteem, but it is nowhere near as bad, and the characteristic self-accusation and self-hatred of the physically depressed are less crippling. There are anxiety and fear, rather than numbness and apathy. There is likely to be a sense of inferiority, a lack of confidence, an inability to express aggression. This type of depressive will find it hard to cope with criticism or to feel wanted, or to feel of any significance at all. These symptoms, lodged as they are in the essential personality, will not abate after the depression has passed. Such so-called mood disorders might be responsive to psychotherapy in the way that the first kind of depression would not.

These two models of depression are crude, to put it mildly. Symptoms more often than not overlap and in assessment are highly subjective. What a doctor thinks is disastrous – say, a poor home, a badly paid job, low status – may not be seen as such by the patient. But it was as far as doctors in the 1930s had got, and it is along this spectrum that types of depression are still measured – or, more correctly, guessed at.

Art, so far as anyone knows, was a victim of the second kind of depression. Despite not seeking any kind of treatment, the inertia he suffered as a result of Cissy's death did eventually lift and did not seem to recur. Given the treatments on offer, it was perhaps just as well that he showed no interest in consulting a doctor. Anyway, if there is a spectrum between mourning and melancholia, the place Art occupied in 1939 was very much away from the pole of pure illness. And yet he was sufficiently disabled to lie in bed while the business he had spent his life building up collapsed around him; to face the indignity of being looked after by his children rather than the other way around. Wells and Lott was going out of business and there was nothing, apparently, that Art could do to help it. Depression had struck for the first time at the open, unknowing face of my family.

Chapter Seven

'They have a horror of abstract thought, they feel no need for any philosophy or systematic world view . . . they have a certain power of acting without taking thought . . . the phrase "a sleepwalking people" that Hitler coined for the Germans would have been better applied to the English' — George Orwell, *England Your England*

My grandfather's breakdown did not endure. After a hiatus of several months, he had collected himself enough to rise from his bed and attempt to reconstruct his life, so suddenly imploded. His dignity, conducted through the sheets, earthed into the bedspring blocks, sought regeneration. The first step at least was clear enough, the almost-instinct of the English when faced with disaster: *bury it.* So it was that the breakdown was never spoken of again.

The house in Essex Grove, with its cigarette machine and snooker table, its squat radiogram and Citroën Tourer, was a lost option: the business had *gone West* and there was no way any more of paying the rent. Art's eldest son, Ken, had moved out already to live with his wife, Rene. A dapper man, so meticulous that he insisted on having his underpants and pyjamas ironed before he would wear them, he considered that his responsibilities were now for his wife. Anyway, the job at Hey Presto! was coming to an end, as war coalesced at the edges of vision. It was a simple war, light facing down darkness.

Ken volunteered for the army, eventually to fight in the Burma campaign. Jack was thirteen years old. Arthur, fifteen, prematurely tense, less handsome, was already working at Cox and Co., a manufacturer of car spare parts in Croydon. The immediate family might be *in extremis,* but it was protected by the larger family, which felt the ripples that the disaster transmitted from its epicentre, as if all were held in a tensile web. For the time being Rose, one-toothed and wild, had moved in to look after Jack. It was plain, though, that the sweet, accustomed life that had floated them miraculously through the economic depression of the 1930s was at an end.

Sanctuary came a few months into the war. Ken was now posted abroad, while his wife, Rene, slutted enthusiastically, rumpling and desecrating the geometrically folded sheets. Once she even tried it on with Arthur, climbing into bed with him, pretending it was all a game. She was a no-good, decided Jack, slightly jealous nevertheless, since he himself was too fat, and too shy, for girls. Also he was fond of Rene. He liked them all, his family, his friends, even his neighbours, and now he would have to leave them.

Hetty, my grandmother's well-to-do sister, lived in a large Victorian house in St James's Avenue in West Ealing, bought by Emil de Villemieur. Emil had died from a surfeit of German hock, and her son Arthur was also gone, agitated into extinction by epileptic fits. Her second son, George, was at university, something unique in the family, and was shortly to train as a pilot in the RAF, while Ladybird, her only daughter, was a Land Girl, an agricultural labourer in uniform. The posters showed them laughing, throwing corn sheaves under the fat sun. Women, wanting of rationality, were not fit to slaughter. So now Hetty was by herself in the big, gloomy house in the self-styled Queen of the Suburbs. Three rooms were empty and she offered them to Art.

He accepted, almost immediately finding a job as a delivery man at Chibnall's, the local bakery. Jack found the old house gloomy and strange. It was inhabited by the scraps and traces of Emil de Villemieur, who stared down from a large oil painting in the darkened front room, down at heavy, age-soiled furniture and a variety of small, filigree hanging cages.

There was a craze for exotic birds in the 1940s – they had, along with miniature poodles, become immensely and inexplicably popular, easily outnumbering all other varieties of pet. The budgies were, by mass habit, named Jimmy or Joey, and inhabited nickel-plated palaces with mirrors, bells and tilting ladders, while they attemped to frame epithets and curses through prissy horned beaks that they sharpened on cuttlefish.

Hetty, perhaps in some kind of exercise in emotional displacement, had taken to these small, cacophonous birds. She had constructed an aviary at the rear of the house, where Jimmy would copulate with Joey, producing multiples of both. Their squawks and trills penetrated the gloom whenever Jack made his way to his new room upstairs, which he shared with Arthur, while his father lived at the back of the house, overlooking the garden. Sometimes the birds would be set free from the cages and flap around the darkened rooms like fat, highly strung moths. Downstairs, away from the front room with its birdseed and pelmeted and curtained fireplace and down a long dark corridor was an equally odd room, covered from ceiling to floor with dark, lugubrious oil paintings featuring Stags in the Glen, Misty Mountains and brooding, overcast landscapes. They looked down on an upright piano that was never played.

The house had a smell, of loss and birdshit and Hetty's fancy Du Maurier cigarettes, and a kind of Victorian dolour. Jack escaped as often as he could, heading at weekends by bus and train back to his friends in Crystal Palace, but the trips were arduous. Gradually, they became rarer and he tried to fit himself into this new life, riding out with his father on the bread van to Notting Hill Gate and the Portobello Road, which was, as chance would have it, Art's designated territory. The schools had closed down when the bombs came, but Jack was more or less at the end of his school life anyway, having now achieved fourteen years of age. His education was absolutely rudimentary, but then what was the point of accumulating facts about alluvial deposits and logarithms and forgotten battles, when there was money to be earned, a life to be survived?

He applied for a job on the assembly line at the Strand Electrics factory at the end of St James's Avenue, and was accepted, wage 12/6 per week. There was to be no teenage interregnum, for teenagers did not exist, even as a word. Jack simply passed from childhood into manhood. Now he would be offered cigarettes and beer, sworn in the presence of, if there were no women around. You could cuss, but never, ever with a girl in earshot. This was a part of the vast patchwork of rules, particular to men, that Jack understood without being told.

Entertainment had been circumscribed by the war to a certain extent, although some cinemas were still open and at home they could gamble – rummy, pontoon, Newmarket – in secret, as Hetty, a puritan by nature, disapproved. But then the war itself was entertainment and a kind of fulfilment. As in every other participating country, the suicide rate dropped sharply. Even in the worst imaginable of environments, the Nazi concentration camps, it was bewilderingly low.

Since, as Jack knew, there was no chance that they would lose, or that he would die – he was English, he was young – the black-outs and bomb flashes became a lark. Walking home from the Northfields Odeon, you would thrill as the sirens sounded, duck and run as the big ack-ack guns sent a spray of razored shrapnel raining into the street. The barrage balloons and searchlights decorated the night sky, better even than the Crystal Palace firework tableaux.

There was an Anderson shelter in the garden, but after a while Jack didn't bother to get out of bed when the siren sounded; he just put his head under the covers, reducing the dangerous world by the trick of invisibility. *If it's got your number on it* . . . You always half-hoped a big one would drop near you, just for the drama of it. And, in fact, early one morning there was a rolling *whooom* that had Jack sitting bolt upright. Shifting red and orange light made the wallpaper unfamiliar.

It was five-thirty and almost time for the factory anyway. Jack peeled back the counterpane, put on his work overalls and made his way downstairs. Emil de Villemieur looked particularly sanguine this morning, reddened by the reflected blaze. Where was it? Who'd *bought it*? Out in the street, cathedrals of smoke were rising from the end of the road, at the junction with the Uxbridge Road. Jack strained to see something. There were shapes, pressed by gravity and the force of the blast horizontal on to the pavement. He moved closer, a slight nervousness now intruding on his excitement, an apprehension that slowed his walk. There was glass and brick and tile, rubble all over, but other shapes, more disturbing, spread across the street, piled against kerbstones, for ten, twenty yards from where the explosion had taken place.

A sickness hawked in his throat, as a cumulus of fog moved upwards and away. Now Jack could see clearly, his eyelids stretching to take in the enormity. There were the shapes of arms and legs, torsos, heads separate from the body, some black, some apparently melting, some on fire. Could a body burn? He wanted to turn and run, but an ancient fascination pushed him closer, his stomach acidic and in contraction.

Amazingly, there were people standing by the scene *laughing*. Jack rubbed his eyes as if to erase what was impressed on his retina. Was war just fun, scaled-up fireworks after all? The bodies were so blackened, yet where intact, strangely perfect. He moved closer, the laughter still sounding. Were there madmen here? A bystander kicked one of the bodies and it moved with an impossible lightness across the street. Another lifted a head and threw it lightly to his girlfriend, who caught it with a giggle. Other bodies on the ground were becoming liquid.

When the *snap* in his head came, Jack began laughing too, though it was an awkward laughter, risen from a well of relief, and laughter at himself and his too-primed imagination. He moved forward with a different step now, unworried. He picked up an arm and waved the hand: *cheerio*. It was so light, the sticking-plaster pink of the mannequin quite unlike human skin. The sign above the shop was punctured by the blast but still readable: *Bur* – here there was a gap – *ns, the Tai* – another gap – *ors*. The clothes inside – three-piece suits, shit brown and slate grey – were still burning. Jack kicked at a few more dummies and, eventually bored, turned on his heel back towards Hetty's house.

Hetty's once shy, wind-soft face was stiffening again, gaining angles and small, crushed lines around the mouth. Jack could almost see them emerging, a watermark on old paper. Even her legs, mottled like those of all middle-aged women of the time, impressed by the heat of open fires, seemed newly sad. The smell of loss was more acrid now, since the telegram had arrived – George was missing, shot down over Germany. She still had hopes of course – sunny side up! – but they were thinning, becoming transparent. The caged birds wittered like morons, ignoring the pointless swivelling mirrors.

Arthur was working with Jack at Strand Electrics, but was on unpaid leave now because he had developed rheumatic fever. For three months, Jack brought him dinner – pig's liver and onions, pies with ersatz meat filling, potato, mash and gravy, oxtail soup the colour of wet khaki, anything off the ration that wasn't whalemeat, barracuda or horse – from Bert's Caff in St James's Avenue. Rheumatic fever affected the heart; it would store itself up in the mulch of Arthur's history and kill him four decades later, in conspiracy with Arthur's careful, over-conscientious personality. But for the time being, it was simply an inconvenience for Jack, having attended to the recovery of his father, now to be nursing his older brother.

Arthur was finally restored to good health well enough, or so it seemed. Jack and he were friends now, beyond the bullying that had hectored the younger boy's childhood, when Arthur had teased his fatness and thrown darts at him as a joke. Arthur's illness, while weakening him, putting an invisible bracket around the far end of his life, made Jack still stronger, accelerating the slide into manhood and responsibility.

Jack's transition to adulthood had a culminating rite, serving in the armed forces, which he embarked upon in 1943, applying for admission to the navy for no other reason than that he liked the uniform and felt it would make him more attractive to girls. Jack was excited, and of course patriotic, but not without shrewdness. He knew call-up was coming to him and he understood that to volunteer now was to provide him with a choice that otherwise would be unforthcoming.

At dawn, on the day of his departure, he put his clothes together in bundles, in a kitbag, and made his way downstairs. The American breakfast – wheatflakes and milk instead of fried bacon and egg – was consumed. Art, awkward with emotion, saw him to the door when he'd finished up and drunk his heavy tea.

Good luck, said Art. *Behave yourself.* He slipped him half a crown, shook his hand and went back inside. They did not hug, now that Jack was a man.

Nervous, Jack caught the bus to the training camp in Skegness – *It's So Bracing*, declared the Jolly Fisherman on the seaside poster. He wept that night, his first time away from home. There were to be twelve weeks' basic training, as an aircraft technician, an electrician for the Fleet Air Arm. *What a cock-up*, thought Jack, who could barely change a plug. He was transferred to Harlow, innocent of its post-war new-town future, just a rural hamlet in Essex. From there he was posted to Cornwall, then Wales, to wait out the war, never seeing active service. Of course, he tried, volunteering for some of the excitement abroad. They were asking for members of the Fleet Air Arm to build bases on the Japanese islands before the Allied landing. It would be like a holiday, with secrets. The newspapers did not show cadavers, so death was hard to imagine. The war was a cartoon, against Musso the Wop and Hitler, who had only one ball. It was music hall with bullets and distant, always heroic death. Jack, to his disappointment, was rejected.

The outfit he had volunteered for were wiped out to a man by the Japanese. George was confirmed dead, Hetty's face settling into engraved stone. Ken was in Burma, starving and shitting water in the jungles and bogs, in the so-called 'Forgotten War'. In the letters he wrote home to his cousin Rita, suffering was excised, out-of-bounds by habit and custom.

After the war, Ken would hate the Japanese until he died, but not so much as the Americans, who stole the war for themselves in *Objective Burma* with Errol Flynn. That film would blind him with rage: *Fucking Yanks*. Other than that, he would not talk of his suffering; talking like that was for poofs and women. There were rumours of German horror camps, where millions were slaughtered. Armour was sought, and found in myth. People were basically decent. Everything would come out in the wash. Everything was just common sense, in the end.

Jack was happy in the navy, happier than he'd ever been in his life. A deeply conformist man, a uniform particle of his class and generation, he loved the camaraderie, operating as part of a larger unit; he loved having everything organized for him. No need to *decide*, that most irksome of mental chores. To tell true, it was more like a themed holiday camp than a war station, a kind of elaborate play-acting. Although they were land bases, they were imagined as ships – HMS *Vulture* in Cornwall, HMS *Goldcrest* in Wales. To leave base, an array of Nissen huts, was to go ashore. *All ashore that's going ashore*, murmured the Tannoy, as if through a veil of catarrh, ashore being an array of sand dunes outside the perimeter fence. VIPS were piped aboard the Nissen huts. A large shot of rum was served up at noon. Six bells was called instead of six o'clock. There were endless sports – rugby, hockey, football, cricket – and girls in the seaside resorts, at a time when men, like everything else, appeared to be on ration, while women were in glut. Maybe there would be a kiss, or heavy petting, a feel. Nothing more, they weren't slags.

A clutch of snapshots from the 1940s show Jack smart and cocksure in the uniform of a matelot, arms forward in a slightly simian pose, cigarette lolloping from the side of the lip, crooked smile, the fat melting under navy training, leaving the residue of a sleepy, handsome face framed by auburn quiff. The faint, knowing arrogance was more pronounced than ever. The navy *did* have the best uniforms, better than the coarse mud serge and shapeless tailoring of the army. The rangy bell-bottoms were folded seven times to indicate the seven seas; there were nonchalant, cocked caps, triple-striped scarves, all in blue serge, bleached pale by the ensigns to suggest experience, war hardness. Mocked as a *sea-going WREN* by the lumpen stokers and grease monkeys in the bellies of the battleships, Jack was nonetheless proud in his uniform. He learned to dance, finding unexpected nimbleness and grace. His gauche, awkward boyhood was slipping away. By the time the war finished in 1945, he was touched by military poise and fresh, boy-next-door good looks.

The family began to collect, droplets into a pool, once more as the centrifuge of peace operated. Ken, intent on ditching Rene now – how had he known about the jumbled sheets? – was still in Burma, toughened by betrayal and the war, and nostalgic for

England. He wrote to Rita on VE Day, 8 May 1945, from 2342092 Corporal Lott RA, South-East Asia Campaign:

> Very many thanks for the letter received a few days ago. I am glad to hear that you and all at home are in very good health and plesed to say that this few lines have me feeling very fit and well. It is now 7.45 pm, which is 1.15pm in England and the PM has just given his 'V' Day speech, the boys are nearly going mad with joy. They all feel sure that now with all the troops that can be sent out hear it will not take long to finish off the Japs and us boys with over three years service out here can come home soon, thank god it will soon be over.

Jack was demobbed in 1946. He chose from four demob suits: a sports jacket and flannels, a single-breasted worsted, a grey pinstripe single-breasted and a double-breasted pinstripe. He took the double-breasted pinstripe plus a Raglan herringbone overcoat. There was also a hat on offer, a trilby or a flat cap, but Jack passed it up; no one wore hats any more. Self-expression, the atomic force of its latency quite unguessed at, could be demonstrated through the style of the hair, the placing of the parting, the swell of the quiff. In the new homeland, the class slurry would be swept away.

The civilian England that Jack returned to was a place hopelessly confirmed in its sense of itself. Any doubt that it was the greatest power, the hero of the world, had been burned away. Plucky, tough little England, the fount and saviour of civilization, the ancients rooting for us down the centuries. *If only they had listened to Plato, Jesus, Socrates*, said David Niven, the pilot-hero in *A Matter of Life and Death*, as he crashed in flames.

Newsreels appeared in the cinemas, showing the horror of Nazi concentration camps, bodies being bulldozed by the ton into lime pits. The atom bomb reduced Japanese babies to a salt cellar of ash, their shadows burned on the ground. Jack briefly shuddered, then explained it, shuffling the images until he could tell himself a bearable story about them. This story had to be true or else . . .

The Germans had been tricked by a mad genius and then –

reluctantly – forced to follow his orders on pain of death. The A-bomb had been necessarily launched against the brave but wasplike Japanese to save more lives in the long run. Hiroshima, Nagasaki, they were acts of mercy. Now atoms – what were they exactly? – would be used for the good. Electricity would be free. Already the novelties were being planned – atomic vacuum cleaners, atomic cars, atomic pudding!

England would go on and on, stretching into the future, as it stretched into the past. Of course, the class fissures had to be closed now, the remittance to be paid for the agony and loss. The eggheads and the nobs, they had their place, looking after us, making sense for us – J. B. Priestley, George Orwell, C. E. M. Joad, William Beveridge, icons for rich and poor alike – but the common man would come into his inheritance. They would run the pits, the railways, the hospitals, the power. It was only fair.

There would be stability, safety, unity, the same sense of unity that thrilled them at Dunkirk, that saw them whistling through the flames. Britain can take it! There would be freedom, not to do spectacular things or conjure pots of gold – there had been enough excitement, the stretching of limits. No, there would be freedom from, not to. Beyond this, the Englishman didn't want that much. As Ernie Bevin complained, *The trouble with the English is that they suffer a poverty of desire*. And now there would be also freedom from *doubt*, for everything had snapped into place, as the stories predicted, as faith always promised. The gears of history had meshed and proved that good triumphed over evil after all. Everything comes out in the wash. It's a lovely day tomorrow. England, the lionheart, the – in a not-much-fuss-about-it way – decent, the safe, the straightforward.

But, if that was so, why did it feel so hard now, when they had won, beaten down the Devil after all? Facts were facts, the right thing was being done for the workers, for the ordinary bloke. It went without saying. Yet it was still so drab, and tough and poor and frigid. No one had realized how poor and frigid, until the Americans came over with their dollars and their white teeth and their rubber johnnies. Rationing was still on, digging deeper than ever. The cities were a rubbled mess. There was no colour, no fashion, only sludge green and puddle brown, grey, black. Only twenty-two types of government-approved, dreary furniture designs. There were fuel shortages, as the bitter winters descended on God's country. Were they sent by God? Women queued for hours every day. The food was ersatz, gristled or stale.

Jack read his *Reveille*. The headlines were bright enough – Face Panties! How I Grew Tall Drinking Blood! Luscious Lovelies! – but the story they did not tell was that of a country still under siege, in the grip of puritan frenzy. A West End milliner's in court for the crime of embroidering roses and butterflies on camiknickers. A gang of men prosecuted for making illicit jellies in Barnsley. It was funny, he supposed, but sort of funny-sad. Jack Priestley, whom he would listen to on the wireless, got it bang-on, didn't he? *We are trying to do a wonderful thing in this country, but not in a wonderful way.*

The books, the wireless, the songs, the movies – *everything* that floated down from on high – told a different story, of a world where all things turned out for the best, where there was promise and perfectibility.

Now working at Berkal, the scale-makers in Park Royal, Jack ruminated as he calibrated the machines. Everyone had a job who wanted one, and if you got fed up with the one you had, people were queuing to give you another. The National Health was a good thing, had to be, even though it got a bit silly. *Reveille* had particularly singled out the National Health wigs for ridicule.

There was no crime to speak of, despite the gang panics in the *Daily Mirror*, the lurid headlines telling of the Cosh Boys, the Elephant Boys and the Knife Boys of the inner city with their knuckledusters, bicycle chains and flick knives. It was all exaggerated; in Ealing nothing was stolen, no one was hurt. Anyway, there was nothing to steal. Also, wages were climbing, 80 per cent higher than in 1936, it said in the *Herald*. Art and Arthur were both making OK money, especially if you counted the fiddles. And there was still fun to be had, they couldn't put that on the ration. Sometimes Jack went to the variety shows at the Chiswick Empire to see Max Wall,

Wilson, Keppel and Betty, Jimmy James, Katrina, Jimmy Wheeler, Leslie Walsh the Memory Man, the Bernard Brothers and their Miracles of Mime. There were jugglers, trick acts, stand-ups hinting at the great secret of sex. The high point – of course – was Phyllis Dixie and her Nude Tableaux, a *dozen naked lovelies*, all of them still as stone. The slightest movement – an eyebrow, a foot – could mean prosecution. They had pasties and stars to cover the nipples.

But mostly Jack went to the dance halls, which were sucking in hundreds of thousands every night, from the prefabs and back-to-backs. The Hammy Pally, the Montague Ballroom in Ealing Broadway, the Odeon in Park Royal. Jack had learned to dance in the navy and he was good now, on the floor before anyone, while there was space, doing the fishtail and the half-chassis, those tricksy variations on the quickstep, plus also the foxtrot, the tango, the paso doble, the samba, the rumba, the new jive and jitterbug, the girls slitting their skirts and losing their tightened, careful selves for minutes at a time. Some dance halls banned jitterbug, a coon dance, filthy. There still remained some English scraps, novelty dances mostly – the hokey-cokey, the Lambeth Walk, the Muffin Man, the conga – but the Americans had freshened England, individualized it, sexualized it. The old dances, the St Bernard's Waltz, the Lancers, the polka, the sequence dances, severe, the flow broken to circumscribe intimacy, the dancers at arms' length, these were dead now, dead as Musso the Wop, hanging by his heels with that whore by his side, and Adolf, that *dastard*, a bullet in his brain and good job too.

His mantle of fat completely gone now, Jack began dating regularly, but didn't go steady until he met Thelma Taylor. She lived over the bike shop in Southall High Road. Well off, the Taylors even had a television. Thelma was willowy, tall, great pins, a brilliant mover. They danced to Oscar Robin, Kathy Stobart, Lou Praeger at the Palais, the Montague, the Odeon. She played around, Jack suspected, sitting at home wringing his hands. He fancied her like mad, not that she would let him do anything in the way of, you know . . . Maybe a kiss. There was nowhere to go to do anything else, no privacy.

They danced three, four, five times a week, Jack now in two-piece, single-breasted barathea suits, plain brown, or pinstripe, or Prince of Wales check, cream shirt with arrow-point collar, Prince of Wales tie and knot, all bought on the coupon. Turn-ups were permitted on the trousers now. Monk shoes with a buckle, also brogues and suedes. Thelma wore the New Look, dominant collars, plunging neckline, the nipped-in waist, the sloping shoulders, the fancy bows. Her pleated skirt flew up under the rotating mirror ball, throwing out spangles of coloured light.

She dumped him in the end. Jack was hurt, but he was a practical man and a stoic, not much given to highs or lows. He had never proposed to Thelma – she was a no-good, not to be trusted. Love didn't come out of the sky and hit you, that was rubbish. Love was something you learned.

On his twenty-first birthday, Art gave Jack a gold watch and some money that had been put aside for him over the years. He celebrated by buying a motorcycle, a Vincent Comet HRD, 500cc, black and chrome, 100mph, single-cylinder, top of the range, almost; there was the Vincent Black Shadow, a beast, too rich for Jack's blood. Jack drove it right out of the shop, first time on a bike, then parked it out the back of Hetty's, and brought it into the room full of oil paintings when it rained.

When he wasn't at the cinema or the dance hall, Jack played snooker at the end of St James's Avenue with Ronnie Van Den Bergh, a wolf and a bit of a villain, and Derek Beard and Freddie Wade. He learned all the trick shots: spin-backs, leap-overs, double screws. They played for hour upon hour, Jack with his Players cigarette staining the fingers that made a bridge for the maple cue to rest upon, Ronnie with his Capstan Full Strength glowing with undreamed-of death. They talked, about nothing in particular, complained a bit, but not too much. Derek had read that two-thirds – imagine! – of young people wanted to leave the country for the Commonwealth. This was a higher figure than for any other country in Europe. A queue of half a million to get out. *Why don't we give it a go?* Jack agreed there and then. Ten-quid assisted packages to Australia. In what seemed no time at all, they had made the reservations, done the medicals, got the visas, said their goodbyes. It all fell through of course, Derek Beard backing out at the last moment, not wanting to leave his mum. Jack couldn't face going out there with just Ronnie, he was too much of a pain in the backside.

So Jack remained in England, in Ealing, working Saturdays now at Terry O'Dwyer's greengrocer's shop in Notting Hill Gate, just for the extra cash. He'd met Terry at Berkal and they got on as mates. One day in 1948, Terry said, *Jack, give up the job and come and work with me, full-time. I'll see you all right.* Okey-dokey, thought Jack, why not? And that was it, that was his future, his entire working life machine-pressed out, a groove, cut deep and immutable. Jack would spend his life working in the greengrocer's. It was OK, he supposed. *Don't expect much and you won't be disappointed,* he told himself, as he would also tell me further down the years.

As the 1950s turned over, a vast motor trying to catch, awaiting some spark, England appeared as a ball at the height of its parabola when thrown into the air, apparently motionless. The restrictions and rationing still weighed down heavily. Jack danced, and worked, and went to the movies, and worked, played snooker, and worked. He read his books, Peter Cheyney, Neville Shute – the dull, decent Englishman winning through – Agatha Christie and his favourite, Dennis Wheatley, *The Devil Rides Out.* Anything a bit sexy, a bit murderous. The job at the green-grocer's was working out well. A bit of bunce on the side, it was a cash business, understood. Arthur was married now, to Olive, who worked in a chocolate shop, Joy Day in Ealing Broadway. Ken, catching on to the vast wave of post-war divorces, had given Rene the Big E and taken a job as a salesman, at which he acquit-ted himself with near-genius. Hetty worked at teaching the birds a new pointless word or two. Art was in love with another woman, whom he would one day marry and produce a Down's Syndrome baby.

Jack's life ambled along on automatic. He could sense things loosening around him; the clothes were becoming more casual, the directives rarer, the coupons less often required. Wages were still rising and there were new items in the shops, 'contemporary' they called them, inspired by atoms and science, new colours, new shapes. It was all at the Festival of Britain. Jack went to see the Skylon, the Dome of Discovery, laid out on the South Bank like a window from *Eagle* comic. They served tea in polystyrene cups; he hoped that wouldn't catch on.

The festival was all very well, about time the country looked forward for once. But England still felt the same somehow – safe, dull, unenthused by the prospect of change, clinging to the muddy soup, the dingy colours, the heavy wood.

Chapter Eight

Now, for the first time, my mother begins to take on definition in the deep blur of family history, as she moves into a time when those who can testify still survive, a time when her image begins to stamp itself on to photographic plates and prints, on to memory traces lodged somewhere magical in the slab of brain, on to that which we think of as heart.

For no particular reason that I can fathom, there is an absence of photographs of Jean between babyhood and teens, but I see nothing sinister in this, only the casual entropy of history. For the most part I can only guess at the ages, except in one portrait, which is dated 1945. It is printed by the Home Counties Press, 246 King Street, Hammersmith, and is copyrighted. Home Counties Press own this image of my mother, it is on loan, I suppose, although the inscription on the back, in the barely joined-up print of Jean's handwriting, reads, 'With Love to Norman. Jean.' There is a number, Wax 3668. 'Wax' is an abbreviation of Waxlow Manor, the ward of Ealing in which Jean lived with her parents.

The print shows her as a pin-up, as cheesecake in *Photoplay*. She is fourteen years old, but looks sexually mature. She is wearing a tartan bow around her throat and a dark blouse. She looks slightly beyond the camera, as if at the future. To look right into the lens would be brazen, invitational. Her expression is one of expectation and confidence, the face innocent of any pain. Although it is not soft-focused, the sense it conveys is of something imperceptibly blunted and rinsed. Her hair, a magnificent auburn, is side-parted and flicked back to show a high forehead. Her nose is too nubby to be beautiful, but her eyes are spectacular, gentle, easy to hurt. The imprint of them, those orbits of old ink, ache and dart inside my chest as if black, tiny birds are working there, trying to crack something open.

In none of the other photographs is she quite so beautiful; sometimes she is merely pretty, other times even plain. The impression of her face varies widely with the light and the angle of pose, endlessly vulnerable to impression. Here, in milky light in front of a thatched cottage, she seems knowing, a faint sexuality that is not neutralized by the folksy gingham dress and plain cardigan. Perhaps it is the cigarette she is smoking, something I can never remember her doing in my lifetime. Here she is on an English beach, her long hair cut back to shoulder length. She looks dark as a gypsy and she holds a blade of long dune grass, as if it has been requested, for the purposes of prop. Her short-sleeved, striped shirt, piped with white, is cut close to emphasize her figure, which is spectacular. Hetty swears she must wear contour support (*a fuller figure – confidentially*) but it is all hers, the stature and curve of Jane Russell, but without the decadence; somehow the stateliness of cleavage suggests an instinct for motherhood rather than passion.

Once again, as when an infant, in this photograph she is perched on a dustbin in the back garden of the house on Rosecroft Road, covering her face as if fake-shy. Evening shadows reach out towards her like pianist's fingers from the rough pathway. There is an air-raid shelter and an old garden sieve in the background.

Here she is, on an empty pebbled beach, in a bikini, which must date the photo to sometime in the 1950s, after the Bikini Atoll A-bomb tests. Her hair, again, is shorter. Perhaps she is beginning to lose it now. She is wearing heavy, unflattering sunglasses. So this one, with her best friend, Irene Downhill, must be earlier, for her hair is at full length again. She is wearing a light, single-breasted A-line coat, just above ankle length. Irene stands to her left, her toes turned slightly inward, flesh showing through the criss-cross straps of her flat leather shoes. For some reason this makes her presence seem sad. Yet, as in all the other photographs of this time, both women are smiling; for some reason, to not smile at a camera becomes taboo about now, in mid-century England. The camera, and its ephemeral product, are being sapped of gravitas.

Here is her mother, Grace. Just as there are no pictures of Jean as a child, there are none of Grace as a young woman. She is always old, as I remember her, with a pronounced nose and a figure like a pillarbox in a sack. Her hair is scraped back and gathered into a bun the shape of a ring doughnut on top of her head. She looks tough, and I remember that she could be astringent, unlike Billy, her mild, dutiful husband. And here is Billy, standing in the back garden. It is a dull photograph, in which he wears a plain sports jacket and buff slacks, and a diagonally striped tie, but something has gone wrong in the processing and there are two white flashes exploding on either side of him, as if something celestial is unfolding.

Here are the first photographs of Jack and Jean together, Jean burnished into teak sitting on the back of the Vincent Comet. Grace, looking like a game OAP, would also take rides, urging Jack to greater speed. Jean is wearing an overcoat and what look like Doc Martens shoes. There is a field of thistle in the background.

Jack and Jean in a hotel by the look of it, Jean in a white blouse with a spray of white carnation on her breast, a lick of hair playing down on to her right eyebrow. She looks luminous, perfect, except for the slight hook in her nose, inherited from her mother. There is the smallest gap in between her two front teeth. Jack, his collar scruffily overlapping the line of his lapel, holds her through the crook of her arm with his big left hand. The other encloses her smaller, unworked hands, in the soft singularity of his palm.

Here they are on their wedding day. Jean has a small crucifix around her neck and is holding a spray of slightly desiccated roses. There are white flowers in her hair and her pulled-back veil falls to her elbow. She is smiling up at Jack, showing her big

97

teeth. Her neck is good, clearly defined from the chin. Jack gazes down, his face a mass of satisfied lines, his quiff improved by Vitalis, his tie a satiny flap beneath his shirt. There is a white carnation in his lapel. They hold hands. Although the photograph is obviously posed, according to the photographer's cue, I imagine, I know, that the sentiment was real and true. This, then, was the happiest day of their lives.

Jean met Irene Downhill the year the pin-up shot was taken, in 1945. Both worked in the rag trade, at the Berkertex factory in Southall Broadway as machinists, production-line seamstresses. Irene made sleeves, Jean made bodices. Although she was only fourteen, this was my mother's second stab at a job. Her first had been as a hairdresser; she had been briefly apprenticed after leaving Dormer's Wells School in Dormer's Lane. Unlike Jack, she had been offered no scholarship on leaving the elementary school, Lady Margaret Junior. Perhaps some seed of future self-doubt was sown here, in this most routine of failures.

Irene did not talk to Jean while they were at the factory. She had noticed her, with her hair, and her bust, and her slightly prim yet self-confident face. But Jean had not really mixed with the thirty other girls working there; she was very young, maybe slightly shy. One day, Irene noticed that Jean had not been in for a while. *She's poorly*, said the foreman, grimacing politely. *Pneumonia. You could die from it*. Someone organized a whip-round for her, poor thing. They pooled their coupons and sent Irene to buy some chocolates and a bunch of daffodils. She had to queue, of course; you had to queue for everything, whether it was bacon or Bile Beans, or Iron Jelloids, or Bovril, or Virol – Convalescents Need It! – sometimes for hours. Irene was given the afternoon off to shop and to drop them over, although she hardly knew Jean.

She was greeted by Mrs Haynes, Jean's mother, a kind woman, big, lovely, thought Irene. Her own mother, it turned out, knew Grace, from the Silver Threads club at the church in Allenby Road, where they played housey-housey and went to beetle drives, and from where they took charabancs to the seaside. Mrs

Haynes showed Irene upstairs to Jean's tiny bedroom. She was a tad nervous at first, afraid she would find Jean at death's door. But Jean was sat up, bright as a button when she saw the flowers and chocolates. Irene sat down for a natter and a cup of tea, it was rude not to.

They found themselves talking nineteen to the dozen, letting the tea go cold. Irene, looking at her across the Singer machines, bolts of cloth and white wax markers of the workshop, had imagined that Jean was a little bit hoity-toity, being so pretty. Also she talked very precisely, very just-so. But she wasn't stuck up, not at all. She was *nice*, that most prized and sought-after quality. Boys touched up bad girls but married nice ones. And she was cheerful, perky, not bolshie or too smart. That was a big plus too when it came to men.

Jean told her about her big brothers, Alan, a little simple but sweet in his heart, and Norman, smart as anything, he was away at the moment, she wouldn't say where. She was pleased as punch at the flowers and had already eaten half the chocolates.

Irene resolved to come again. It was funny how they just hit it off, and soon it was once or twice a week, bringing biscuits, fruit, magazines – *Woman* or *Woman's Own*. She flicked through it on the bus, the 105, on the way over. *There is a unanimous acceptance,* read Irene, *that to be loved and loving is better than being brainy, rich or nobly born.* Signed, the editor. *Hear, hear.* She hopped off the bus, before it had properly stopped, the way you did, for a giggle.

The more she talked to Jean, the more they seemed to have in common. Of course, Jean was different in a way, more at ease with herself, while Irene was always a bit edgy, on the touchy side. But they both loved clothes, and dancing, and sport. Boys as well, she supposed, though they didn't talk about *that* very much; they were only after one thing.

Jean was back at work in no time at all. By now they were tight, firm friends in an exclusive, sealed unit, within which they would remain until one or the other got married, when friendship would naturally recede. For now, though, they were together, not even another girl to interrupt or dilute the friendship. It was normal; you got a Best Friend – always female, for neutral male friends were unknown, since upon contact they converted alchemically into 'boyfriends'. Then you waited for the man to turn up. They were not teenagers, they were girls, and would remain so until they became wives and mothers. Even then they would still be girls, but they would have earned respect, having done what was required, done the right thing. Life was prescribed, immovably, linearly, in this way: school, work, best friend, marriage, housewife, mother, then grandmother. Then death, painlessly, in your sleep, although you never talked about that.

What *did* they talk about all those hours? Silly, really, but it was hard to know. Where they were going, where they had been – the Pally this week, or the Montague, or Ealing Town Hall. The boss at work, *that great lummox*, the weather – the coldest for fifty years – the bright vermilion colouring of Jean's new skirt, she made it herself, a dirndl, she would wear it with a taffeta underslip, and a nice off-white blouse with a Peter Pan collar and leg-of-mutton sleeves. Utility was fading now, those neat, puritan lines, designed by Molyneux, Hardy Amies, Hartnell. Square shoulders, boxy, straight with skirt just above the knee, regulated pleats. Good riddance. The queuing, the dance steps. The way that boy looked at them, he was a wolf, they were all wolves. The movies, especially the romances, not the war ones, there had been enough of that. Jean hated to see or hear anything *horrid*. Relatives and what they were up to. Where was Norman? She still hadn't met him. Their dreams, of course, half-formed, tiny. A week's holiday in a caravan at Brighton. A house of your own with a front and a back garden. Nothing intellectual, or clever, not s – e – x, nothing at all really. Just chit-chat, gossip, filling the warm spaces in the air with words, out of habit or embarrassment. Waiting for the man to turn up who would look after you for the rest of your life. You had until you were about twenty-five before the worry set in, before your assets began to fade away: the shape, the hair, the skin.

Bored with the repetitiveness of the work at Berkertex, they moved, together, to Camps in Perivale, an American firm – the Yanks were everywhere nowadays. *Got any gum, chum? Pennsyl-*

vania six five thousand! Top of the world, Ma. Frankly, my dear, I don't give a damn. They made foundation garments, bras and corsets mostly, and some surgical wear; everything seemed huge for some reason. But it was a laugh, better than Berkertex, and better paid for that matter; you could pick and choose your job up to a certain point, the point when you started to get in the way of the men. Funny to think during the war of the women doing men's jobs. That was all in the past now, the genie back in the bottle, thank goodness, not that everyone could accept it. There was a demonstration, it said so in *Woman*, for equal pay. In the picture the women all wore black masks. They were ashamed. They were probably ugly, couldn't get a man. It is better to love and be loved.

Jean was dating now, after a fashion, a boy from the Southall football team, Ted. But she and Irene still went dancing together and always came home together, leaving each other at the door. The funny thing was, after Jean's illness, they never went in each other's houses, not even for a cup of tea. You kept your distance, up to a point, you minded your own business. Only so much could be said, only so far could be gone, even among the very best of friends. Especially for Jean, she never said anything in particular, really. Anyway, what do you want to *talk* for, when you could be having fun. And they did have fun, it was great, though they never had much to say; it was hard to explain. Ted met her at the factory gates and cycled home with her. They didn't hang about on the doorstep, kissing, because Grace would be yelling from the window, *When are you coming in then?* That was all there was to it, as far as Irene could make out. Jean wasn't telling, of course. Oh, she was a dark horse, was Jean.

Ted came and went, then there was one other boyfriend before Jack, John Watts, a matelot. He came to visit when he was on leave, which wasn't often. That didn't last long either. So Jean and Irene carried on waiting. Jean could design and sketch and tailor clothes, make them on a Saturday and wear them in the evening, but it was never going to be a career, because girls like Jean didn't have careers. That was a given. The designs were copied from patterns in magazines, never customized, not even a touch. You didn't want to stand out. Everyone just did what everyone else did – it was one of the secret rules, of which there were thousands. Irene and Jean thought, wildly, of getting a flat at one time, but they knew their parents wouldn't stand for it. It wasn't even worth asking.

Two or three times a week, they took the bus over to the Empire Snooker Hall in West Ealing, full of boys – they were the only girls ever there – most of them on the rough side, off the barrows; some of them, one in particular, not that bad actually, a bit dishy. But Jean and Irene didn't go to snare boys, although they were always ogling Jean in her tight sweater and shorts; they went to play table tennis, Jean crouching over the table almost fiercely, determined to win. She hated to lose. Such a silly game everyone thought, ping-pong, but it wasn't, there was the cut, the chop, the topspin lob, the smash, the drop, the backhand flick – it was a whole world. The boys glanced up, pretending to be casual, as they picked off the reds, then the colours, swearing softly when they cocked it up so the two girls wouldn't hear.

Norman, Jean's oldest brother, so mysteriously absent, was in fact expertly weaving baskets in borstal. A petty villain, he had been disqualifed from serving in the war effort.

He had started *behaving antisocial* at school, at Dormer's Wells, having failed the scholarship exam, a lot of stupid questions he didn't even understand. Norman was repeatedly caned for trivial misdemeanours; not even misdemeanours, six strokes once for not being able to do his algebra. The teachers seemed to enjoy it; one of them, a middle-aged cripple with a club foot, waited around a bend on the concrete stairs once and tripped Norman up with his cane, laughing out loud when he took a tumble, cutting his face open. The woodwork teacher flung the work at your face if he didn't like it. Norman skived off, and when they caught him, he was caned in front of the whole school. So Norman began to resent authority, what with one thing and another, began to get an attitude, although they didn't call it that then – it was just showing some cocky. The school bully, Ken Haydon, was the straw that broke the camel's back, picking on

Norman after yet another caning. Norman hit him so hard, he broke his nose, then followed it up with a kicking. After that he was the school hero.

His kid sister, Jean, disapproved of course, she was always inclined towards the conservative type of thing and was never in trouble in school or anywhere else. They were very close, he and Jean. They went dancing together, or up to London for the day, or for a week in Southend. They'd take their own food and the landlady would cook it. Jean was a bit shy, he thought, a home bird: making doilies with Mum, or sewing, or taking romantic novels out of Jubilee Gardens library. Despite his bad reputation, Norman imagined Jean was secretly proud of him.

Of course he didn't tell her everything, or anything much at all really. Not the time he whacked the foreman at his first job at the AEC bus factory, or the time he knocked out the one at the Crown Cork Company, his next job. Of course, she must have noticed when he punched the bloke who stared too hard at his girlfriend, because this one hit back and knocked him silly. By the time he got home he was covered in blood. It wasn't something you could shrug off really. Jean hated it when he got into fights, but he couldn't help it, especially when people took the mickey.

Also it did something to break up the boredom. England was so ruddy boring, no colour, no money, not much to do. For fun at weekends, he'd go to the Northcote Arms in Southall to drink ten pints of mild and bitter: gnat's piss, you didn't even get drunk on that, just relaxed enough for the fight when the barrow boys from the White Hart in Acton came for that week's bust-up. When it got too hairy, Norman hid under the snooker table.

Anything to brighten things up. And it didn't help that Dad was so mean, he had to go to job interviews wearing wellingtons and Billy's tennis trousers. Someone laughed at him in the get-up, so he floored him. He didn't get the job. Where was life? A mate of his had an idea. The new Ealing Studios, where they were making movies, the security was non-existent, so one night – he was only fifteen – he broke into the studio village, climbing over a twelve-foot fence. Inside, he nearly fell over. The rooms were filled up with racks of clothes, and the colours! Instead of everything being black, or brown, or grey, there were colours: screaming reds, cool ferny greens, plum, chartreuse, electric blue, powder blue, an orange shirt – imagine! – jazzy socks, violent purple ties. It was like nothing he had ever seen. Norman stuffed as much as he could down his waistband – a pair of plum trousers, George Raft black-and-white shoes, two sizes too big, a pink shirt – and ran for it. When he got home, he hid everything in the loft, taking it out and dressing up when Grace and Billy were out, clumping along in the floating shoes. Now Norman saw, as he primped himself in the mirror, that there was a way out after all.

The next time he went to work – he was mending fridges now at a place in Perivale – he closely inspected the factory opposite, Guerlain's Lipstick. That same night he broke in, with an empty suitcase, and came out with it full, walking down the main road at twelve o'clock at night.

A while later, he met Fingers Colleta, who'd had half his hand chopped off in a gang fight. *Soho's the place*, said Fingers, and so Norman went uptown, standing on the corners of Wardour Street, his suitcase full of lipstick, rouge, eyeliner. They went like hot cakes, they loved him for it, called him a spiv, although he wasn't really, just a hound, a hound that ran with the pack.

Now, for the first time, Norman had money, and it was a wonderful thing. He went to Lou Sicandelphi in Wardour Street, got a Tony Curtis haircut, then splashed out on a double-breasted grey drape suit, wide shoulders, it was the bollocks, off the ration from a sharpie in Shepherd's Bush. Jean made him a spear-point shirt to go with it, worn with one of the ties from Ealing Studios, as bright as you could crank it, Windsor knot. *Ooh, you look like the dog's dinner*, said Jean. Grey snap-brim fedora with the peak steamed back, a double-breasted camelhair coat with wide belt, pointed shoes with micro-soles, wide trousers, a Players drooping from the lips. That was class.

They always got you in the end, though, first borstal, then, in the end, the Scrubs. It was a pig for Mum and Dad, and for Jean. He supposed Jean was ashamed – how she hated anything that caused a fuss! – although she never said anything. Jean never did, never did say anything really.

After noticing her at the snooker hall, through the blue curtain of smoke, Jack began to see her around, because the world was still small then. The absence of choice bound everything into place. She was there at the Palais, jiving with her spivvy brother, his scrawled-on pencil moustache – you could tell, burnt cork or boot polish. Black-and-white shoes, where on earth did he get those? Not such a bad mover, this girl, though heavier than Thelma; a bit of heft around the thighs and rump gave her movements just a shadow of consideration, of forethought. Not lost in it quite, but she was a trier, a hoofer, that much was sure.

She was there at the cinemas, the Odeons, the Gaumonts, the Empires, usually with this tense-looking one, not bad, taller, not Jack's type though. And then once she was at the hall at the Lady Margaret pub. Jack watched, tending a cup of tea and a ginger nut – no hootch allowed in the dance hall, of course, unless you smuggled it through in a teacup or a Tizer bottle. She was dancing with the other girl, coyly, a little aloof, in what looked like a Crimplene dress, blue, flared from the waist, a cute bow tied across the neckline. Mother-of-pearl necklace. She had made the dress herself. Black highish heels, about two inches, but heavy. She moved with a style that suggested will rather than grace, but it was OK, it was good.

Jack was with Ronnie Van Den Bergh, who was as wide as a bus and a bit of a wolf. He had a reputation. As they moved in on the two girls – Jack in a plain brown single-breasted suit, turn-ups, single-pleat baggies, nothing flash – Jack was centred, calm, the unselfconsciousness that the best dancers had by right. It was no big thing. They didn't need to say much, just a nod towards the floor, an outstretched hand, a *Would you care to?* It was a small band, Kathy Stobart, a six-piece. She played the saxophone. 'Sunny Side of the Street' melted away as it did, no big gesture to mark the final reprise, then it was 'Can't Get Started'.

Ronnie took Irene's hand, though she held back – *that Ronnie!* – but Jean just slid over, adopted the position: hand round waist, face six inches away, eyes focused across the right shoulder, eyes merely catching each other then letting go, silver fish in nets too wide. The perfume, he could swear, was Evening in Paris. A slight gathering. Then Jack took her off, the fishtail, the half-chassis, the whole kit and caboodle. It was easy, it was right. She kept up.

Trumpets did not sound, nor did lightning sheet and fork. As Jack chatted over the curving and slipslide of the light, wistful music, he felt no reverberation from the future, of a lifetime in each other's company, of children, and worry, the shared bed, achievement and loss. But, he thought, she was nice, though not in that dull, apologetic way, where niceness edged out spirit into the murk. Jean, yes, Jean was OK. They would meet again, if she would agree to it, and she did, readily enough. But Irene was less keen on Ronnie – who knew what he would try?

Jean turned down the lift home on the Vincent Comet as he expected. Still, he knew she was impressed by the line and slip and cut of the machine, which was enough for this first time. Instead they walked the two girls to the bus stop. Jean's dress rustled like a cornfield as she walked, with that stumpy, purposeful step. They said goodbye, without a kiss, though Ronnie tried with Irene, of course. Ugh. But still – See you soon. The Montague? Saturday? Sure.

And they turned up, that following Saturday, as if it were a given. And soon, soon enough, without anyone really stating it, or designing it, Jack and Jean were going steady, that netherland of testing, assessing, of cautious touching. Jack paid for everything, of course, although a lot of the boys thought this was old hat, a con. For Jack, the boys – Ronnie, Derek Beard, Freddie Wade, Cyril, Terry, Derek, Phil, the Empire mob – began to take a back seat, while for Jean, Irene was edging out of the picture, especially since she and Ronnie couldn't hit it off. As always – always! – nothing much was said, nothing that got to the heart of anything in particular. Everything was expressed through action, and inference, and intuition. Perhaps there was a knack then, before the talk show, before the therapist and counsellor, of feeling your way through life, of charting some course without stating the coordinates. And perhaps that is lost now.

But for Jean and Jack, some conviction, some invisible imperative, was working its way into palpability. They went to see the Andy Hardy movies and *Sunset Boulevard* and *Strangers on a Train*. They went to see the Ralph Reader Gang Shows, Jimmy James and Ted Ray at the Palladium. They went to see *Annie Get Your Gun* and *Carousel*. And then they parted, and Jean returned to her Singer and Jack to his paper bags, his beets and snips and toms and pots, and all the while, under the surface, choice was turning into fate, will into a kind of unconscious necessity.

It was 1951 and England remained frozen, dull and silted down in the past. Possibilities had yet to develop; poverty and the force of the guardians of the state – *behave, stop that* – pressed down as insistently as ever, although there were flashes of a different future, like premonitions. Jack read about them in the *Herald*, and the *Sunday Express* – the New Edwardians of the West End, the Teds, with those narrowed trousers, the brocade waistcoats, the velvet collars. The slipping of the formal, the press of the individual, thanks to the Americans and the Italians – blue jeans, slacks, windcheaters, coloured raincoats. Rayon, Crimplene, nylon. What was once simply *understood* was beginning the long decay into particles of choice, of expression. Women's hairdressing salons on every street. The new self-service Sainsbury's that had opened. The bouffant and the backcomb. The milk bar, with frothy coffee that tasted like hot speckled nothing, too hot to taste. Leicester Square, lit up for the first time in ten years. The bonfire of controls, at least the external, visible, legal controls.

Still, these were just coloured specks on a blank backdrop. They did not even seem to be what they were, seeds pregnant with future. England hugged you close, warming and suffocating, constricting and securing. It stretched back, it would stretch forward, storm-cloud grey, cold and sticky and pale as a Wall's briquette. The stories it told, the stories you needed to survive, were the same as ever, the motifs like well-worn rivets holding them in place. King. Tea (always warm the pot). Bread and suet (pudding). Great. Sun that never – Stiff upper – England can take it! Dull. Decent. Brave. Best country in the – Marmalade and Bovril. Bread and dripping. *Never have so many – A home fit for – Vivat. Vivat.*

Jack went to meet Billy and Grace at the house in Rosecroft Road, roaring to a halt on the Vincent, bracing himself against it, leaning into the weight. Propping it and then shaping his hair, disordered by the wind (no helmets then). He rang the electric doorbell that sounded the fanfare of the new suburbs: *bing-bong.*

Grace was intimidated at first; he seemed a cut above, to have such a vehicle. Norman, back from one of his secret absences, gaped at the machine. Norman went dirt-track racing at the White City with Norman Staple, who lived around the corner in Rutland Road; he loved the thrill. So Jack had his vote. Alan talked nineteen to the dozen but only about and to himself, poor Alan, so it was hard to tell. Billy – well, Billy thought what Grace thought. And Grace was pleased.

Such an extraordinary event – the arrival of this charming man, on his Vincent Comet, with his navy overcoat flapping around his knees like a schooner sail – demanded particular treatment. The front room was opened! After the preliminaries of tea, and Garibaldi biscuits and some Madeira or seedcake, and nervous hellos and chitter-chatter, Jean and Jack were led into the front room, to *court.* The hard three-piece suite, the knick-knacks in the glass-fronted case, the best carpet scrap laid over the dun lino. Beige wallpaper, cheap mirror over the open fireplace, unlit. Two cups of tea, a small sherry, they were left alone, to hold hands and to talk. Maybe a hasty kiss, not a kiss that penetrated but one that touched and teased and suggested, that inferred instead of pronounced.

There were other marker posts to be passed, other approvals to solicit. Arthur, Jack's brother, was living with Olive in one room over a shop in Chiswick. The roar of the cycle engine announced them in an otherwise quiet street – all the streets were quiet then, in subtopia. This time Jean was on the back, hair enclosed in a gypsy turban, face tanned by the wind. She wore a second-hand leather jacket. Oh, she was attractive all right, thought Olive, and she knew it. She could see what Jack saw in her. The hair, the bosoms. Could they be real? Olive was still working in the chocolate shop in Ealing and this impressed Jean no end. *Ooh, I couldn't do that. Haven't got the brains for it.* She gave a little laugh, at her own expense. But actually, Olive didn't take to her, not at all. She seemed spoilt, full of herself. Almost the first thing she said was, *Ooh, that lipstick. It doesn't suit you, you know.* Cheek. But Olive said nothing, she wasn't that sort of person. Anyway, Arthur seemed to like her. *Nice, isn't she, Ol? I suppose so.*

Jack was sure now that he was in that condition, that epiphany, the singers and actors and writers were so preoccupied with, the condition of love. They were just – good together. She was everything he wanted: beautiful, intelligent, practical – that was important – and physical, sporty. He could see no flaws, no bad side, just as the songs suggested. And she loved him too, he was sure, although she never said so. They never discussed what it was they liked in each other, at least not with each other, not in words as such. Those things were only for the voice inside, and, even there, were wordless.

In the late summer of 1951, Jean and Jack performed a final rite, a testing, on their progress towards matrimony. They went on holiday together, for a week, to a boarding house in Weymouth, with the blessing of Grace and Billy. They were trusted to keep within limits, and they did so, Jack sleeping in the lounge downstairs, while Jean was lodged in the bedroom upstairs. The owners insisted that he did not go upstairs at all and he kept his word.

They motored around the town on the Vincent, stopping, going for walks, eating ice-cream, swimming, playing the arcades. Kissing, more forcefully now, the initial coyness retreating. They walked under the stars in England and they were happy, they supposed – it wasn't a question, then, that you asked of yourself – and they knew now what must surely unfold.

On 17 January 1952, Jack took Jean to see *South Pacific* at the London Palladium, to celebrate her twenty-first birthday. They were late, pushing into the row through shushes and tuts. But it was marvellous, Mary Martin and Ezio Pinza reprising their Broadway roles as Nellie Forbush and Emile de Becque, the stage transformed into paradise. It was corny, *corny as Kansas in springtime*, with the knee-slapping and slushy ending, but Jack and Jean loved it, the tunes, already seeming like standards, forming like foam on their lips. *I'm in love, I'm in love, I'm in love, I'm in love with a . . .*

Walking on the streets afterwards, Jean got to talking about how much she liked Olive and Arthur and, quite casual, Jack said, *How would you like them to be your in-laws?* And Jean said, *Oh, Jack, yes,* and that was it. They carried on walking, the most natural thing in the world. Jack gave her a ring, platinum with a single solitaire. They would be married in July. No point, as Jack so straightforwardly put it, in hanging about.

The day was set for 12 July 1952, at St James's Church, a few yards from both the Empire Snooker Hall and Hetty's house. Jean set to making the dress for herself and for the bridesmaids, Irene and Bud's daughter Betty. Hers was to be white satin, full length, with a lace surplice and septagonal neckline, a headress and a veil. There would be white flowers in her hair.

They spent the night before preparing the wedding feast for the thirty or so guests – cooked ham, salads, cheese, fresh raspberries, a few bottles of wine – and made up the trestle tables in Hetty's back room. Billy and Grace had no money to make their contribution, but Billy baked the cake and Grace gave some loose carpet as a gift.

The ceremony was simple, C of E. Arthur was the best man. Jack wore a blue single-breasted suit, made by Jack Gay at Northfields, with a carnation in his lapel. Jean carried a bouquet of red roses. Hymns were sung, vows made, to love and worship and honour. To obey. These incantations bound them for ever, this they knew; marriage was for life. As Jean left the church, she was given the gift of two lucky horseshoes. She threw her bouquet and Irene caught it.

They walked from the church to Hetty's and ate that simple lunch. There were no speeches, for, being English, all were ill at ease with ritual. Every last penny had been spent on the wedding, but Terry O'Dwyer had given Jack a wedding bonus of £40, to see them through the honeymoon.

At about four o'clock, they set off into the afternoon sun, a small crowd cheering as the neighbours peered, heading out towards Cornwall. They had put a deposit on a caravan, for Jean, as she told Irene, had always dreamed of a holiday at the seaside in a caravan. Jean had a knapsack on her back and wore an army-surplus black leather coat.

They stopped on the way at a hotel in Shaftesbury for their wedding night. In the bedroom, a four-poster. They were both virgins, a little nervous to be having sex for the first time, she twenty-one, he twenty-six, with the one and only person they would ever sleep with. And it was a sacrament, and it sealed and bound their marriage.

The next morning they arrived at the caravan, which they had yet to see, near Watergate Bay. They had imagined something spacious, perhaps made of painted wood in a wide field of grass, with nothing but the blue air and the far horizon. When they saw the caravan, they struggled to stifle their disappointment. It was a tiny, dirty box in the closed backyard of a house. It was a slum on wheels. Jean sat down and cried.

Without so much as a word to the owners of the caravan, they set off again, to find another place to stay. Like Joseph and Mary, they knocked and pleaded and begged, but there was nothing; it was the height of the season. It was beginning to rain. Along the far coast at Watergate Bay there were a few more boarding houses. Jack revved the Vincent, as if its power alone could lead them to sanctuary. As the rain settled in and they drove along the beach road, Jack saw a colour, a flash at the edge of his vision. Stopping, pulling back, he saw there was a saint, Mary perhaps, a stained-glass glint above a door. He swung the Comet in that direction and pulled up before the beach hotel.

Up a flight of stairs, a middle-aged woman welcomed them. No, she had no room, it was the height of the season! But then she saw Jean, and she heard the story, and she thought. A friend of hers . . .

And so it was that the friend put them up for a few days, and after that there was a vacancy in the hotel for the rest of the fortnight. There was a beautiful room to rent, within their means, overlooking the yellow beach. As they left the hotel, the rain stopped and the sun cleared some scrap of raincloud and did not once go in again. And it was perfect, as the Virgin Mary smiled down upon these newlyweds, upon my pert, pretty, not-quite-sure-of-herself mother, Jean, and upon my solid, handsome, almost-arrogant father, Jack.

Chapter Nine

Thus far, this true narrative seems to me to have acquired the air of fiction, a short story that might have appeared in one of the pulp magazines Jean would have read as a girl, *Peg's Paper* or *Secrets* or *Glamorous*. Perhaps the story was called 'Stolen Joys' or 'Dangerous Bliss' or 'Passionate Nights'. A pretty girl, swept away by a handsome sailor who arrives not on a white steed but, better still, on a black and chrome Vincent Comet HRD. Love, a white wedding, a honeymoon saved at the last minute from disaster by a glittering Madonna. Happy endings and a future that seemed to glow with all the essential ingredients of the perfect denouement: horizons, broad highways, new dawns.

And this, for the time being at least, is how the story continues, as if underwritten by benevolent myth. Jean and Jack make up a flat at Hetty's, where they will live until they've *got enough behind them* to have children. To have a family is not a decision; it is the grain of life, with which Jack and Jean know they must accord.

Jean has not as yet given up working, but she will when the children come and without a second thought, for it is not a wife's role to make money, that's an *accepted thing*. She sews, from patterns in magazines, or bought at Rowses in West Ealing, which depict, in pastel sketches, graceful, modern women, in yellow dirndls and plum slacks and oatmeal jerseys. And knits and crochets, and chooses floral print curtains and pictures of cathedrals and landscapes, and china knick-knacks for the flat, to make it cosy, to make it their own. Nothing is bought on the knock, because the Victorian habit of thrift is too inbred to be dislodged by the new, bright and brittle appeals in *Reveille* and *Tit-Bits* and *Woman's Own* to buy now and pay later.

They save, cash put into a Post Office savings account, for there are no bank accounts and cheque books, no stocks or bonds or 'investments'. Jack, the wage earner, rises at six every morning to go to the shop, where he will put on his starched dun coat and prepare for opening by scraping caked ice from the freezer, boiling beetroots, cutting back and cleaning the filthy soft lettuces, trimming slimed cabbage. Maggots and worms and tropical spiders crawl from the cos lettuces and the Webb's Wonders and the great boxes of bananas. There are rat traps on the floor, where, on some days, fat vermin are extracted, their necks, or legs, or backs broken. At night the rats sometimes scamper across the window display: pyramids of foil-wrapped satsumas. Hanging paper advertisements for Outspan and Fyffes and Jaffa are the only decorations in the shop, apart from a cheesecake calendar in the dank back room, the pubic hairs blotted out. The twelve women – August is black, the rest are Mateus pink or the colour of weak porridge – each smile cheerily as if about to offer a cup of tea and a plate of Garibaldi rather than their airbrushed, depilated bodies.

The range of produce is by and large modest, English and seasonal, but this being Notting Hill Gate, there are occasionally fruits and vegetables still on the borders of vocabulary. There are avocados, courgettes, calabrese, capsicum and mange tout, lychees and kumquats. In winter, there are hothouse grapes, Belgian Colmar and Muscats. They sell garlic, which Jack would never take home, for herbs and spices are still considered an exotic continental embellishment to food. There are tiny bottles of Sasso olive oil, V-8 vegetable juice, Epicure pineapple chunks and Del Monte mandarin pieces in syrup, and cobnuts and Ogen melons. In the freezer, a scanty selection of frozen prawns, frozen orange juice, fish fingers, cod steaks, a few luxury items from Young's: Coquilles St Jacques or Sole Bonne Femme. Outside, plastic buckets of flowers by season.

Each day is hard graft, with much lifting and bending and cleaning and cutting and serving. There are deliveries to be made in the Commer van, with its face as blunt and kind as a pig, up flights and flights of stairs to dowager duchesses and unemployed thespians and jazz beards in mansion blocks behind Holland Park. In the winter it is bitterly cold, even in the closed-off part of the shop in the back, and fingers are always numb and blue. But Jack likes his job, even loves it, because it is a *people job*. He gets to meet all sorts – actors, singers, lords and ladies, villains and tarts, you name it. And they would chat for ages about things you never got to talk about at home – politics, the scandal, what was on up West.

At around twelve o'clock, Dennis, Terry O'Dwyer's cousin, would cook a full meal in the tiny back room, or Jack would have dinner at one of the new Italian cafés that had opened around the corner, the Piccolo or the Varsi Grill, maybe one of these new pizza pies or a lasagna with chips, and some cassata or Neapolitan block for pudding, with a frothy coffee. Or maybe he would go to the Galleon in Pembridge Road and eat pork chops with cabbage and jam roly-poly, or shepherd's pie with sprouts and rhubarb tart with custard, washed down by a cup of tea. As he ate, he would read: Ed McBain, Dorothy L. Sayers, James Clavell, Harold Robbins or short stories by O. Henry. After exactly one hour, he'd be back, sweeping the floor, folding and stacking boxes, trimming, cutting, weighing, measuring, serving. On his feet all day long, stamping to keep them warm in January and February when you could see your breath turn into clouds even with the one-bar electric fire turned on. But the wage was good, six pounds a week plus whatever you could trouser, within reason of course. At six o'clock he'd leave for home on the Vincent, arriving back at Hetty's about six-thirty. Jean would have his dinner ready for him on the downstairs table.

Jack now had two weeks' paid holiday a year, and in the

summer of 1953 they decided to take a caravan holiday in Mawgan Porth with Olive and Arthur, and their two kids, Jilly and David. Olive and Arthur were bringing them up in a rented two-bedroom flat in Chiswick on Arthur's salary as a factory worker at Jantzen's Swimming Costumes in Brentford. It was hard to make ends meet; Olive envied Jean, who seemed to have everything she wanted, spoilt by her parents and now spoilt by Jack. Ah, well. Olive had no clothes to wear; she even had to borrow those off Jean.

The holiday went well, even though the weather was iffy, mackerel skies mixed with thunderstorms. The caravan smelled of Calor Gas. Jack and Jean took the double bed, and the children had bunks, while Olive and Arthur slept on an inflatable Lilo that gradually, every night, lost all the air through the valve and left them sleeping on the hard floor. They didn't let on, of course. Olive tried hard to get on with Jean, but it wasn't always easy. They all played cards, but Jean wouldn't join in and wouldn't try to learn. She wouldn't go for walks in the evenings because, she said, the flies got in her hair. She had tantrums when she couldn't get her own way; Jack would not respond, would simply walk away. And one time – and this really got Olive's goat – she slapped David hard on the legs when he accidentally kicked sand on her. Olive never said anything – you don't, do you? – but Jean had no right to do that.

Shortly after the end of the holiday, Jean missed her period and for one of the rare times in his life – for he was not given, at any time, to extremes of emotion – Jack felt elated, for Jean was pregnant, in the family way. In March 1954, Jack and Jean's first boy, Jeffrey Stephen, was born in Perivale Maternity Hospital. He was perfect, without a blemish, with dark hair and eyes, and even, handsome features.

It was another twelve months before Jean fell pregnant again. But something was wrong, as I unfolded, fish, then newt, then frog, then weird homunculus. Jean could not sense it, she had no instinct for disaster or omen. But a sort of omen there was, as, instead of the lush and lustre of her mane of hair growing as the months played out, dabs and clutches of growth began to stick in her widetooth comb and her peppermint mother-of-pearl brush.

She started to fret, for what were a woman's assets in this world, what was her capital? The breasts, the hair, the legs, the smile. In fact, Jack didn't mind, thought physical attraction superficial, but it was hard for a woman to believe it. Already her figure had broadened and inflated below the waist from the first birth – *Tree trunks, Irene, that's what my legs are* – while the six months of breast-feeding had stretched and neutered the tilt of her most vital statistic. If the hair went, she would be a monster, a circus lady.

The doctors didn't really know what was wrong with her. They called it alopecia, something to do with the nerves perhaps. Maybe it would recover on its own, but best be on the safe side. They gave her handfuls of pills, even though she was three months gone. Jean feared for the child, but they knew best.

The moment I was born, on 23 January 1956, at 8.05 a.m., it was obvious that some kind of mistake had been made. They pulled me, all vernix and crimson, out of the womb and I panted without screaming and shivered. My colour under the ick was strange, not so much blue as gunmetal grey. There was a bloody gap where the centre of my upper mouth should have been. I was weedy, just under six pounds, and fretful.

They didn't cut me open right away, because they didn't know that so hard on being born, I was dying. But I vomited up my food, my mother's milk, so they X-rayed me and found something black where there should have been only shadow.

There was a chance, but it was finer than lint. Too sickly, too fragile to be held, I was wired up in a pink plastic incubator, tubes forced into my day-old wrists and ankles, as thick as children's crayons. After three weeks or so, perhaps I would be strong enough to survive the operation which would open my gut. Such an operation had never been performed on someone so young.

Jean cried for sorrow and shame as the hospital priest, gauze-masked, in black, performed the rite of baptism, as I screamed and kicked, untouched by my watching mother, the proteins and warm fluids seeping into me through tubes like anchoring ropes. I kicked with outrage and punched the air to make my claim on life, with purple fists as small as monkey nuts. My hare lip was warped into a sneer, a parody of my father's.

Having no choice in the matter, Jack continued to work, while Jean sat helpless in the pink enamelled steel-frame bed and the doctors, the doctors of the still-new National Health Service, waited and probed and measured and pinched, brooding behind clipboards like judges' lecterns. After three weeks it was decided, *now and no longer*. The priest, having provided the first bracket for my life, was now ready to supply the last, a sad sermon of analgesia; suffer little children to come unto me.

So it was that my first real experience of life, beyond the instincts of breath and tears, was not my mother's touch but the cut of a surgeon's knife, opening me from chestbone to groin. They sought for the kidney that they knew to be raddled, but it had more or less gone, only a husk remaining that had not been consumed by cancer. It appeared that from my very conception, in and before my birthing, my bones and skin and organs had coalesced around a pivotal inclination to blankness, the size of a peachstone.

But England saved me, in the shape and hope of the National Health Service, with its banks of doctors and new technology, all paid for by what would one day come to be known, with strange contempt, as the nanny state. After my hours under the tiny knives, the priest standing by with his magic book, I came to and began to scream once more. Jean watched as I kicked into life again behind my glass bubble, her arms folded, unable to hold what she had made.

I would not let go of my life, although the trauma and bruising of the operation left me wounded and mottled, although my wrists and ankles were punctured. There was a gash half the length of my body struggling to heal. My open lip now wore a steel cage to protect it from my feeble punching. I was only partly there, my one kidney doing the job of two, as it would have to for the rest of my life.

I was too weak to leave hospital and still close to death. Each day my mother stole sleep when she could, and in each awakening expected a stony silence and stillness in the crib. No one other than my father came to see her. Grief was private and to be quarantined, as if communicable by touch. Olive, all earlier reservations forgotten, made the effort on one occasion, to find Jean bored and wan. She was hooked up to a machine to extract her milk.

Jack came every evening after work, to try and talk it out. What to do with Jeffrey Stephen? Eighteen months old now, he needed his mother, but Jean could, it was said, be in there for weeks. *What it boils down to*, as my father was fond of saying when he determined to reach the nub of a matter, *is this*: if Jeff was brought in once a week to see his mother, it might simply upset him, so it was decided that mother and firstborn would be separated for as long as Jean was in hospital, and that Olive would take care of him at the flat in Wolseley Gardens. It would be for a short while only, after all.

As it turned out, Jean stayed in hospital for three months, separated from Jeff and with her second son still trying not to die.

The family snapshots of my childhood are hard to decipher, fenced off as they are by the conventions of pose, lark and grin. I watch myself grow, still in monochrome, leaping by self-conscious smile and shy grimace towards adolescence. My clothes are lumpy and plain, and I am, in all honesty, an unattractive child, eclipsed by my handsome father and neat, Roman brother.

There is just one photograph of me in my steel face-cage, which I was required to wear for more than a year after my discharge from hospital, to stop me picking at my wrecked lip. I am looking dumbly at the camera, apparently ungrateful that such a record is to be made of my disfigurement. Jean is holding me on her knee. She is not smiling as requested. She seems to look pained, even agonized.

The remainder of the photographs of my childhood are more or less archetypal and with little to distinguish them from those of my father a generation before. There are donkey rides and petting zoos, long dune grass, buckets and spades, pulled faces, sack races. The cars are Fords, Mini Clubmen, Austin A30s, Morris Traveller Shooting Brakes. Here are Jack, Jeff and I posing with our heads in the stocks outside Corfe Castle. Here is my gaolbird uncle Norman with seaweed draped over his hair on the Devon coast. Here is Arthur carrying me in a hessian sack across an empty beach in Cornwall, with his too-small mouth, an unscarred copy of mine, stretched in a grin.

As I get older, I grow fatter, some predetermination inherited from my father. My hair is white blond, shaved roughly at the sides. It occurs to me wanly that my mother made the right decision in abandoning hairdressing as a career. I look thoroughly piqued and there seems already to be bagging under my eyes. I stand at the centre of a cold fountain, holiday chalets, the size and shape of garden sheds, framed in the background. The half-tone photographs make it impossible to guess the weather.

In later childhood, the holiday photographs switch from seaside boarding houses to inland holiday camps, which Jack and Jean discovered in 1963, and became enthusiastic about. We did not go to Butlin's or Pontin's, where, Jack imagined, you would get the hobbledehoys, or real working class. Instead, our camps styled themselves 'Country Clubs' or 'Halls', and offered a slightly less regimented, brassy regime than Billy Butlin or Fred Pontin. We mainly holidayed in Devon, at the Torbay Chalet Hotel, or Barton Hall or St Audrey's Bay, which admitted that it was a holiday camp, and the Devon Coast Country Club, which pretended it was not.

It was about this time that our class was beginning to discover the attractions of southern Spain, as charter flights boomed throughout the 1960s and factory workers and plumber's mates brought back wire guitars, wineskins, ornamental maracas and flamenco dolls to place on G-plan shelves. But we stuck to England, a country still loved by my parents and their friends in a quiet, insistent way.

So our souvenirs remained map tea towels, inscribed clogs, lucky Cornish pixies, Welsh slate etchings, novelty pennants, mottoed keyholders, layers of Alum Bay coloured sand in a glass tube. Or, from the holiday camps, nickel-silver badges and trophies for ping-pong or badminton.

The pattern of each of the country clubs was much the same – bluecoats, or greencoats, or greycoats, urging participation from the wake-up call announced through the barking PA. *Roll out of bed in the morning/with a great big smile and a good, good morning.* Jack and Jean were treated as hybrids of adult and child, as evidenced by the signs on the toilets, 'Lads and Lasses', and the gamesmasterish invocations to 'have a go'. We swam in unheated pools, secretly pissed in by children and stuffed with chlorine. There were card rooms and snooker halls, ping-pong tables, rooms full of dartboards and communal televisions. There were egg and spoon races, tugs-of-war, treasure troves, day trips, beetle drives, paper chases, crazy golf and gorgeous granny competitions.

By now, my parents had progressed from badminton to tennis, although Jean still held her racquet as if for badminton, using too much wrist, wielding it like a saucepan, face always set in absolute determination to win. Underneath, the ever-present fear that a sharp gust of wind or a stray ball would knock her wig to one side, leaving her exposed, bald-pated. Jean, with this in mind, was always on guard, for she could imagine nothing worse than being exposed as what she was, the thing that people always – unwittingly – made jokes about over the cherry brandy or bottles of Stingo: chrome-domes, slap-heads, coots.

In the evenings the main meal would be slightly continental – perhaps paella, or cannelloni, or curry with raisins – and the wine was rosé or Asti Spumante or Liebfraumilch. Then Jeff and I went to bed in monitored chalets, little more than beach huts with beds, Goblin Teasmades and nylon sheets that issued tiny electric shocks. After nightfall, ballroom dancing and novelty competitions – lookalikes, knobbly knees, fancy dress.

In one photograph, engraved in copperplate 'A Souvenir of Our Holiday Torbay Chalet Hotel', my mother, Irene and her husband, Bob, are dressed up in pyjamas and nylon nighties, holding candles, for the theme of 'Wee Willie Winkie'. A showgirl stands off to the left and Rory Blackwell, a bluecoat, to the right, his face screwed up in a showman's smirk. A three-piece show-band is in the background in jackets and ties, playing 'Spanish Fly' or 'Que Sera Sera' or 'Volare'. Later they will accompany the ritual singsong that ends the evening: 'Run Rabbit Run' and 'Lily of Laguna' and 'Hello, Hello, Whose Your Lady Friend' and 'Ta Ra Ra Boom De Ay' and 'I've Got Sixpence' and 'Mairzy Dotes' and 'How Much is that Doggy in the Window?'. Always the evening will close with 'Goodnight, Campers' sung to the tune of 'Goodnight, Sweetheart'.

As I study the photographs, I begin, lazily, to intellectualize: *it may be that the holiday camps prefigured and reflected, in their tired brightness and choreographed bonhomie, an emerging England, one where community was by agreement rather than instinct, a kind of pre-arranged herding, and where the insistence on fun, and vitality, and zest drowned out all other appeals to self-reflection and quietude.*

This, I then realize, is a defensive thought, the reflex distancing of a full-grown parvenu, ashamed of the fat boy in the corduroy jacket, plaid wool tie and paisley shirt, doing the conga and the twist and the March of the Mods amid the sparkling ballroom lights.

Most of the snapshots are of these successive, brash holiday camps, but there are a handful from the family home, purchased by Jack in February 1958, when I was two years old, for £2,100. He had been offered a workman's cottage behind the shop in Notting Hill for £500, but turned it down as slummy. Instead, there was the house at 31 Rutland Road, next door to Bertha Staple, whose son went dirt-track racing with Norman, Jean's brother. Billy, Grace and Alan were two streets away, at 4 Rose-croft. Jean, dutiful in daughterhood as in everything else, would visit every day.

The house that Jean and Jack bought was more or less replicated hundreds of thousands of times over in post-war Britain. It was part of a six-house terrace. There was a coal fire with a back boiler with wooden panelling around it. Plain lino was ready-fitted. French doors at the back led on to a small garden. A wire fence between concrete posts in turn led to the garage, anticipating a car that would not arrive until the mid-1960s. There was a connecting door in the living room to a small kitchen, the doorknobs brown Bakelite. Upstairs, a copy of Grace and Billy's, two largish bedrooms, maybe ten foot square, one box room, and separate toilet and bathroom.

Jack and Jean furnished the living room with a maroon velour, cord-effect three-piece suite and put up wallpaper showing cornstalks and wild flowers. There was also flock wallpaper and standing lamps with prissy fringes. The only evidence of the new scientific age that the newspapers claimed they were living through were classic, geometry-driven 1950s scatter cushions, depicting molecular shapes. Upstairs, Jeff and I slept in an army-surplus bunk bed, him on the top, me on the bottom. On the ceiling, night-blue paper dotted with yellow stars at which I would often stare and pretend that I was in the open, looking up at the firmament.

The photos show a neat rear lawn being dutifully mown by my father while I sweep the path. There were rockeries, and concrete woodland animals, and snapdragons, and mind-your-own-business, and ivy and honeysuckle snaking along wooden trellises. Next door, at Bertha Staple's, there was a pond with frogs, goldfish and dragonfly. I kept a tortoise for a short while.

Here I am pedalling a tricycle along the path towards the garage. And here, years later, I pose in my County Grammar School uniform from Abernethies in Greenford, the prize for my sailed-through eleven plus. Around the same time, I stand confronting Jeff; we are caught like two boxers, which is apt, for there has been tension between us ever since Jean arrived home after a three-month absence with a squalling, mutant rival. Sometimes, I wish him dead.

Out of the fifty or so photographs of this time – the late 1950s and 1960s – only three are colour, all from the fag end of this era, as it shades into the time-burb of the 1970s. Suddenly my past does not look elegant, muted, dignified, but lurid and vulgar. Jack and Jean, Olive and Arthur, stand in front of a bar decorated for Christmas, Olive in a navy blue trouser suit, Jean in a red cable knit sweater and a miniskirt. Arthur is smoking a Manikin cigarillo. Both Olive and Jean have blue eyeshadow, betokening the 1960s, as does the short, piled-up hair. There is another colour snap of my elder brother, hair down to his shoulders, the beginnings of stubble on his chin. The flock wallpaper has gone now, to be replaced with bright pine veneer and violently purple curtains. The colour of history, the spectrum of England, seems to have suddenly changed, to have become as brassy and vivid as the 3-D shock of a plastic Mattel Viewfinder.

And this is the story the newspapers told, of a country beginning to emerge from its perpetual Victorian mourning and formality around the time of my birth, and becoming Technicolor, Sensur-rounded, free, flippant, classless, guiltless and disco-bright.

My intellectual twitch recurs: *the contours and content of the decade and a half after 1956 have been haggled over ever since, claimed by one faction as a disastrous prolequake, the beginnings of corruption and decadence, and by the other as the awakening of liberty and classlessness.*

But in Southall, in all the horizontal, racing spread of subtopia throughout England, the 1960s was little more than a rumour, indistinguishable from other forms of entertainment. Here, Viet-nam or Grosvenor Square or the moonshot was no more, and perhaps slightly less real, than *Danger Man* or *Compact* or *Our Man Flint*, and less significant than a new flavour of crisp. If Jack thought about it at all, he would have been in favour of the bomb rather than Bertrand Russell, the police rather than the pro-testers, the Americans rather than the Vietcong. Despite lifelong socialism, his reflex was always to support authority. And it was a reflex; any serious moral thought – of which, in a way, there was much – was confined entirely to the private, the intimate, the local. So we did not protest, or grieve for Kennedy, or debate Betty Friedan. We just got on with it/took life as it came/did what we had to do/put up with it/just accepted it. We did not see *Blow-Up* or *Zabriskie Point*, but *The Swiss Family Robinson* and *The Sound of Music* and *Zulu*. For Jean and Jack, and the families of the new towns, and creeping green-belt housing estates, and the flat, ubiquitous edge of city developments, the 1960s was not 'events' but a sort of vaguely felt process that expressed itself largely through vacuum cleaners, glittering soapsuds, rising wages, Cyril Lord carpets, ever-lengthening holidays and, above all, television.

The new, framed, packaged, spectral community magnetized people out of the dance halls and pubs and into overlit front rooms with deliberately parted curtains which would display to the street the largeness of their screens, each night, beckoning more like a hearth than their log-effect gas fires. Mr Wall over the road – whose Christian name, hilariously to me and Jeff, was Walter – had the largest, closely followed by the snobby Mrs Pugh at No. 37, who always wore elbow-length gloves. Acquaintance was no longer through bothersome neighbours, but through Eamonn Andrews, Michael Miles, Millicent Martin, Val Parnell. The cocooning, the particle-by-particle separation of England had been sparked. It would later be flamed, intensified, by, in turns, the car, the telephone, the walkman, the PC and simple fear.

Families were imperceptibly becoming partial, flyaway; but the life of my family, a cell of a much larger interior common-wealth still bleeding out from the inner cities, stayed firm, if nuclear rather than extended. There was no sense of gathering entropy; we were lulled by a gentle, growing security and confidence, and a decaying of work's tyranny.

The pattern of existence was traditional and conservative, a life more accurately reflected in 'The Gambols' than Cathy Come Home. Jean was a Daz housewife, a Gibbs SR mum, worried about the cleanliness of clothes and the neatness of home and children. She took pains to be bright and optimistic. She left money matters to Jack, since she considered herself innumerative. She stuck to what she sensed she was good at. With pinny and novelty oven glove, she prepared dinner every day for Jeff and me. We walked home from Lady Margaret Primary School at midday, to be met with skinless sausages, fried luncheon meat, liver sausage, boiled potatoes, bubble and squeak or leftovers from the previous night's tea.

Jean did not consider that her function was to hold opinions, or hanker for a larger life. Her particular job – apart from child-rearing and hygiene – was to keep the threads of the family together. It was she who would remember birthdays, who would carefully pick a card from Forbuoys in Allenby Road, one with a soft toy or a sunset on the front. The sentimental rhymes were carefully and seriously examined for relevance. The love they spoke of, in copperplate decorated with fluffed clouds, was the solvent for all ills, all disadvantage. This, I imagine, was her great and deepest belief, and, by the ubiquity of these cards, she was not alone in it. The thought that all could be redeemed through love was perhaps the closest thing there was to idealism in the endless dull and practical blur of subtopia, unless you counted the closely related aspiration of 'niceness'.

Perhaps she would add a poem of her own, agonizing to get the rhyme and metre right. Her job, her role, was to maintain relationships, to smooth wrinkles and resolve quarrels. There was an almost complete myopia for anything outside the family.

She went shopping once a day at the Top Shops, where she would 'pop' rather than 'go'. Popping was the fundamental verb of suburban life – you would pop down the shops, pop in for a cup of tea, pop round the corner. Popping tended to be confined to small, informal journeys (despite the fact that to die was customarily simply to 'pop off'). Jean did not pop when she did her once-weekly 'big shop'; she simply went, or 'schlepped' in a scrap of Yiddish that had found its way into our vocabulary for some reason. She travelled to Bentalls or John Sanders in Ealing Broadway, stores that were filling up with novel objects and materials – Melamine, polythene, polystyrene, Bri-nylon, Terylene, Pyrex, Orlon and Banlon and Dacron, Crimplene and Perspex, Formica, aluminium, thermoplastics, tubular steel.

Her chores were completed without complaint or resentment, with, in fact, pride. Jean did not consider herself a drudge and never seemed to be sapped of her childlike brio, her slightly taut 'perkiness', by the endless round of tasks. The women's movement – *women's lib* – did not register, let alone find a place in domestic conversation. If brought up, it would be left to one of the men to suggest, artfully, that he was thoroughly in favour of bra-burning. And that was as far as it went. Feminism was something 'out there', in a larger world which was ruled, and engaged in, by 'them', or more accurately, 'they'. It was 'they' who shouldn't allow this or that, 'they' who knew what they were doing (I suppose . . .), 'they' who made a lot of fuss about nothing. 'They' were sometimes benevolent and wise, sometimes hectoring and selfish, often stuck up and with no idea what 'real life' was about.

'They', never precisely named or defined, were the people who knew things, who were 'experts', who had power and money, who lived in a distant, invisible world that was as unchangeable by people like us as the weather. They held dinner parties, ate in restaurants that had candles in Chianti bottles, went to public schools and 'knew all the right people'. There was 'one law for them and one for us'. But by and large, 'they' were tolerated and not particularly resented – *Good luck to 'em. I'd do the same in their shoes.*

Our England was to the naked eye, if perpetually lowly, slowly getting better. There were the new grammar schools, our local being Greenford County, which, if you were brainy, would see you through to your A-levels and maybe a job as a middle manager or computer programmer at Glaxo or Honeywell or EMI. Unemployment was practically non-existent, and much of London was clean and new, rebuilt from scratch. Rutland Road was as much subrural as suburban, with every house carefully tending its privet and close-cropped front lawn. Crime, though rising, was not a serious concern.

Jean and Jack occasionally went to see the new wave of films that were meant to tell them about their lives: *Saturday Night and Sunday Morning*, *Room at the Top* or *A Taste of Honey*. But the people they saw, the words that were delivered, belonged to a class that was already antiquated and on the verge of extinction – the back to back slum-dwellers of the northern cities or, in *Play for Today* or *Armchair Theatre*, the East End of London. To Jack and Jean, the kitchen-sink dramas presented people unrecognizably feral, crude and 'gritty'.

In these fictions, there was something conveniently observable and distinct, but the great endless, cultureless, billowing suburbs of the true, emerging England, made by the internal combustion engine and the arterial road – the Southalls, the Hemel Hempsteads, the Dagenhams, Staines, the Sloughs and the Sudburys – were largely ignored, perhaps because they were too vast and amorphous to get a grip on. In truth, the reality and aspiration of England was more likely to find an echo in Fred and Wilma Flintstone, Lucille Ball and Desi Arnez, Dick York and Elizabeth Montgomery in *Bewitched*, than in the terraces of Salford or the tower blocks of Hoxton. Only Galton and Simpson with *Hancock* and, later, Clement and La Fresnais with *The Likely Lads* teased out the real, subtopian England – aspirational, uncertain, displaced, ridiculous, perplexed and, above all, with lives increasingly out of focus.

This England, my England, was no longer held together socially by geography or class, in the way that had been true for Art and Cissy, and Billy and Grace. The great lumps of English life were flying apart. All that held them together now were – apart from TV – clubs, societies, evening classes, community centres, coffee mornings, Tupperware and lingerie parties, Avon ladies, bridge nights, sports centres run by the LCC or Ealing Council. Jean learnt to upholster, to flower-arrange, to practise yoga, to draw, to 'appreciate' classical music. Jack taught himself bridge and played competitions with Arthur at municipal halls. Every Sunday, whatever the weather, we went to the new open-air swimming baths at Chiswick, and played park tennis at the courts at Duke's Meadows next door, leaving for tea at Jean's, or Olive's, or Irene's when it got dark.

If at any time the 'high sixties' that happened on television was to be discussed, it would be at these communal teas, over the cheese footballs, jammie dodgers, silverskin onions, large split tins and Cornish wafers. But any sort of sustained conversation was a rarity, and analysis tended to splutter out after a few exchanges, damped down by lack of hard knowledge. A heart transplant: *amazing what they can do now.* The moon landing: *who'd have thought it? Isn't it marvellous?* The Aberfan disaster: *terrible, isn't it? Yes, but what can you do?* But everything serious tended towards the private, and everything else towards a relentless, generalized commitment to frivolity and a gut tolerance: *you can do what you like so long as it don't harm anyone else.*

In the dull, pebble-dashed sandwich between the A4 and the A40, the high sixties hardly touched at all, unless you counted Olive's daughter, Jilly, perched on the back of her boyfriend Tony's Vespa in black and white chequerboard smock from Biba with Mary Hopkin droopy-dog hair, the Vespa farting its way to the Boathouse in Kew or the Ivy Shop in Richmond or the Hammersmith Palais. They would not, of course, sleep together until marriage.

The families I watched on our Ekco sixteen-inch black-and-white television, people in cinema and TV dramas, did something strange and, to me, artificial. They picked up a subject or idea, ran with it, twisted and tweaked and manipulated it until some conclusion was squeezed out, some platform for action. But the conversations at Southall were truncated, purely functional. On the occasions they went beyond practicality to the realm of philosophy, it was largely a brief, confused sally with an end bracket of well-rehearsed aphorisms: *these things are sent to try us/we live in hope/worse things happen at sea/there's good and bad in everyone/you take people as you find them/money can't buy you happiness/might as well look on the bright side/there's got to be some purpose or else we wouldn't be here.*

Yet my family and their friends were far from being stupid. My father and his brother swiftly became experts at bridge. Some of their friends were professionals: Johnny Amlot was an architect, his wife, Helen, was a maths teacher, Bob Downhill was a computer designer. But they were not middle class, or even lower middle class; they were New Subtopians. They did not have much use for abstraction, since their inherited instincts for sniffing through life were so much more effective than some sort of vague process which might have robbed them of those lodestones, those gut sensibilities. They had good instincts, Jean and Jack, Helen and John, Irene and Bob. They understood the value of friendship, and home, and family; they did not overvalue freedom or money; and they respected, and trusted, the police, the law and, to a lesser extent, 'them'. The fact that 'they' sent their children away to boarding school, that 'they' sometimes got divorced, that 'they' drove their children with their own ambition, was thought of with pity as much as outrage. 'They' were seen as cold, arrogant, neurotic and, as such, unfortunate.

So, in the world of appearances, of processes and events, life in Southall was safe, dull, secure, reassuring, in slow forward motion. We lived enclosed in the dream of our own community. Yet other, half-hidden processes were taking place which we did not mind, or did not notice, a faint almost invisible fog of choice and movement, counterpointed by a sodden centre of ersatz, separation, drifting. The newspapers were blindly full of it, with their hints and headlines of a new age dawning.

Thus it was said, in roaring feature headlines, that Jeff and I were the New Elizabethans, a unique generation in history. Our minds were to be shaped by Admass, a convocation of television and advertising, and we belonged to a class that even then was being called 'the endless middle'. Instead of our parents' wish for security and stability, our desires would be inflamed and our attention span limited by the cheap, glittering world around us. We would, within ourselves, find new instincts as we ingested the new world – ambition, freedom, possibility instead of stoicism and a willing entrapment. We would have opinions. We would count.

The New Elizabethans – so the newspapers explained – were set quite apart from old stodge of England. We could all be vital, creative, original, sexy! We would own things, and they would be different shapes, made of different materials, than what had gone before, and the sensation of ownership would fulfil us. We would have fun, and time to have fun. We would be clever, with bagsful of qualifications from red-brick universities and white-tile techs. We would make more science, which would free us still more, and make Anything Possible (well, they said you could never get a man on the moon twenty years ago . . .).

So the *Herald* and the *Sketch* and the *Daily Pictorial* had it, in ever spreading headlines, crammed between ever larger pictures and ever softer news. The posher papers – which, of course, we did not take – sounded a more doubtful note. The loosening of solid reality. The endless burgeoning of desires. The powerful, ill-defined longing for sensation. The mad scramble to be first under the deferred death sentence of the bomb. A no-tomorrow generation, a no-yesterday generation. A generation too sophisticated for the Bible, but too stupid for Freud, or Heisenberg, or Darwin. A recipe, in short – said the voice of 'them', the voice that still entirely populated the airwaves, that was authority – for disaster, for rootless and sullied confusion.

Chapter Ten

'Man is the storytelling animal . . . He has to go on telling stories, he has to keep making them up. As long as there's a story, it's all right' – Graham Swift, *Waterland*

And they, as usual, were wrong. Or perhaps they, as usual, were right. I wish I could tell which it was. I wish I could tell a story, a single narrative, like my father has, instead of this snakepit of narratives that compete, and eclipse each other, then slide mutely back into darkness. For my father, like all the fathers and mothers before the Great Flood that began around 1956, seemed to have a common story, with a beginning and a middle and an end in the right places. The story was a lie, of course, all the stories we tell ourselves are lies, but it was a good lie, a sustaining lie, and, above all, a single and comprehensible lie.

My life, on the other hand, has been just a thin patchwork of disconnected impressions that seem to disable me since I am not sure which are true. If they are not true, some of them are actually quite bad lies – that is, unsustaining, cruel, self-defeating. But worst of all, none of them ever really comes into focus or takes on permanent shape. I wish for my father's ballast. I wish for his quiet certainty, his sense of the shape of his own life. But I have only scatterings of impressions that light up the landscape like flares, then disappear again into the great, bubbling unconscious. We have no common story now, to hold them in place. We make it up as we go along, then forget it, and make up something else, because we cannot live without stories.

My childhood, for instance, is it a story, in which consciousness grows, maturity is achieved, stages are accordingly approached, reached and passed – events that will teach me, wisdom that is passed to me? I do not know. I imagine so, as this is what I have been told, but I cannot even guess at the shape of it for myself, except that it seemed to be happy, more or less, and devoid of obvious cruelty or neglect. In the story I have told myself, my mother is loving, energetic, resourceful and inclined to easy laughter. My father is strong, essentially patient if sometimes tetchy, and always reluctant to praise. Jack believes, like many of his generation, that to praise a child is to spoil it. Yet he seems easy and confirmed in his idea of himself, and kind. In accord with Jack's memory, there are never arguments between husband and wife, either publicly or privately.

Beyond these vague, arching principles of which, I suppose, I am fairly sure (and if they are lies, they are lies I have confidence in), there are only scraps. These scraps are like random out-takes from a very, very long film. I hold them up to the light, I examine them. What they tell me is infinitely open to interpretation, but holds my attention nevertheless, because these scraps are the last relics of a time when I imagined myself holy, master of my fate, fitting tightly into a larger story.

I am in my bedroom in Rutland Road, Southall, facing on to the street. For some reason, I am on the top bunk, which is strange, because I always sleep on the lower bunk, to my infant pique – it seems lower in status than the higher one, from where you can stare at the yellow stars on the ceiling paper and imagine yourself in a spaceship speeding across the void. Jeff is in the bunk below, sleeping. The sun has set and the room is illumined by a too-bright overhead bulb (unlike Grace and Billy, Jean no longer feels the need to economize by installing forty-watt bulbs throughout the house). Outside the bay window, there are a few cars parked in the street – Zephyrs, Anglias, an NSU Prinz – and the glow from the windows opposite – Mr and Mrs Jones, Mrs Van Breda, Mr and Mrs Wall – is reassuring, as if the transmission and reception of our electric lights connect us fundamentally. I can hear the sound of a train, from track which must be at least a mile away. This, too, helps to moor the night into something safe and cocooning. A rag-and-bone man shouts incomprehensibly.

Buses clatter at the end of the street, heading east towards London, inscribed with their interim destinations – Perivale, Hanger Lane, Park Royal.

I am wearing pyjamas made by Ladybird, and decorated with sprigs of green holly. On the floor there is a scattering of toys – a tin piano, a toy soldier, a stuffed bear, Noddy in Fuzzy Felt Toyland, the Magic Robot quiz game. There is a ragged pony on wheels that I call Neddy and ride fanatically for hours, like the possessed boy in *The Rocking Horse Winner*. There is Richard Scarry's *Best Storybook Ever* and Arthur Mee's *Children's Encyclopaedia*. Downstairs there is the murmuring of adult conversation. The view out of the windows is unfocused because, in an attempt to warm the chilly room, my father has nailed sheets of transparent polythene across the struts of windowframes. Every morning they drip with condensation and leave pools on the windowsills, which my mother has to wipe dry with a linen tea towel that has shillelaghs and leaping leprechauns printed on it.

I am jumping up and down on the mattress of the bed frenetically. I am four or five years old, and not yet tired out by the day. Soon, I know, my mother or father will come from the living room, their tread threatening on the stairs, to remonstrate with me and insist that I sleep, but I am lost in a particular fantasy in which I am Punch and a cushion is Judy. I thump and stamp and shout, and bash the cushion with my fist. Perhaps, although quiet and shy, I am an angry child – much mirth is made of the fact that I sometimes tie my stuffed bear to the bedpost and hit it for minutes on end. I am also inordinately fond of guns, with which I annihilate invisible enemies. There is still a livid scar on my stomach, and scars on my wrists and ankles from the feeding tubes, and a twist to my lip where they sewed it back together. But in every way I am strong and, it seems, normal. Certainly, my energy has not been stifled; I throw myself back and forth, controlled by an imagination that habitually takes possession of me entirely. Junior school teachers would note this absence again and again, in manila-enveloped reports, in scholarly resignation: *Timothy lives in a little world of his own.*

I imagine myself to be on a trampoline, thinking that if I go high enough I will be able to touch the ceiling, the stars. I know it will be only minutes before my father, stern, will put an end to it all, so I push higher and higher, determined to touch the blue and gold of the paper. Jeffrey stirs underneath, maybe seven years old, but habitually impatient with his younger, disfigured embarrassment of a brother. I jump again, still inches away from the ceiling – it can never be reached – and as I drop, I lose my footing and tumble into the air.

I sense my flight quite distinctly, as if it were 100 feet rather than maybe six, but I do not feel anything when I hit the sisal carpet, and I am silent for perhaps a few seconds. I raise my hand to my cheek and feel that it is soaking wet. Still, I do not cry. Jeff is awake now and staring at me with a detached curiosity. By this time I realize that something serious is wrong and I begin crying distractedly. Perhaps my parents will not come – Jean's one child-care book, by Dr Spock, suggests firmly that children should be left alone to cry. But I can hear footsteps thundering up the stairs and shouting. Blood marks the already purple carpet.

My father and mother run in, my mother first. She picks me up, blood soaking into her blouse. My father picks up the toy soldier on which I have torn open my face, the edge of the soldier's cymbal having acting like a scalpel, leaving a flap of skin hanging from my cheek. There is no telephone to call an ambulance and no car to drive to hospital. My parents' shock feeding and multiplying my own, I scream louder still. My father hurries next door to see if Norman Staple is there with his mother; Norman has a car. I can feel no pain, only amazement at the disarray and fear of the grown-ups, which stun me more completely than any physical reaction.

In the back of Norman Staple's car, I am wrapped in a tartan travelling rug and my father holds me tight enough to stop me thrashing about. I am in a panic now, a panic that worsens as we arrive at the hospital, when a man in a white coat separates me from my mother and father. Now terrified, I fight back, but a posse of nurses, six in all, hold me in place on a metal gurney, clamping, in turn, my ankles, my chest, my arms, hard against the surface. Someone approaches my face with a needle that reflects beams from the raging lights above and I scream for my mother, but she does not come, and as the stitches go in, I feel the pain, not of the needle, but of something sharper, invisible.

I am around the same age, perhaps slightly older, and we are taking one of our pre-holiday camp trips, to a farmhouse in Scotland. We stop off first at Arthur and Olive's council house in Acacia Avenue, Brentford, where they have recently moved from Chiswick. Inside, their house is more modern than ours – Ercol chairs with splayed beech legs, artist's palette tables, a rod-and-ball sunburst clock. There is a Pacific maiden in the hallway and Tretchikoff's Green Lady upstairs. In the bathroom, an Ascot water heater and pastel, multicoloured, wide-gauge Venetian blinds. Downstairs in the living room, a picture of a green sea that turns into white horses at the crest. A red soda siphon which is never used rests on the top of a miniature bar in the corner, decorated with sketches of cocktails. There is a ship in a bottle and a polished wood plaque that Jack and Jean gave Arthur and Olive as a souvenir from Tiverton or Swanage. It reads, 'I may not always be right, but I'm never wrong.'

Olive and Arthur load Jilly and David into the car in which we are travelling, an Austin Cambridge shooting brake – it seems enormous to me. It is borrowed for the week and there are stickers in the shape of acute triangles on the back window that proclaim visits to Clovelly or Cowes or Folkestone.

The journey is arduous and boring. Jack drives; Arthur has not passed his test. The rest of us try to fill the hours by singing 'Ten Green Bottles', or 'Some Enchanted Evening', or 'She'll Be Coming Round the Mountain'. We play games, I-Spy and Animal, Vegetable, Mineral. The car radio plays Semprini, or Mantovani, or the Mike Sammes Singers, scatting blandly. We have to stop from time to time because Jilly becomes nauseous.

Half-way into the journey and we are driving across flat, endless moors touched by brushes of heather and rough grass. The car is in silence, as we have run out of diversions, and the sky, far larger than in London, is the colour of pencil lead. I stare out of the window at the electricity pylons strung out across the landscape like mechanical giants and thrill at the thought of the mysterious power that thrums down the lines from one tower to the next.

All of a sudden, it seems, there are two mysterious shapes on the horizon, so outrageously at odds with the surrounding landscape that they must have been placed there by the invading aliens that I have read about in imported copies of *Amazing Stories*, or *Tales of the Unexpected*. We draw closer and my eyes widen. Everyone else in the car seems indifferent or asleep. The shapes are clearer now; they are massive globes, metallic, which shine with reflected light. They unnerve me for some reason; they seem sinister. In their shadow, there are vast, rotating silver scoops pointed towards the sky.

I try to get someone to tell me what this apparition is amid the gorse and faint drumlins, this ridiculous conceit. People yawn, seem uncertain.

What is that, Jack?

That? Must be Fylingdales. It's around here somewhere.

Oh.

And it is Fylingdales ballistic missile early warning station, for we are traversing the Yorkshire moors. Arthur informs me that it is a scientific system, for detecting incoming nuclear weapons, ICBMs. My curiosity is fired. How much warning do you get? Where do you go to be safe when the warning comes? What does the warning sound like? Will the bombs come on planes or on rockets? Is it the Germans who have the 'new clear' bombs, for I know they are our enemies from the comics I read, *Commando* and *Captain Rock*.

Jean laughs at my concern – *such an imagination, that boy!* – Arthur and Jack are vague, though, not embarrassed or worried. They are pro-bomb – *It's a deterrent, isn't it? No one will ever use it.* I learn that I have three minutes, and that the Russians have rockets which can reach as far as America, but not to worry because the authorities will make sure that we are safe. They have secret shelters everywhere. Then, it seems, the subject is closed. I turn my head as the domes retreat into the distance, and the radar dishes swing endlessly around, feeling for impulses from space. Eventually, Fylingdales disappears from view entirely, but these shapes are in my head now and I cannot banish them.

In bed that night, every time I hear a plane pass overhead I hold my breath, for fear that it is carrying an A-bomb or an H-bomb, though I do not know the difference. These nights continue, from time to time, when I return home to Southall, and for years after; somehow the lights in the street and the distant sound of the train and the cry of the rag-and-bone man can no longer protect me. I work out time and again where I can get to in three minutes, and decide that the coal shed at the back of the garden will be safe. But how will we all fit in there? And will the radiation get in through the cracks under the door? Perhaps it will be best, like my father later says, to just go and stand in the street – *Get it over with. You won't know anything.* Yes, perhaps that's best. After all, we go to heaven anyway, as long as we've been good, and I have, I have been good, except for when . . . and that time when . . .

For the first time, I am going to the shop where my father works in Notting Hill Gate. It is a winter Saturday. At five in the morning we go to Covent Garden Market, to where my grandfather, Art, also travelled every morning. The market is packed with small, tough, loud men, pushing great hemp sacks of fruit and veg loaded on to porter's barrows, which people scamper to move out of the way of, since once they have momentum they are hard to stop. The pubs are open, and dinner-jacketed spill-outs from Boodles and the Ritz mix with tattooed, grizzled costers. The impression is of chaos, and the air is stiff with *fuck* and *cunt* and *fucking cunt.* Effing and blinding, my father calls it; he rarely uses any word stronger than 'ruddy', at least at home. The smell is alternatively fragrant and foul, of flowers and decay.

We set off for the shop, the van loaded up. I am too young to do any proper work and so I loaf around, getting under the feet of the other employees. These are Doug and Mick, rougher than my father; they drink too much at the Uxbridge Arms at lunchtime and think that Jack, who is more or less teetotal, is a bit of a snob. Doug takes longer on his deliveries than he should. Jack suspects he is paying special attention to the society tart Janie Jones, who takes an order once a week.

My father tries to make me do some work, folding and stacking boxes or trimming lettuces, but I am slow and clumsy, and he becomes irritated, feeling that I am showing him up, so he consigns me to the storeroom upstairs, where I listlessly stack cans of tangerine pieces in syrup and processed peas. When he comes in to check that I am doing something useful, he finds me staring pointlessly out of the window into the street. Irritated once more by my sloth, he insists that I come on to the shop floor and help serve the customers. My father is keen that I acquire a work ethic and has offered me a small sum of money, five shillings or so, if I make myself useful.

Before starting on the task of bagging up quarters of button mush or toms or pots or snips, or wrapping flowers, he sends me next door to pick up some change for notes from Mr Salik's delicatessen. Mr Salik is a sprightly Pole, mean with money, who works with a florid East End Jewish assistant, Wally. The shop amazes me, with its yards of tiles and racks of continental breads (cholla, pumpernickel, caraway rye, beigel) and marbled sausages and cheeses that smell of used football socks. There is nothing like this in Southall, only Wonderloaf and Wensleydale and chipolatas made of marrow-scrapings and brain-waste. Jeff, my brother, helps out here sometimes, but I am too useless and lazy and shy. Mr Salik is busy, so I spend what seems like ages staring at the displays, reading the packages and pronged signs stuck into the produce that seem to have a poetry all of their own: *bockwurst, bratwurst, cervelat, provolone, prosciutto, apfelstrudel, stollen, Lindt Milka, pretzels, lox, gravadlax*. These names, and smells, bewilder and attract me. But Jack, who will not even export garlic to Southall, never brings anything home from Mr Salik. He is content with his boiled gammon and cold lamb and corned beef salads – *none of that foreign muck*.

Mr Salik, who always seems on the verge of being angry, notices me, takes my notes and carefully counts out some florins and half-crowns to match the value of the notes. I am hoping he will offer me something to eat from the cake shelf, some mysterious cream gâteau or marble-cake, but he simply hands over the change and goes back to work. Wally winks at me and ruffles my hair. When I return back to the shop with the change, I ask my dad if I can have some Stollen, and, looking at me as if I am mad, he says:

What am I, Joe Soap?

What am I, made of money?

Who am I, old muggins?

Then he asks me what Stollen is, when it's at home. I blush, for I do not know. Jack laughs and goes back to serving a customer. Yet I know somehow that whatever Stollen is, and provolone, and cervelat, and Chocoleibniz, I want them, and at the same time, obscurely, I know that it is not the food itself that I desire but . . . I cannot put it into words or systematic thought. It is simply a craving for *other*, for difference, unfocused, unnamed.

I spend the rest of the afternoon working in the shop, trying to learn the distinction between nectarine and plum, Sturmer and Cox, Webb and cos. At one point a tall, distinguished-looking man in an aquamarine suit with elegant, brilliantined hair walks in. He has with him a young boy, about my age, with the crimson clouds on his cheeks that so many of the young rich seem to possess, tailored shorts, a crisp white shirt and a bow tie. The father and son are talking in loud, plummy, unselfconscious voices that advertise confidence, power, success, stretching back generations. I help my father prepare their order; I sort through filthy potatoes and soaking cos.

The young boy, when he turns in my direction, looks straight through me as if I were invisible. Then I realize that I *am* invisible, I am nothing, because I am a shop worker, and to this boy – younger than me, I think now – I am simply one of the large army of service personnel that make his life run smoothly on the way to Eton or Harrow. The boy, I realize, is talking to his father, in measured, analytical tones, about the production of a particular opera by Puccini – its strengths, its weaknesses, its moments of catharsis. A wave of shame and rage engulfs me. I do not know who 'Poo-chini' is. I hardly know what an opera is, let alone catharsis. My father hands the tall man his order in a plastic bag, and the man pays peremptorily, without saying thank you, still talking to the small boy as if there were no one else present. My father hands him his change, indifferent, easygoing – *good luck to 'em!* – and smiles, and the man and the boy leave the shop, still braying, eternally oblivious to the world beneath.

We are on holiday again, at a boarding house in Ventnor on the Isle of Wight. We have crossed on the ferry from the mainland and I have been sick over the side of the boat four or five times.

Now we settle into our holiday routine, of breakfasts accompanied by tiny glasses of orange or grapefruit juice, which are also served as a starter in the evening as an alternative to Brown Windsor or vegetable soup, followed by cottage pie, or Cornish pasty and crinkle chips, or suet with steak and kidney. The days are made up of swimming in a cold sea or walks along windy bluffs and sand dunes. There are visits to amusement arcades, where you can play bingo or skittles, or shoot tin ducks to win worthless pink rabbits and Chinese alarm clocks.

I am soon bored with the routine, and spend hours on benches, or in the back of the rented shooting-brake, reading books and comics – the *Topper* and *Beezer* annuals, Billy Bunter and Jennings books. As a special holiday treat, someone has bought me a full-colour American D C comic. Intriguingly, it is entitled *The Death of Superman*, and its cover shows Superman, the Man of Steel, laid out in a stately coffin, with Lana Lang and Lois Lane and ace reporter Jimmy Olsen weeping over the noble cadaver.

I imagine, even as I am handed the comic, that there will be a trick ending, that the cover is a dupe or a teaser. I take my super-heroes religiously and, in a child's way, can enter into the pages of a comic entirely, as if I were myself Mr X, or the Green Hornet, or the Flash, or Plasticman. There is no irony in this reading; the precious trick of entering entirely into myth, forgotten by adults, had not yet been lost to me.

There is a strapline on the comic that announces, gravely, that

The Death of Superman is a one-off issue, an 'imaginary' happening that might or might not take place one day. This means nothing to me, for Superman is as real as Jesus or Santa, an absolute inner fact.

I sit on the beach as my parents sunbathe and become engrossed in the comic, following the narrative and oblivious to the sand stinging my face. Lex Luthor, as happens from time to time, has gained access to a quantity of green kryptonite, a glowing rock that has the capacity to kill Superman (significantly, the deadly rock is a scrap of his home, an element of his past). In previous episodes, although Superman was weakened, or made ill, or stripped temporarily of his powers, he always emerged triumphant, leaving Lex Luthor to curse to the heavens the fact that good endlessly triumphed over evil.

As I approach the end of the comic, I wonder vaguely how Superman will escape this time, as he was exposed, in a dark cell, to the opened lead casket containing the kryptonite, its eerie glow bathing him with death itself. Superman weakens and turns pale, as Luthor leers. He falls back on the ground. He closes his eyes. And Luthor rejoices.

I turn the final page and the tableau that greets me, full-bleed, in lurid blotting-paper colours, is simply a development of the one on the cover. Superman is in his coffin; Luthor rejoices; Lois, Jimmy and Lana weep. There is no let-out. The final panel reads, 'Not to be continued'.

My mother arrives, back from swimming, floral bathing cap still in place, to find me weeping bitterly among the dunes. Her face transforming from mildness to concern, she bends down to my level. The comic is lying in the sand, being slowly covered by the edge of the sandhill.

Timmy, what's the matter?

I cannot speak, because something permanent in my imagination has changed, something triggered by this cheap and trivial comic book with its grey pulp paper and spreading out-of-register inks.

Timmy, why are you crying?

I look up at my mother. Now there is embarrassment at the

edge of my mind, because some part of me senses that adults will think me ridiculous. But a switch has been thrown that cannot be pulled back. Jean holds my gaze, waiting for an answer, so that she can help, so that she can comfort. I cannot find the words to express what I have discovered, so I blurt out the bald fact.

Superman, Mum. Superman is –

Jean notices the comic and picks it up, brushing off the sand. She glances at the cover and her face breaks into a broad smile of relief that something worse has not happened.

Don't be silly, you daft ha'p'orth. It's only a story.

But it isn't, it isn't only a story. Superman is dead. And if Superman is dead, then . . . then . . .

You and your imagination! Here, Jack – you'll never guess what . . .

But I am still lost in unnameable sorrow, oblivious to the growing laughter of the adults. For I have discovered something I had not known or suspected before. Since, in the story, I had become Superman – as I could as easily become Batman and Green Lantern and Thor – I have discovered what my parents had once known but had forgotten already: *everything, one day, even if you were Superman, even if you were an eight-year-old boy, would come to an absolute and final and unstoppable end.*

I am in my school assembly at Lady Margaret Primary School, which my mother attended before me. The headmaster, Mr Turnham, presides. There are perhaps 200 of us, in smart grey uniforms. My shirt is made of grey Bri-nylon and makes me sweat. There is an Osmiroid fountain pen in my top pocket with which I am learning Marian Richardson handwriting. The children in my class are called Steve, Dave, Mike, Sue, Jenny and Julie, these modern names having superseded Bert, Fred, Alf, Vi, Dot and Gladys.

We sing, as we sing every morning, hymns to a God who is invisible, and everywhere, who watches over us and judges our actions and secret thoughts, each second, every minute. We sing 'All Things Bright and Beautiful' and 'Jerusalem' and 'Immortal, Invisible' and 'I Vow to Thee My Country'. The words to the

143

last hymn are so powerful, I cannot sing for the choking of emotion.

> And there's another country
> I heard of long ago . . .

Day after day, the teachings of the Bible are read to us, in assembly and Bible class, in nativity plays and harvest festivals, rituals and traditions that still, more or less, hold England in a common envelope. As an adolescent, I recognize the stories as fairy-tales, like death and Superman, but as a child I breathe them in, and perhaps they enter my bones, beyond my later mocking denials. I learn, much as my father and mother have learned before me, that goodness is rewarded, not only in heaven, but within, with the elevation of the soul. Wickedness leads to spiritual death and damnation. I learn that there is a hidden order of things that is not to be transgressed.

I hear of the Good Samaritan, the Gadarene Swine, the Burning Bush, the Healing of the Lame, the Feeding of the Five Thousand, the Rebirth of Lazarus and of Barabbas and Pilate, and Jesus on Calvary. There is much I cannot understand. What is the Holy Ghost? Why do the Jews hate Jesus? Why does God not save him? What happens to the black babies in Africa who die of starvation not believing in Jesus? Will they go to hell? But all the stories, massed together, tied and underlined each day by the muttered incantation of the Lord's Prayer, convince me of this: that there is something called Sin, and it crouches within us, waiting for an opportunity to strike and damn us.

So that night, as I drift into sleep, I make a decision, because, like a TV American, I believe that the decisions I make in my head will change everything, inside and out, that my will is decisive. And I am unhappy, because I am being bullied by a larger boy, from whom my mother cannot protect me. So the decision I make is this, prompted by the assemblies and prayers and hymns. I will be good, always. If someone strikes me, I will turn the other cheek. If a child is cruel to me, I will forgive them. I will be kind to the weak and ugly, to the misfits in the class. I will do as my parents tell me. I will love my older brother, although he does not care for me. I pray to the stars on the ceiling that I will be like Jesus.

And I wake with the resolution still in my head, and carry it out. That morning, my brother pins me down under the covers of my bed, which terrifies me, and will not let me out. But I do not cry and I refuse to become angry. Later on, the bully in school attacks me, but I do not fight back. In the evening, my mother asks me to wash up when it is not my turn and I perform the chore without complaint.

This strategy I follow, doggedly, for days, even weeks. I lend other children my pocket money and do not ask for it back, and when they want more, I give it to them. When my brother steals my toys, I let him do it and try to smile. One night I offer to clean my father's shoes and, bewildered, he accepts.

It takes some weeks before I realize that I am not entering into the promised condition of holiness and reward. People at school take advantage of me and laugh at me behind my back. The weak and the ugly children cling to me, and I realize that they repel me. The bully goes to greater and greater lengths to humiliate me. My parents do not even notice or comment on my strenuous efforts towards virtue. My prayers go unanswered.

The next day the bully follows me home again, taunting me with a thin branch that he lashes at me. A gaggle of mates look on and laugh. After the fourth or fifth lash, some gear inside me turns, shifts lower. I turn around, swinging from the waist, and punch him full in the face. He stops dead in his tracks and looks astonished. I punch him again, this time in the stomach. He doubles over and begins to cry. The crowd of silent and sullen observers then suddenly begin cheering. The boy cries bitterly and I feel sorry for him and want to apologize, but the children laugh and cheer even more. The next day, everyone in class wants to be my friend; I am popular. When the weak, ugly children approach me, I shun them. I have realized, dumbly, wordlessly, that, as my father has always suggested, the world is not a gentle place and I must play its prescribed games with this in mind.

That night, I do not pray to God. In fact, I never pray again, not until I am thirty-one years old and hoping to die.

It is a Sunday morning in late summer and, as usual, we are at the open-air swimming baths at Chiswick Lido. There are rows and rows of wooden changing cubicles which, on one famous occasion, I emerge from having actually forgotten to put my costume on, until the amazed glares of hundreds of bathers alert me to my absence of mind. But that is years in the future. On this day, I am noticeable only for being unusually over-weight. There are towels and Lilos spread out to cover almost every square foot of the paving stones, and transistor radios, made in Hong Kong, broadcasting chatter and chart hits that are somehow increased by the tinniness of the speakers, punc-tuate the perimeters of the rectangular towels. On this day, they are playing 'Have I the Right?' by the Honeycombs, and 'Con-crete and Clay' by Unit Four Plus Two, and 'Telstar' by Jet Harris, and 'Runaway' by Del Shannon. The shouting and music and chatter make an astonishing row. The air smells of cheap hotdogs and Westler's hamburgers, which we do not buy, preferring to economize with packed lunches of white bread with Sandwich Spread, pilchard and salad cream sandwiches, followed by rock cakes. We will drink squash rather than Idris or Pepsi or Corona.

I am plucking up courage to jump in the pool, for I know that the temperature – it is chalked up at the entrance – is only fifty-seven degrees and that the shock of the initial cold will knock the breath out of me. Today is what I have christened Flying Ant Day, for I have noticed that one day in the year the air is filled with winged ants who disappear the next day, not to be seen again for another twelve months. If this day takes place while I am at home, I boil water and try to exterminate them as they teem through the rockeries of our back garden. But today, Flying Ant Day takes place at the pool, and the bathers swat and wave their hands in frustration, and guard their Zooms and Fabs and Jublees against the clouds of pests. Simply for the enjoyment of it, and to delay the plunge into the pool, I stomp around the paving stones with my flip-flops, killing as many ants as I can. But it seems to make no difference; the flying ants just keep coming.

Finally bored, I make my way towards the edge of the pool and try to pluck up the courage to dive – or belly-flop, since I am clumsy – into the icy water. There are two stone lions erected at the shallow end that spew out water in constant streams. Where these streams strike the surface of the pool, children gather to douse themselves and tamper with the cascades, filling buckets or empty crisp packets. I climb to the top of one of the lions and look for a gap in the crowd of flapping arms and kicking legs. I decide to break through my fear. I jump.

The clutch of the water is as shocking as I knew it would be and I pant for breath. I have struck a small boy below me in my fall and he looks at me, offended, then shrugs and swims off. I strike out into a shambolic butterfly stroke in order to distract myself from the chill and make my heart pump so as to raise my body temperature to something tolerable. This takes several minutes, and at last I feel I am beginning to enjoy my swim. On the edge of the pool, my brother throws a beach ball to my cousin, David. I change strokes, breast, then Australian crawl, then backstroke, which I have to abandon because the packed crowds get in the way. The stench of chlorine is overwhelming and my eyes will smart for hours afterwards. Somewhere in the middle of the pool is my mother, keeping her chin just at water height, her bare head encased in a rubber bathing hat which she never submerges. She is always terrified that someone will knock it off, but I do not know this. I do not even know yet that my mother is bald.

I now do the doggy paddle, keeping to mid-shallow end, because it seems less crowded. I begin to imagine, faintly, that people are staring at me but dismiss the impression as ridiculous. I notice that there is a faint redness around the patch of water I am swimming in. I look up and see my brother pointing to his chin and gesticulating wildly. I do not know what he means. He is shouting something, but the noise of the bathers around me makes it impossible to hear. Screaming boys are doing torpedoes and belly-flops all around, and I feel as if I am under artillery attack. My brother is still yelling something. I make my way to the chrome ladder at the far side of the shallow end.

As I climb out, my brother's face is a mask of excitement and suppression. He blurts out his secret. *Your chin!* I look down and see that my chest is doused with a crimson liquid. I raise my hand to my chin and it comes back dripping with pink, chlorinated water. Everyone is staring now and my mother has left the pool. The blood makes patterns on the flagstones. I am embarrassed rather than in pain. They rush me to hospital and sew me up, in a two-inch wound under the chin. I now have seven scars in total on my body and face. It seems sometimes that I am a child whose central instinct is one of self-damage.

My father has brought home a box of records, old 78s that a customer has given him and he in turn has given me. I am excited, for I do not own any records, even though we have a second-hand Dansette, bought from Harvey's Exchange and Mart in West Ealing. My father has a couple of Music for Pleasure albums of top chart hits, cod versions of real records that sell for a fractional price and feature exciting go-go dancers in chain-mail bikinis on the cover. Also – perhaps later – an album by Manuel and his Music of the Mountains, and Big Ben's Banjo Band. Neither my mother nor my father is very keen on music, except for 'background'.

I sort through the records one by one and load them on to the record changer. The sound they issue is tinny and thin, the music disappointing: covers of 'Little Brown Jug' and 'Alexander's Ragtime Band', piano medleys by Russ Conway, light instrumentals by defunct showbands. At the bottom of the pile is a record with a black label, quite badly scratched, that I force on to the turntable without looking, for I am bored now and ready to give up. The needle strikes the groove and a sound issues into the air quite unlike anything that I have ever heard. The chords, instead of being brassy and upbeat, overprocessed, are melancholic, bare and stricken. Through the hiss and scratch of the record, a clarinet sounds.

I sit, rooted to the spot. Then the vocals begin, and I feel a tear form and run down my cheek. The voice is incredible, worn, razed and busted up, with a moan that tugs at my chest. It is a woman and she does not sing so much as drawl, in a voice stretched out and punctured and sad. I can just about make out the lyric through the pop and bustle of the stricken quality, and this, too, is mesmeric and strange. Out of the world I live in, which is made up of gameshows and toothpaste ads and *Sunday Night at the London Palladium* and Alma Cogan and Helen Shapiro and Max Bygraves, I hear, it seems to me for the first time, something that is real.

The song is 'Strange Fruit'. I read the label, which bears the legend 'Billie Holiday'. I assume this must be a man. And perhaps for the first time I begin to realize, though without word or conscious thought, that there are two worlds to inhabit: the ersatz and the authentic – avoidance or involvement, denial or engagement. To be lost in one is to be numb and to be lost in the other is to be in danger. Or perhaps, as my mother suggests, as I play the record time after time, until the groove is worn to nothing, I am simply morbid and more fascinated by death than is healthy for a child.

It is nine o'clock in the morning and I am eating my breakfast, a boiled egg with bread soldiers that I dip distractedly into the yolk. As usual, it is overcooked and I have to scoop the whole thing out with a spoon. I cover it with salt. I sip at a cup of Camp coffee. There have been no comics delivered this morning, so I pick up my father's *Daily Express* and begin to read.

The first thing that strikes me is a double-column black and white photograph of a man whose face is so creased and melted by pain that it is hard to look at. He is wearing a trilby and his eyes are drooped and deep-set. They stare at the camera and the camera reads the despair within them. The eyes are completely indifferent, lost. The mouth slips downwards at the edges. The impression is of someone completely broken inside, whose face is so heavy with grief it appears that gravity itself has forced each line of jowl, cheek and eye downwards towards the earth. I recognize the man, but cannot place him until I read the headline:

I cannot take my eyes from the page. Tony Hancock was my hero, my favourite comic. Dad and I would watch him on the tiny screen, doubled up with laughter at his pretension, his conceit, his puffed-up, tragic pride. We laughed because he was us, because he was true. He had gone to his hotel room in Sydney, Australia, swallowed too many barbiturates and lain down to die. His suicide note read: *This is quite rational. Things seemed to go wrong too many times.*

I am bewildered and cannot eat my breakfast. How can anyone be so sad as to want to take their own life? It is an unfathomable mystery to me. I carefully tear out the photograph, take it upstairs and paste it into my scrapbook. I cannot forget the look in his eyes. What strikes me is that Hancock is even now dead, as he stares mutely at the camera. The suicide merely confirms what is already true.

It is a Saturday, and for the first time in my life my mother is allowing me to go to the cinema by myself. She is nervous and takes much persuading, but she believes, as does Jack, that to be too protective of your children does them more harm than good.

As I board the 105 bus at the junction of Rutland Road and Somerset Road, I feel excitement at this new freedom, this barrier crossed. The future will be full of such crossings, into new territories, new freedoms. The bus conductor takes my fare and hands me my ticket without remark. The strangeness of going unaccompanied is invisible to everyone but me.

I sit at the front of the bus upstairs, my favourite position, and the AEC engine churns and wobbles like a cement mixer. The bus travels past the council estates, where they eat Stork margarine instead of butter, never watch the BBC and come to school with dirty mouths and wild hair. The bus travels past the flat scrub and canal of Durdan's Park, past the endless plain terraces of subtopia, all dun-pebbled, accompanied by garages, crowned in red tile.

The bus arrives at the Palace Cinema; I can see its great golden dragons in the distance. I jump from the bus before it stops and run towards the entrance, past Southall Town Hall, which is immaculate, mysterious and imposing. Southall Community Centre is half a mile over the bridge, and the trains I can hear faintly at night sound clearly here. Living, as I do, in the suburb of a suburb of a suburb (London–Ealing–Southall–Rutland Road), Southall High Street contains a fleck of the excitement of an imagined West End, imagined because I have never been there, Jack and Jean not seeing the point of London.

The film I am rushing to see is Phil Silvers in *It's a Mad Mad Mad Mad World*, part of the *zany* cult of the time. I pay sixpence to get in – decimalization is still several years away – and take my seat, by an aisle. I already have a small packet of fruit pastilles and watch the invocations to buy Kia-Ora, Sun-Pat peanuts and Paines Poppets, and to visit the Golden Orient Chinese Restaurant in Hanwell Broadway, with mounting impatience. As the film begins, the cinema goes completely quiet, for there are no videos to convince people that film is a private experience, allowing for private manners. The experience is to be silent, collective, apart from the outbreaks of laughter or intakes of breath.

The film is not as good as I had imagined from watching Phil Silvers in *Sergeant Bilko*. It seems stupid and chaotic, and tries too hard to be funny. But I am pleased to be there, unaccompanied and, for a few hours, quite free.

There is a rustle as someone sits next to me. I think this odd, as the row is more or less empty, but ignore it, although I notice through the darkness that the size suggests a man rather than a boy. He wears a hat and I cannot see his face. A faint wave of laughter transmits around the auditorium as Phil Silvers pulls one of his terminally exasperated, disbelieving looks at the stupidity and naivety of the outside world. I feel a creeping sensation on my leg. The man has put his hand on my knee.

I am corrugated with terror. Of course, Jack and Jean have told me about 'perverts' and 'flashers' and 'weirdos' and 'homos' who occasionally populate cinemas and municipal parks, but as a child I imagine myself immune from serious misfortune of any kind. I have been given a prescription for what to do in circumstances like this: go immediately to the manager and report it. But I feel transfixed by shyness and cannot bring myself to seek out anyone in authority to tell them that someone is trying to mo-lest me. Anyway, what does the manager look like? I could tell an usherette, but she is a girl; she will laugh at me. Instead I rise from my seat and the hand falls away. I go and stand at the back of the auditorium, wondering if I should tell 'them'. But the embarrassment is too great. Assuming that, in the dark, if I move to a new seat, the man will not be able to find me, I move along the side aisle and into a space ten or twelve rows back on the other side of the cinema.

After a few minutes, I begin to find my way back into the film and relax, but then I feel a movement beside me and the man sits down in the seat next to me once more. The terror redoubles now, immobilizing me. My small palms, holding the empty packet of fruit pastilles, are wet. I feel the man's hand again, this time in my lap, questing for my zip. I can hear his breathing. He smells of wet earth. I cannot see what his other hand is doing.

Still too intimidated to go to the manager, I rise again and run, but, in a panic, I do the thing I am always told not to do: I go to the toilet. I think that if I lock myself in a cubicle, the man will not be able to get to me. I rush into one, but the lock is broken and there is unflushed crap in the bowl. The toilet is otherwise completely empty. Fighting the panic, I dart into the second cubicle. This time there is a lock and I slide it closed. I stand on the toilet seat, so that if the man looks under he will not see my feet. I am not thinking straight. I fear that I am about to be fucked and murdered, although I do not know what fucking is, will not even pronounce the word in my own head.

I hold my breath. I wait minutes and nothing happens. Then there is a footfall outside and someone tests the door. I realize how completely vulnerable I now am and berate myself for my stupidity through the fear. I hug myself with crossed arms; my Viyella shirt is cold against my skin. I do not know what to do.

What seems like hours pass, though it is probably five or ten minutes, and I listen for the sound of either a single movement or a loud bustle that will betoken the safety of a crowd. Neither happens. A hope in me begins to swell that the man has gone away, given up. I peer under the door and can see no shoes to suggest a hovering presence. Gathering myself, I unlatch the door. The smell of piss in the air strikes me. There is opal light from the overhead window. I can hear faint traffic.

Outside, I immediately see that the toilet is empty. Tense and blank now, I head towards the door and pull it open. The man is standing in the hall between the toilet and the cinema. He is in shadow, I cannot make out his face. He is reaching out towards me and is speaking in a low, cocoa-warm voice.

I only want to give you money . . . I only want –

I thrash out. I once saw my father take a football in the groin and he was nearly sick with pain, so I hit blindly towards the man's crotch. To my surprise, he grunts and doubles up in agony, and I force my way past him in the narrow corridor and into the safety of the cinema. Even as he doubles, he is imploring me.

But I just want to –

What is it that old men want to do to children? I do not know, but I know that it is terrible, and a secret. Phil Silvers is bellowing, ten feet high, behind my head and the crowd is laughing idiotically. I race out of the cinema, into the light, not checking over my shoulder and run, run, run.

I am sitting at the kitchen table in Rutland Road, alone with my mother. She is cooking shortbread and I am bored, dithering at the table over a plate of cherries, which I consume indifferently. I put the pips back on the plate, until there are twenty or so. Then I begin playing 'Tinker, tailor, soldier, sailor, rich man, poor man, beggar man, thief'. I have an odd faith in these portentous games, like reading the numbers on bus tickets to find out how many times I will be married and how many children I will have.

The cherry pips decide that I will be a rich man. This excites me and I wonder how it will come about. I ask my mother what she thinks I should do when I grow up. She is silent for a moment and puts her finger to her lip. It is clear that she is taking the question seriously. Her eyes are filmy with faint confusion.

A draughtsman is a good job. Perhaps you should be a draughtsman.

Mum, what's a draughtsman?

A draughtsman? He does . . . drawings.

But I can't draw, Mum.

Well, you can learn. You can learn anything.

What does he draw pictures of?

Jean is still, as if scanning through her memories for the answer. It suddenly becomes clear to me that my mother does not have the faintest idea what a draughtsman is, that the thought is borrowed, picked up like static takes fluff.

Buildings, I think.

Jean turns back to her shortbread, pulls it from the oven and begins to stack it in a biscuit tin. The tin is decorated with a picture of two white Scottie dogs perched on a wicker picnic basket draped with a tartan rug. The shortbread smells delicious, as always.

Arthur and Jack have lent a boat from a friend at the badminton club (grammatically, of course, they have borrowed it, but the terms in our argot are reversed). The order of consumption in subtopia is this: first a terrace, then a semi, then a caravan on Camber Sands or at Folkestone, then a boat, which you would park in your front garden and take out twice a year for a doodle on the river. There are several of them in the streets around Southall. My father thinks they're a waste of money, but on this occasion has decided it will be a laugh.

The boat, when we see it moored at Teddington, is a bit ropy. It is squat, small and ugly, a cabin cruiser that is little more than a tiny caravan with a hull. The paintwork is peeling. Arthur is wearing a little sailor's cap. None of them knows anything about the river, but they decide to give it a go.

Can't be that difficult.

No. Just like driving a car. Only you keep to the right. Is it the right?

Yes, I think so.

We board the boat, me and Jeff, Jack and Jean, Olive and

Arthur, and set off down the Thames. The outboard motor is weak and makes a noise like a lawnmower. Our progress is slow, but the water is calm and the weather reasonably pleasant. I settle into a sort of disinterested torpor and half doze.

After a while I open my eyes. There is a loud rushing sound in my ears. I look at the adults. Arthur is fiddling furiously with the motor. Jack's and Olive's faces are tight with fear. But I am not unduly worried, because I know adults can do anything, solve any problem. The sound is getting louder and Jack is barking at Arthur.

For Christ's sake!

Arthur is silent, struggling with what looks like a gearstick. He is white and his lips are pushed tight together. He is sweating. The sailor's hat is still in place, but pushed to one side precariously.

I look over the bow of the boat, to see the source of the noise. There is a huge weir in front of us that crashes down into a great spume of white water. It is immediately clear to me that if the boat goes over, it will be smashed to pieces. And yet the weir has the boat in its grip and the motor is too weak to pull us out. Gradually, inevitably, we are slipping towards this boiling horizon.

I can feel quite clearly now, stronger than the spray of water, the air of panic. I begin to understand that the adults have lost control and look around for my mother. She is not there. Arthur grunts and cries out. With a last desperate pull, just as it appears we will go over, he has shifted the lever into reverse. The engine catches and the boat holds still, then very gradually starts to move backwards, away from the weir. The relief is thick as tar. Shaken, we decide to turn around and head back to the jetty.

I wonder what has happened to my mother in those moments when it appeared that her whole family, including herself, was about to drown in the freezing Thames. I ask my father where she is, but he seems busy with something. Eventually, when she reappears, I have forgotten the question. I do not find out until much later that my mother, as catastrophe approached, went down to the tiny cabin, closed the door, laid her head on the pillow, put her fingers in her ears and closed her eyes tight. She remained fixed in this position, hiding, until Jack came and told her that the danger had passed.

Chapter Eleven

'In the animal kingdom, the rule is eat or be eaten. In the human kingdom, it is define or be defined. The struggle for definition is the struggle for life itself' – Thomas Szasz

It is the 1970s, a short, stupid non-time bracketed between two distinct eras: the long 1960s and the longer still 1980s. Everything once loose is being packaged, everything once fresh is being recycled. Hyper-reality spreads like a secret fog. Imagineers conceive themed shopping centres, construct heritage out of history and lifestyle out of life. Things, it seems, must be more than, or different from, what they are.

Collective memory fades, consensus fractures, nostalgia is epidemic. In popular movies, buildings burn, the earth splits apart, aeroplanes crash, floods smother cities. In Rutland Road and Acacia Avenue, in Mon Repos and Mon Abris, the sense of progress and security begins, for some, to be fringed with doubt. There is inflation, decimalization, oil shock, IRA bombs, industrial strife. Mass immigration is changing the face of England, nowhere more than in Southall. These things are not distant, like the floating silver bubbles of the 1960s. They hector and threaten a whole raft of what once were certainties: civility, stability, money's absolute value; whiteness, and superiority over what are politely referred to as 'our colonial cousins' or 'coloureds'.

The National Front march in Southall in the 1970s. Although it is an axiom of Jack's and Jean's philosophy that everyone has a right to say what they think, they dislike the NF as *bolshie* and *troublemakers*, and wrong. *Everyone's the same, wherever you go,* Jack would always insist. At the same time, they are uneasy at the speed of what is a remarkable transformation of their world.

There are rumours that whole families of Asians are tunnelling through the walls and living secretly in lofts. And there is the smallest part of both of them that believes it.

Nevertheless, the protective faith that is Jean and Jack's inheritance – *Everything'll come out in the wash* – is, like all habits, not prone to easy decay. Entropy and change are played down, advancement and continuity teased up. And this is not an altogether difficult trick for them, since in many ways things remain on the up and up. They have a car now, one of a series of Morris Travellers, and a telephone on a telephone table with seat, and a colour television edged in black plastic rather than cedarwood or mahogany. They begin to eat out in the new Greek, Indian and Chinese restaurants for the first time, and likewise for the first time they holiday abroad, in Majorca and Malta.

There are accumulating amounts of pine and white Melamine in the house. They have extended the kitchen, had fitted, co-ordinated cupboards installed. Jack has put in a lopsided serving hatch. There are concrete rabbits and hedgehogs in the garden, and a honeysuckle arch.

For the first time, the enduring icon of their class has appeared on the mantelpiece. This ornament is owned almost without exception by every householder in subtopia, more ubiquitous even than ornamental egg coddlers or Guernsey cable-knit sweaters. It is a carriage clock. No one, it seems, can ever remember where it came from or who bought it. As if by sorcery, they just begin to appear in living rooms at this time, between the framed family portraits and dry-flower and peacock-feather arrangements. They vary slightly. Some, a sub-genus known as 'anniversary clocks', are confined in glass domes. Some have tiny brass feet, some have black-and-white paddles that drive the clock by heat energy. Some have revolving, irrelevant pendulum balls. But otherwise they are identical: about five inches in height, brass or brass effect, roman numerals on a white or gilt clockface, with a small horseshoe handle on top. They are usually driven by a quartz chip and keep perfect time, without noise. Along with log-effect gas fires, they are as specific to subtopia as the Aga and the Barbour are to the Home Counties. The year before my mother dies, she sends an outsize Christmas card to my father, wishing him *Happiness for the coming year*. The illustration on the front, standing in for nativity angels and decked with bells, holly, ribbons and mistletoe, is a large, mahogany-faced carriage clock.

I develop an aversion for our particular carriage clock out of proportion with its squat ugliness. Its artificiality, its reverence for the past, its mysterious ubiquity, annoy me. I have become, mysteriously to Jack and Jean, something they never were or dreamed of being: a disaffected and restless teenager. I have lost interest in the fortunes of Queen's Park Rangers and playing club ping-pong, and have sunk into a dull ballet of so-what shrugs.

On the whole, though, the family remains strong, integrated, and the network of friendships they have built up – a core of about five married couples with children who do everything together – easily survives the inevitable squabbles and rivalries. A new pair has joined the circle, Bert and Barbara, he a wealthy, self-made man, gregarious and a bit of a card, she nice, slightly neurotic and shy. They live in Bickley, near Bromley, which, like Ashford or Chalfont St Peter, is the next ladder step from the London inner-outer suburbs.

Jean has a new child, James Allan, two years old in 1970, who roots her life and keeps its story consistent and, in a way, simple. There are glancing blows in this decade which stretch and fray Jean; perhaps they weaken her, and somehow root the sad future. But there is more than enough cause for optimism: most notably, both Jeff and I have made it easily to grammar school, which will guarantee us a low-level white-collar job.

The grammar is modelled on an English public school, although it is coeducational. The head, a diffident woman known only as Miss Smith, wears a mortar board and gown, and the school is divided into houses, St Patrick, St George, St Andrew and St David. We wear green uniforms and peaked caps. The school motto is '*Loyal au Mort*'. In the main corridor outside the assembly hall, there is a wooden plaque with the name of university entrants inscribed. It is a very short list. Most of the pupils, myself included, have never even met anyone who has been to university outside of our teachers and doctors.

The school smells of school dinner cabbage and floorwax. Its teaching approach is traditional and there is a large population of late-middle-aged teachers, furious or bitter or resigned, as they sense the wind of change blowing from the 1960s which will render them redundant or archaic when the school goes comprehensive the year I leave. Most still view knowledge as an unpalatable but necessary medicine which must be routinely administered to wild children, by force if necessary. We learn about kings and queens, about the Empire whose collapse is unacknowledged, for the Empire was benevolent and is indivisible from the idea of England itself. Great store is set on the formation of oxbow lakes, the application of cosines and logarithms, the periodic table. By the time I leave, almost all of it will be forgotten, although I am reckoned a good if slapdash pupil. Despite my final achievement of two mediocre A-levels, I am mired in willing ignorance.

The dry, sexless air that the teachers trail after them, a dim vapour trail, confirms the pupils' suspicion that education is a mysterious confidence trick at their expense, that it is not the product advertised. On one occasion, someone writes on a blackboard, to the annoyance of the Religious Education teacher, a quote from Ecclesiastes: 'He who increaseth knowledge, increaseth sorrow.' And although it is merely a joke at the teacher's expense, it seems true to us. The impression is further confirmed by the generalized contempt of pupils for the clever or diligent. The untrained but somehow instinctive absence of glottal stops and dropped aitches in my speech provokes suspicion, as does my inflated vocabulary.

You swallow a dictionary, cunt?

This much has not changed since my father's cousin, Rita, was ostracized for achieving her scholarship and Jack rejected his grammar school place. Thus it does not take long for my natural habit of reading to decay. My voluntary trips to Jubilee Gardens library to read novels – a few modern classics plus a raft of yellow-jacketed Gollancz science fiction – become rarer and rarer, as I realize what the world demands of me – that is, the efficient passing of exams and the wholesale pursuit of experience, sensation, unprovoking leisure and salary. My father's instinct for conformity, in this matter at least, is passed on.

I have abandoned my childhood persona of being shy, introvert and bookish and have reinvented myself as an extrovert, a loudmouth and a joker. My body has changed now, is no longer a child's. I have developed an average-size cock which provides me with a hobby which I have come to find more fulfilling than nomination whist or Subbuteo. To this end, I hide, under a Marley tile in the toilet, a single pornographic photograph of an out-of-focus peroxide blonde performing oral sex on an anonymous man (he is anonymous because his head has been cut off by the photo crop). It is the absolute limit of my ambition to one day be in receipt of this tantalizing favour. But my hopes are circumscribed; the sexual revolution does not appear to have reached Southall, and girls, so far as I then understand it, remain mainly interested in getting married and procreating at the earliest opportunity. Most have not yet been given the confidence to do otherwise.

My other preoccupations are transatlantic, drawn from the fading shadow of the American counter culture, but this is already in terminal decline. The 1960s have entirely run out of steam and a vacuum ensues. I am vaguely aware that I am picking over the leftovers and bones of a past epoch and that my time, as well as my place, is unformed, ersatz, penumbric.

Like my father, my generation has lives governed by aphorisms, delivered like a virus by one acquaintance after another from schooldays onwards. They are different from Jean and Jack's, more relative. Now they show the loosening of everything, the lack of interest in consequentiality, the seizing of the present: *no one knows anything/everything's just opinions/why worry? we could all be dead tomorrow/it's not a rehearsal/money can't buy happiness, but it can buy a big car to drive round to look for it/just do it/today is the first day of the rest of your life/anything's possible – they said you couldn't put a man on the moon/go for it.* In a real public school, it would perhaps be *Memento mori* or *Carpe diem*.

I am popular at school, although not with my brother Jeff, who is two years above me. The rivalry between us has not abated; if anything, it has worsened. Jeff is the most fashionable boy in the school. He has an earring, which is unprecedented, and long, layer-cut hair. He is persecuted by the teachers and one of them, a Scottish puritan by the name of Jim Hall, nicknamed 'Jock', strikes him periodically on the top of the head with the flat of his hand and publicly humiliates him for the acne on his back, which he sarcastically ascribes to the length of his hair.

Apart from the cod-hippie of my brother, the only other fashion is skinhead, which is more widespread, this school drawing largely from the working-class estates in the area. Haircuts range from a number one (shaven) to a number four (mod-short). The skin girls have feather-cuts or crops with bangs left at the side. The skins wear Sta-Prest, brogues, braces and Ben Shermans, and talk about Paki-bashing, which, to my knowledge, they never actually execute.

Jeff and I wear studded cowboy shirts under our blazers, flared grey flannels, loosened knots in our regulation ties. We are not into peace and love; it is merely fashion. In Southall, no one is idealistic; they are uninterested, or ironic, or mocking. No one goes on demonstrations against nuclear weapons or Vietnam. We are selfish, we have our own lives to kick against. My protests are limited to fits of minor violence. On one occasion I punch the English teacher and only narrowly escape expulsion.

Jeff, unlike me, is meticulous and careful and, in his own way, conservative. He dislikes drugs, dirt and mess, and seems indifferent, so far as I can tell, to sex. He files his records – Jackson Browne, the Byrds, Emmylou Harris, Gram Parsons – in strict alphabetical order, whereas mine are left in a random heap. He hides his comics so I cannot read them, since he has paid for them and considers it unjust that I should benefit. I suspect that he irons them. I search them out and leave them dog-eared, which sends him into a fury and one of the many fights which he invariably wins, being eighteen months older. My impression is that he dislikes me intensely and, in self-defence, I have adopted an identical attitude, although beneath this struck pose, I vaguely recognize that I am desperate for his perennially withheld approval and acknowledgement.

On one occasion we start a fist fight and to my amazement it becomes clear to me that I am for the first time stronger than my brother. I am sporty, he is not, and the muscling on my upper arms and shoulders is beginning to count. The punches I throw are finding their way through and my long pent-up rage gathers within me and achieves critical mass. I feel excitement as I prepare to beat my indifferent, contemptuous brother into submission. I can see in Jeff's eyes that he knows this also and is worried. Suddenly he sits down, shakes his head and speaks.

For Christ's sake. Grow up.

The rage in me magnifies. He has finessed me. At this moment, my father walks in, having heard the ruckus, and pulls us apart. I am speechless with frustration. Jeff complains that I am being immature and my father remonstrates with both of us. But the anger inside me that has waited so long for a chance for expression will not be denied. I dart past my father to where my brother sits, quite still now and defenceless on the bed, and I punch him full in the face with every scrap of strength I can muster. I feel a sense of release.

He grabs at his eye, which is starting to bleed. He will carry now his first scar for the rest of his life, still many short of me. My father starts bawling at me, but I break away and run out in the street, enthralled by what I have done, but shocked also. I feel that I am shaking and I want to cry. My anger still reverberates, as if within a soft, hidden echo box. I wonder what its source is, and why it always seems to be present within me. I wonder what it is I should do with it, for it seems to demand discharge, like the sexual energy that finds its way daily into pristine sheets of tissue.

The blow struck at my brother does not cure my anger. Nothing, it occurs to me, ever does. As I walk down Rutland Road and up the hill towards the Top Shops, the rage transmutes, away from my brother and towards my surroundings. The endless blank terraces and dim skies and flat, dull playing fields enrage me further. The sheer absence of the place. I have seen on television, I have read in magazines, that there are other places, places that have focus and shape and meaning. I think of Notting Hill Gate. I think of Mr Salik's shop. I think of the man in the aquamarine suit. And I think that I have no time, for the ICBMs are waiting to drop, perhaps tomorrow. I am dimly aware, as usual, of a faint but constant panic.

My dreams and fears are mysterious to my parents. They seem rooted and sure, while I am both disconnected from my past and uneasy in the present. Their lives were predetermined, locked into place by circumstance, while I am fired and teased by possibility. This place in my head is unbounded, shameful and absolutely anything can happen. Genocide can happen. The world can be written on silicon. There will be apocalypse, if not now, then soon.

I walk to Jubilee Gardens park, which is empty and puddled with mud and dog shit. I walk to the middle of the football pitch, alone in the park, and shout, as loud as I can, the worst words that I know.

Buggerfuckcunt.

And then, defeated by the silence, I walk back to Rutland Road, with just one thought.

Some day.

Some day what? I do not know. I do not know anything.

The family photographs of this period are badly composed, soft-cornered, often out of focus and disfigured by red-eye and bad fashion. There are also plenty of them, since I now have a Polaroid camera and am prolific with my snaps, which are as shambolic and artificial as my father's. But the required smiles and raised glasses are not wholly false, even if they fall short of the truth. In many ways, things will never be better for our family.

Jean still inclines towards turquoise eyeshadow and her wig guarantees a sort of enduring youthfulness, meticulously teased and restyled into bobs, curls or loose perms. Mostly she favours a helmet-style neck-length arrangement, slightly piled and fluffed on top, inspired by Purdey in *The New Avengers*. The hair turns from black to auburn to slightly grey towards the end of the decade. For Jack and Arthur, for Bob and John, the greying is real and the hair at the temples begins to recede. Their clothes are losing the last traces of formality. There is no dominant mode of dressing any more. Instead, a ragbag of windcheaters, Hush Puppies, floral shirts for men, Guernseys and jerseys and cardies. Collars are long and worn outside of crew necks or wide-lapelled jackets. The ties are shiny, too wide, but shirts are more usually open-neck. Beige and muted orange are popular. Jean wears lime flared slacks with sewed-in creases or slightly frou-frou evening gowns, self-tailored or bought from the Grattan's catalogue, for whom Olive is an agent. She has a pair of Dr Scholl sandals, which she swears by. There are peasant smocks, purple midi-skirts and bell-bottom British Home Store denims.

Both Jilly and David, Olive and Arthur's children, are married now. Jilly has married Tony, her mod boyfriend. He gradually converted to hippie after smoking marijuana. In the wedding photograph, she wears a floppy hat, and her hair is still unmodified Mary Hopkin. He has extensive sideburns and a dark grey suit and white tie. They will move to Yorkshire and spend seven years on the dole. Tony will become active in the local Labour Party, then leave in despair when it becomes dominated by *middle-class wankers*. He cannot understand why they choose to talk about *blacks*, *women* and *gay rights* rather than wages and jobs. Years later, in the mid-1980s, he will set up his own business, which will briefly prosper and then go bust. Afterwards, Jilly and Tony will divorce.

At David's wedding, to Sandy, an infant school teacher, David wears a three-piece flared suit in light beige with lapels that touch the shoulder seams and platform shoes. He has a Zapata moustache and shoulder-length unstyled hair. Technically minded and fond of gadgets, he will spend his working life with what has yet to become British Telecom. He will shortly make investments in eight-track cassette systems and quadrophonic sound amplifiers. James, defenceless, takes the worst of the 1970s fashions, with overlong flared trousers with exterior patchwork pockets, a too-tight plaid jacket and a brown shirt with an orange fat knotted tie. Jean has pulled out her 1960s purple: she wears an ankle-length waistcoat with Mary Quant-style floral buttons, a high-waisted skirt with maroon flowers and a matching cravat. Jack's suit remains formal, narrow-legged and thin-lapelled. He and Jean are standing in the front garden of the council house at Acacia Avenue on scrubby grass edged with a creosoted picket fence. They toast with Babycham.

There are photographs from package trips to Majorca and Malta, from a camping trip to the Continent. Jack still insists on posing in his Jantzen swimming trunks, with his increasingly ample stomach very obviously pulled in. Jean is wearing skimpy bikinis, and on one occasion sunbathes topless, to the horror and embarrassment of James. There are blue pools, cloudless skies. In one photo, in Munich, Johnny Amlot bends to fix his Wolseley, which is always breaking down. German cars, it seems, are far more reliable, and increasingly popular, despite the 'I'm Backing Britain' campaign once supported patriotically by Jack. But *Who won the war, that's what I'd like to know?* is an incantation most frequently uttered by a previous generation. Jack and Jean are not resentful, are generally pro-Europe, and in the 1975 Common Market referendum, they vote Yes. Still, they remain suspicious of foreign food, and make sure to take diarrhoea tablets. In the background, behind Johnny's stricken car, a wall-advertisement reads: *Trink Coca-Cola. Das erfrischt richtig.*

Arthur, now a manager for Dolcis shoes in Wembley, owns an expensive camera and is something of a buff, much concerned with the interplay of F-stops and exposure times. At the end of each holiday he will produce a large box of rectangular slides which he will feed into a viewing box or beam on to the wall with a box-projector. Despite his investment, the photos are bad. The time it takes for the correct camera adjustment to be found means that irritation clearly edges the parade of posed grins.

The domestic photographs are more revealing in the background than foreground. There are leaded miniature arboretums, pine clocks, Scandinavian-style furniture from Ercol. There are mirrors overprinted with coloured etchings of an Aubrey Beardsley girl in pink and Marilyn Monroe in green. The ridged, square three-piece suite has given way to studded, golden bronze velour. A print of Van Gogh's *Sunflowers* is in the hall. There are ridged pine-cladding, purple curtains, lace nets. There is a coffee percolator, which on special occasions replaces the gruel of instant coffee with an overboiled brown sludge.

In the kitchen, Habitat-style half-globe lampshades in ochre. A Morphy-Richards toaster, a Mouli mixer for the sauces that Jean is now learning to prepare for her meats, Espagnole, mornay, curry, followed by Angel Delight, or Bird's Instant Whip, or Charlotte Russe or pineapple pudding with evaporated milk. Not present in our house, but in snaps from some of Jack and Jean's friends, are Capodimonte figures of ballerinas and harlequins, miniature, idealized earthenware cottages, valances for the bed bases, pinoleum blinds, Wharfedale Denton loudspeakers. Jack wears a digital wristwatch. The greetings cards on the mantelpiece no longer always rhyme; often they have stanzas by Susan Polis Schultz, a sort of transatlantic Pam Ayres, whose 'modern' poetry decorates the inside of cards painted with Jonathan Livingstone seagulls and Californian sunsets.

In one picture, Jean poses with Jack in the garden. It is Jubilee year and he is wearing a plastic Union Jack boater. Although he is laughing at himself, and self-conscious, he is still proud to be English, and proud to say so. Perhaps he is right, for at this time there is still a welfare state and education system and a low crime rate that is, in Jack's often repeated incantation, *the envy of the world*. The growing chorus that tells us we are as a people corrupt, racist, colonially brutal and exploitative simply bewilders Jack. For Jack, it is an article of faith that people are basically good, and that the world is sensible and straightforward. When with my father, I ridicule his naivety. But when Jeff makes a visit home from Quebec or Montreal or southern France, I find myself parroting my father, talking insistently about living in the most civilized country in the world, which he decries as a rotting, rinky-dink, penny-ante dump. As is habitual for me, I am not sure which I believe; my opinions change according to circumstance. I ache to own a belief, a conviction, but nothing seems incontrovertible, everything is plausible.

Around the same time, Jean and Jack are on the velour sofa, newly pine-clad walls reflecting a photo flash behind them. Jack is asleep, Jean has her head on his shoulder and is smiling with a look of deep contentment. She loves her husband. It is always Jean who moves to him and says, *Go on, give us a cuddle.* He is pleased, always responds, but never makes the first move himself, not thinking it manly. After Jean is dead, he will regret this and give me one of the few pieces of advice he ever offers:

Always show affection to your wife. Tell her you love her.

There are few photographs of Jeff in this time, because he has fled England at the age of eighteen, never to return except for brief visits with foreign girlfriends. What pictures there are show him boiler-suited or tanned or in ragged T-shirts. He becomes itinerant, working at one time in a French youth hostel, at another as a pony and trap driver in Quebec, kicking the horses with an adopted Gallic indifference. To my parents' bewilderment, he has become obsessed with something called 'authenticity', the quest for which explains the plainness of his clothes, his working man's beard and his labourers' boots. A typical shot shows Jeff in France in front of a Christmas tree with his French-Canadian girlfriend. He is wearing a peasant neckerchief and denim, she is wearing a boiler suit and working shirt. The inscription on the back reads: 'This is us in front of our *real* Christmas tree, Dec 76'. It is a reference to the fact that we have lately taken to buying a plastic one, since the real thing produces too much mess. Neither Jack nor Jean tries to bind Jeff to home by the subtle application of guilt or appeals to self-sacrifice; as Jack repeatedly asserts, *You have to let go.* Jean says that she agrees. In this way, she seems to prove herself strong as well as dutiful.

The remaining photographs suggest that Jack and Jean's life is still good. They live in security and more or less without fear, for the present or the future. They pursue leisure, increasingly available. The pictures show 'relaxation' and 'activities' and 'recreation'. Here they are at the Acropolis Restaurant in Weybridge, on the anniversary of friends. They are drinking retsina. Plates will be smashed later in the evening and Greek dancing attempted. Unlike me, they lack the self-importance to mind making fools of themselves. Jean and Helen pose with roses clenched in their teeth. Here they are at the Old Orchard in

Harefield, where they go for dinner-dances, which have by this time more or less replaced ballroom dancing for their generation. Jack still moves beautifully and is a sought-after partner.

Here is Jean at evening classes, doing yoga and flower-arranging. She goes with Olive and takes the lead, since Jean makes friends easily, unlike Olive, who is slightly diffident and shy. Here's Jack playing badminton, his Carlton, cat-gut-strung racquet poised over his head in an overhead smash. He is a good player, tactical acuity more than making up for his unschooled, improvised style. Like my mother, like me, he will be determined to win. There are shots of more holiday camps, restaurants with flock wallpaper, sun on the fields of France and Germany, of Luxemburg and Belgium.

Occasionally they will glimpse themselves on television, in *Terry and June* or – Jean's favourite – *Butterflies*, with Wendy Craig as a dreaming housewife with difficult but finally lovable sons. Or they will go to the Richmond Theatre or the Alfred Beck Centre in Hayes to see *Jesus Christ Superstar* or a revival of one of their old favourites, *Carousel* or *Seven Brides for Seven Brothers*. They will not go and see Mike Leigh's *Abigail's Party*, that cruel, inaccurate satire of subtopian life – it is 'theatre' and therefore 'arty-crafty' and so not really entertainment *as such*.

Jack and Jean, who have never expected much from life, are in fact satisfied, far removed from Mike Leigh's grotesques. Yet shadows are inching towards Jean, as they did in the photograph of her at sixteen years old, on a dustbin in the garden at Rose-croft Road, across a dry garden path.

For me, this is a time of success, at least measured against the ex-pectations of my background. Jean and Jack are proud of me, but they do not say so, believing that it will encourage conceit. In fact, the insecurity this restraint engenders in me produces exact-ly the effect they hope to avoid. I become increasingly cocksure, almost as an act of defiance; my deeper feeling is quite different.

Jeff does not seem to have an opinion on the matter of my exam success. His unexpected failure in his A-levels has not done much to bring us closer and his self-imposed exile does not give us the time to properly reconcile our childhood rivalries. When we meet occasionally over the following years, the atmosphere of competition and resentment is palpable.

I have developed a defensive arrogance that makes even people who like me dislike me simultaneously. Yet the effect on the whole is what I hope for: people find me interesting and seek me out. I am not ignored, even if I am not always liked. Furthermore, women are attracted to this arrogance, mistaking it for self-confidence.

This expression – apparently self-assured, *bolshie*, as my mother will have it – is the only constant in the photographs of me at this time. Otherwise I am in an endless state of transformation, as if hunting some condition of rest. I am trying to make myself up. I am searching for ballast, the ballast that was my parents' birthright.

Here I am in schooldays, my hair long and girlish, in a mauve satin jacket and a purple yoked cowboy shirt, in platform boots and loon pants with triangles of cloth sewn in to accentuate the flare. I leave school in 1974. I have found a place in further education.

Here I am at technical college in Harlow, where my father trained as a matelot, before it was a new town. I am taught tabloid journalism (thirty-five word intros, give it spin, build the story like a pyramid). Most of the writers on the course will go on to provincial locals, or, if they are lucky, the *News of the World* or the *Daily Star*. One of our chief lecturers is a reporter from the *Sun*. The course chief is a sports reporter from the *Daily Express*.

My hair has been shortened, layered, and I have smartened up into a dog's-tooth jacket, thick tie, polka-dot scarf. I am wearing yellow aviator spectacles and have a Zapata moustache which pulls my mouth downwards into a dimwitted droop. I look like a fool, but then, it is the 1970s. Everybody does.

Here is Debbie, my first girlfriend, whom I meet at college and to whom I lose my virginity. I am enthusiastic about sex, about sensation in general. I want to live in a Bacardi commercial, or Benson and Hedges poster. I want self-transcendence, perpetual delight. My thoughts are not consecutive enough to

170

frame limits; there seems to be a strobe running somewhere. Still, I am happier than I will ever be again in my life, here in Essex, the spiritual home of my class. I have succeeded in deflecting certain unsettling questions into relentless activity. I conspire, along with the rest of the world, to limit introspection. Lights flash. Loud music sounds.

Debbie is an attractive, warm, too-pliable girl from an ordinary family. She is from the inner city, in this case, a tower block in North Kensington. We work meticulously through the pages of Dr Alex Comfort's *Joy of Sex*. I have even sprouted the beard of the Californian-looking protagonist in the tastefully pencil-sketched pages. I wear plaid bum-freezer jackets with fake-fur collars, Afghan coats that smell like damp yak, purple platform boots, Donald Duck shoes, shirts with collars like ox tongues. I have an army greatcoat, bell-bottom Wranglers bleached and frayed at the bottoms, fitted leisure shirts from Michael's Men's Boutique in Ealing Broadway. I have grandad vests, lapels like Dover soles. Everything is inelegant, toylike, parodic without being ironic.

The next set of photographs shows me employed on a local paper in Uxbridge, five miles west of Southall, where I hone my craft of the brief sentence and the artful cliché. I learn a specialized kind of lie which I am trained to understand, in my bones, as being true.

Here the houses are more widely spaced, smarter, and the residents have two cars and garden sprinkler systems. Jean has talked of moving out this way lately, but they are insufficiently well off. The photographs, often newspaper 10 × 8 black-and-whites, show someone unmistakably prosaic, suburban, mildly laddish. My T-shirt and jeans, my haircut and shoes, still tend towards American casual. I drink until I am sick at parties. I have a faint sense that I am doing what is somehow required of me, but it is only faint. I am garrulous, determined, proudly ignorant, on the make. I have given up reading books.

It is 1976, the year of punk, when England begins to reimagine itself as it really is, or as it is becoming. Rage stands in for nostalgia, junk is virtue. McDonald's boxes begin to litter the streets and Covent Garden, where my father and grandfather have plied their trade, has been turned into a covered shopping mall. I am employed on a national pop music magazine, at the heart of it all. I have left home and am living in a freezing basement flat near the Harrow Road, decorated with ironic flying ducks and 1930s knick-knacks. The photographs, Polaroids with faded colours or press half-tones, show that the beard has gone, as molecules of the trash aesthetic rub off. My hair shortens further and I wear black drainpipes, rocker jackets, tour T-shirts, thin ties and lapels, narrow-toed boots. I shop at PX in Covent Garden and buy boiler suits and camouflage jackets from Lawrence Corner.

The photos show me with the celebrities I have begun to interview, my heroes of the time – David Bowie, Bryan Ferry, Kraftwerk. Here is me with Freddie Mercury in his Kensington garden, and here with Poly Styrene of X-Ray Spex, Paul Weller, the Clash. I am frightened of the people I interview, suffer a kind of vertigo each time. I overcompensate for my secret shyness by thickening my patina of arrogance. Yet I am also amazed that they are so unremarkable, so prosaic.

The world has changed for me utterly now. I am flown all over the world. Before this job, I have only eaten in a proper restaurant once, on my eighteenth birthday. Now I eat in restaurants with Michelin stars. I drink bottles of wine worth more than my father's weekly wage which I cannot appreciate, order food from menus which I cannot understand. Here is me in LA in a white stretch limo. Here I am in Barbados, in my own hotel suite. Here I am at the George V in Paris, the Essex House in New York. It seems that my childhood instinct is right: the world is without limits, if you are smart and determined and lucky. And daily perhaps, I ask that question, that burden of my generation, am I happy? And daily, the answer comes, it is not enough. It is never enough.

Here is Marion, my second girlfriend, whom I take up with after three years with Debbie. She is dark at first, then turns bleached blonde, after which she becomes promiscuous, in retaliation for my own unfaithfulness. I find myself living with her after she is made homeless and she moves into my flat. The spreading vacuum within me reaches out to her to look for something solid and finds only more empty space. I push and bully her to elicit some definite boundary, but the more I push, the more she collapses. Like me, she has no opinions, no convictions, no real beliefs, only an instinct to jump on to the next raft of experience. Her reliance, her strategy, is habit, instinct, niceness. We are weak, without self-knowledge, we torment each other, both unfaithful, both too dependent. Overweight, she suffers from bulimia and causes herself to vomit in the toilet. In the end I leave her, as I have left Debbie, with some amazement at my suddenly found strength after years of vacillation. It is 1979 and I am twenty-three years old.

By this time the photographs have changed once more. On cue for the coming decade, I have set up my own business, a news agency, with a partner, again from my background. I am smart, with expensive clothes and sharp, gelled hair. Oh, we are on the rise, my class, the C2s, the Essex Men. We have money, we have opportunity, we have hope. My partner, a clever and garrulous man who grew up in a council block in Islington, has no doubt where the future lies.

Something special is going to happen with Maggie. Yes, you can laugh, but you'll see. This country's going to be great again.

And it is true, it does feel like a new era is starting. Money is coming in. The grammar-school generation are biting the hand that fed them and voting in their millions for an end to soft consensus, slow drift. They want something firm, something they can bite on. Although I am unconvinced and put my cross in the same place my father always has, I feel the change. People believe in fairy-tales now, in anything at all, and are voting for them. People believe that the impossible is possible, that everyone can be rich if they try.

And sure enough, I am soon to be rich and in constant motion forward. How will it feel, I dream at this time? What will it be like to have that special thing? To have money. Will it make me real, bring me into focus? I dream, I plot, I prosper.

Chapter Twelve

'Struggling against impossible odds, surrounded by children, poor housing facilities and little money? These neuroses usually respond best to therapy with Triptafen' – 1970s medical advertisement

Facts, there are so many facts. I have left such a lot out. There must be many more unremembered and still more unknown. If I had chosen differently, it would be a different story, but this is the story I have told myself and I must hold to it. It is a trick I am trying to learn.

I need a story and that is the nub, that is what it *boils down to*, as my father always says. I need one like breath, one that sticks, because they are always coming loose, floating away. Others rise up from underneath and take their place, then in turn fall and fade. They focus, then blur, focus, then blur. It is very – disquieting. It is dangerous, not knowing the shape of your own life. I have made that mistake once. I have had that flaw, if flaw it is.

So I must carve and sculpt, I must select and discard, I must hold fast to the narrative. Perhaps I am indulging myself, lying, writing the autobiography of a nobody, for nobody but myself. It often feels that way. There are few clues to tell me that I will one day go mad, unless ambition itself is a sort of madness. There are few clues to tell me that my mother will go mad, unless connectedness – family itself – is a kind of madness.

Two things happen in the 1970s which loom large in this particular version of my story. They seem consistent, are always presenting themselves to me one way or another as I daily pick over the past, that unfinishable, indigestible feast. Perhaps this means they are significant. I will come to them, these scraps of story, but let me first put these questions, questions to which I do not have an answer. Does the human mind behave like metal? If put under enough strain, does it fatigue and weaken, so that one day the slightest wind will snap it? Or is it like a reed, bending, then flexing back into place, without damage? Is it rigid or is it elastic? Is it soft or is it hard? Does it have a true past which takes action on the present or only an endless, enveloping present in which we simply imagine a past?

It is a beautiful sunny afternoon, a Sunday. Jean and Jack are playing tennis with their friends at Duke's Meadows in Chiswick, as they have done on Sundays for years. I am fifteen years old, with hair down to my shoulders, splitting at the ends, greasy and darkened in the centre parting line. I am bored, for too many reasons to list.

I begin to walk, down towards the Yew Tree roundabout in Hayes. I have taken to idling around the common ground on the high-rise estate there facing the Yew Tree pub, where I have a friend called Donald, who goes to a local secondary modern. It is an ugly estate, system-built, white. Donald and I often stand and share our ennui, as if it were a cheap cigarette. We indulge in minor vandalism or drink VP sherry or Olde England Cherry Wine. There are girls there sometimes, plain ones in postal-catalogue polyester and nylon. We take them into the underground garages and try to find the courage to make rudimentary sexual advances, but fail. I am shy, ashamed of my scars and my oddly refined voice. Instead we kick the ground and skirt the subject. Hours will pass before I go home, nothing achieved.

On this occasion, however, I am not going to see Donald but another friend, Graham, who is older than me, has short hair and wears a parka. He also lives on a council estate, across from the blank high-rises, in a six-house terrace. In later years, he will become an ultra-right-wing Conservative councillor.

I walk down the Greenford Road, over the bridge, past the Taylor Woodrow factory. I do not know what it makes, but some of my father's bridge partners work there. Sweat marks my scoop-neck long-sleeve T-shirt with the flared sleeves. I have an attempted moustache, a faint line of fur. An uncommon feeling of anticipation beats in my chest. Graham has a surprise for me and I have an inkling of what it is. I am very slightly frightened. The sun is relentless.

I reach the Yew Tree roundabout and take a left turn. My Converse All-stars, worn with thin rayon socks bought by my mother, feel sticky. Outside Graham's house there is a Vespa scooter that does not work; the guts of the engine are splayed on the crazy-paving. I knock on the door and Graham answers with a conspiratorial grin. We go inside. A carriage clock sits on the mantelshelf and there is a coal-effect gas fire. We are alone in the house. Graham's parents, unusually in this particular England at this particular time, are divorced and his mother is out for the day.

Graham is a small, stocky boy, almost a man, with an impudent, knowing expression, even when his face is at rest. He moves something like a boxer, in short, stubby shifts of motion. I sense an edge of violence to him sometimes that makes me nervous, but he is on the whole likeable and funny. He also attends a secondary modern, but seems clever, cleverer than me.

I sit in the brown napped and stained 1950s-style armchair, clearly humbler than Jean's neat three-piece. I am slumming it in a sense, a wafer below my class, but I am hardly aware of such things. Graham and his family are not quite respectable and that makes them attractive.

Graham makes me a cup of powdered coffee – I hate tea for some reason – and we fiddle with a couple of Royal Scot biscuits. It is as if some introductory ritual has to be gone through, but we feel the irrelevance of the gesture. I am rubbing my knees, a nervous habit I have picked up from my father. Graham reaches into his pocket and brings out a piece of silver paper the size of a sixpence. He smiles, like a butcher displaying his best cut of fillet.

This'll do the trick.

He carefully unpeels the silver paper and shows me proudly the contents. I can see nothing at first, then, as he waits for my reaction, I notice two tiny dots standing out from the foil. I am not sure what I am expected to say.

Oh. And this is –

Blue Sunshine. Microdot.

They're so small.

I had expected the LSD tablets to be about the size of para-cetamol. I had intended, on this occasion, to take only a half or even a quarter. But the tablets are so tiny, they are virtually in-divisible. It seems that I am bound to lose face if I try and divide it up. Anyway, something so tiny can hardly be very powerful.

Jack and Jean have warned me about drugs, that if I smoke pot I will go mad and become hooked. The fact that this prediction has proved untrue has weakened the scraps of their authority. This is the first time I have been offered LSD, however; the supply lines that once fuelled Chelsea art schools and Notting Hill communes have only just reached the suburbs. The gap between *Sergeant Pepper's* and the Yew Tree roundabout is about five years. In the King's Road now, they have moved on to junk, skag, H, which are still more or less unknown this far away from Charing Cross. Marianne Faithfull is shooting up somewhere in a basement, Mama Cass is dead, Neil Young is writing 'Needle and the Damage Done', Lou Reed is singing love songs about heroin.

The inherited taboo about drugs is still very powerful, even if the barriers to availability have fallen. Also there is a part of me that is sensible and cautious, in a way. I do not smoke cigarettes, for instance, considering it stupid. So as I pick up the tiny dot and place it softly on my tongue, I fight a faint sense of shame, as well as fright. Then the tablet dissolves and I begin to wait, neutrally.

I do not know what to expect, other than a vague idea of hal-lucinations, which I suppose means that I will begin to see things that are not there. Dancing elephants, perhaps, like in *Fantasia*, or hosts of cartoon cherubim. Most of all, I expect to feel sick and slightly disappointed, as I do when I smoke the low-grade cannabis that is sold in the brewery-remade pubs around the estates of Ealing and Hillingdon, where I wash down crisps with barley wine and draught Triple V cider. Sometimes, at par-ties fuelled by Watney's Party Sevens, I am given what I am told are mandies and dexies, or blue bombers. They, too, disappoint.

Perhaps they are placebos, inauthentic like everything else, like me.

For about half an hour nothing happens. We walk over to Donald's estate, where Graham knows a couple of girls. I have met them before, but this is the first time I have entered their flat. Again, their parents are out. They are both dumpy and have dull, unstyled hair. Pictures of a weeping clown and a wide-eyed orphan boy are the sole decorations on their living-room wall, which is on the second floor of a thirty-storey block. A dull thud of music can faintly be heard from the flat above. It is a kind of pop reggae, perhaps 'Uptown Top Ranking' by Anthea and Donna. I feel awkward with the girls and can think of nothing to say to them. They bring me a whisky glass filled with Orange Corona, which I dutifully pick up without drinking.

I notice, after a short while, that the two girls are looking at me curiously, although I cannot imagine why. Graham has started laughing like a loon.

What you looking at?

And then:

What's up with him?

The girls do not know that we have taken LSD, so they can have no idea why I am staring fixedly at a spot on the wall about a foot square. The wall is covered with stippled wallpaper, presumably to cover lumped plaster and stains. I have picked the spot at random and am finding it intensely satisfying. The curve and whorl of the pattern seem to be coiling and uncoiling of their own volition. The sunlight that fires through the oily, metal-framed window catches them in a fascinating way, making the contours stand up and gently vibrate. I follow the beam of the sun to the air in the middle of the room. It seems to have become solid, or perhaps a thick liquid. It exists in a sheet that cuts below the bare light bulb hanging from the ceiling. There are dust motes illuminated by the sun, hanging, rearranging into fresh patterns. My mouth is beginning to drift open in amazement. The motes – there are so many of them and their dance is so slow. They seem to be the loveliest things I have ever seen.

Everything appears as lit by a powerful, hidden strobe. Motion slows.

I am still and my mind is brilliantly clear. There is no reason to move, ever. There is just this shining moment. I let my eyes drift around the room. No longer are the objects out there. It is clear that they are fundamentally, intensely connected to each other and myself.

Noticing Graham's laughter, I look at him and begin to laugh too, not because anything is funny, but because everything is so fresh and new-minted, so absolutely wonderful. It is as if some great leathered covering has been lifted from my eyes and heart, as if some invisible, fogged layer has been pulled back to reveal an always-hidden Eden. When Graham speaks, it is as if his words are bowled to me in slow motion.

Something funny?

Yes. Yes, I suppose you could say that.

Mind telling me what it is?

Mind? No, I wouldn't mind. How could I?

My sentence drifts away. I have become astonished by Graham's face. Little ripples are passing over it at an astonishing rate. It is still recognizably Graham, but it has become more than him, somehow, more concentrated. I hold my hand in front of my face and move it; it leaves a blur of afterimage.

The girls have started to look nervous now, aware that we are both behaving peculiarly. I notice that Graham's eyes are black at the centre, the pupils dilated, as if to allow the world in. Mine must look the same. We are sitting oddly still and attempt to maintain an even conversation, but it breaks down every few seconds, as some new wonder catches at us: a patterned teacup, a crumb of biscuit, the weave of my shirt.

Graham.

Yes?

Graham.

What?

But I have forgotten what it is I have to say.

We remain rational enough to sense the girl's mounting unease and rise as one to leave. The exact coincidence of this makes us begin laughing again, as if some deep mystery has been suddenly revealed. Steadily, we make our way towards the door and out into the estate grounds. It is apparent that the girls are relieved to see us go. As the door closes, they are forgotten.

Well? Fancy a stroll?

Why not?

I don't know.

Well, then. We'll come back later.

Yes. We'll clear up.

Well, then. Tally ho.

We collapse into laughter again. The tower blocks shine like mirrors, and the blue of the sky seems to have concentrated and leaked out into the air, so that everything is soaked in aquamarine. There is a deep, relentless and secret whirr within me, a dynamo which has just been switched on to full power for the first time. I am so full of delight I want to leave my skin and melt. Indeed, I think I am melting into the world around me, and that it is melting into me. There is no barrier any more.

We stand at the bus stop, waiting, though I forget what for, until a bus moves into the middle distance. I have decided to go home and see a friend from Southall, Nick Blong, who lives two streets away from the house at Rutland Road. Suddenly Graham takes it into his head to wander off towards his home, as the bus approaches. I get on all the same. The street is moving like a sea and is coloured like petrol spill. The red of the heaving bus is more red than anything I have ever seen, more deep in its hue than a field of poppies.

What amazes me, as I fumble for money for the fare, giggling to myself like an idiot, is that I feel sure that I am not seeing things that are not there – I am seeing things that *are* there. It has become plain, quite obvious, that the sensible world is simply a construction of my brain, and the brain is a kind of filter that keeps unmanageable, too-large information out. This I deeply know to be true, and know it to be true long after the effects of the drug have worn off. I am in a state of the purest, most concentrated ecstasy and it is the most real, the most truthful thing I have ever experienced.

By the time I leave the bus, in Lady Margaret Road, I have noticed that there is a sort of ratchet effect built into the drug. It builds, falls back, then builds higher, more intensely than before. I presume it will level off after a while, but I do not mind because I assume the greater the strength, the deeper the pleasure I will experience. Certainly things are becoming very strange now. Objects seem to be on the point of disintegrating before my eyes into sparkling, undulating crystals. My eyelids are pushed up, my eyes are round. Matter seems to present itself as energy. The most trivial object is invested with a celestial significance.

When I arrive at my friend Nick's, his parents are home. As a sort of running joke, he calls his mother faggot and his father fag. He calls for a cup of tea.

Faggot! Tea!

I try very hard to make myself appear normal, but it is increasingly difficult. A slight sense of fear is appearing at the edges of my self, as the strength of the drug kicks up another level. Things are becoming so large and encompassing that I fear I will be absorbed, lost. But for the time being, I can politely refuse Nick's mother's offer of tea, and sit and pretend to listen to the Stooges '1969' and 'No Fun'. The intensity is now becoming insupportable. I say to Nick that we should go and he comes with me. He knows that I am on acid and finds it amusing, but I can tell that he is becoming a little disconcerted by the oddness of my behaviour, and my wild, fractured sentences.

We walk the few hundred yards back to my parents' house and I somehow manage to open the door with the key. Nick is recognizable as himself, but he seems increasingly gnome-like and malevolent. The fear within me is slowly turning to panic, as I understand that the whole experience is going out of control and there is nothing I can do to stop it. The flood of images and sensations is becoming a tidal wave that threatens to engulf me entirely. I am only vaguely aware that I have even taken a drug. I begin to stamp the floor with my feet in an attempt to re-establish some relationship with a more manageable reality and shout, as loud as I can, *No!* time and again. But I am slipping away, into somewhere that has no boundaries. Nick is looking distinctly nervous now. When I pick up a chair and throw it across the room, I turn and am just about aware that he has gone, that I am alone. The panic begins to turn to unalloyed terror, as I feel my very sense of self beginning to collapse into the swelling chaos of everything else. I start to walk like a robot, picking things up, putting them down, rearranging them. It is no longer me who is acting, but some much larger, metaphysical force, a force within which I am absolutely drowning. I am negated. I have gone completely mad, although everything is unmistakably, intensely real.

I pick up a piece of cake and it collapses into terrible, rotting, moving heaps. I do not know what to do and in a fear so great I cannot bear it, I begin to smash up my parents' house, throwing picture frames, plates, ornaments. I kick the wall. I pick up the carriage clock and hurl it at the window. It seems undamaged. The minute hand clicks another degree.

My sense of being present in any sort of time – of time itself passing – has disappeared. I have found myself present in a sealed off never-never land, which I believe cannot end. I seem to know that I have plugged into my source and it is burning me horribly. I suddenly need to be free of all that binds me to earth and I tear off my clothes, as if it will release me from torment. Naked, I pace the house, all sense and meaning now sucked out of me and into the heated, distorting air. I stare out of the window, as if I could find salvation there. I want to see Jamie, my younger brother, the only particle of my self that I can remember. In my love for him I see some hope of relief, some tether.

Jamie is two years old at this time and I run out into the hot street, still naked, to see if I can find him. I do not notice the astonished stares of the neighbours. A woman is walking along the road with a small baby, and I rush up to her and pick up the child in the hope that it is my brother. I inspect his melting, drifting face and see that it is not him. The woman is screaming now, but I am indifferent. I put the child down and start to wander, absolutely without purpose.

Walter Wall, who lives opposite, opens his door and comes out. A labourer, stockily built and powerful, he tries to knock me down with a blow to the chin. I scarcely feel it and run instead into his open door and upstairs, where I begin tearing the Walls' bedroom to pieces. Walter, although more powerful by far, cannot find the strength to stop me.

After a while – I cannot tell how long, because I have lost all sense of time passing – I am aware of two policemen entering the room. They overpower me and drag me into a police car. By now, the entire street is watching. I am talking gibberish. They start the car and start towards Greenford Police Station. I feel momentarily relieved that I am being taken somewhere safe.

When I arrive at the station, my panic has returned, more intense than ever. I have decided that I am God and am engaged in a cosmic battle against nothingness, that the world is my creation and I find it intolerable, that it must fracture. I am locked into a tiny cell and left alone.

Now I am nothing but terror and madness. I know that a doctor is coming to see me and I think that if he examines me, he will discover that I am dead, and once this discovery is made, I *will* be dead. I imagine that I am faced with a choice between an eternity in this tiny, barred room or final oblivion. I clearly feel a sensation inside the pit of my chest, like two electric drills being held point to point, two opposed battling energies perfectly balanced. The doctor arrives. I fight to stop him from examining me and the police hold me down.

The cell door opens again. It is my father. I fall into his arms and begin to cry. He holds me, embarrassed, and takes me home in the back of his car as if I am a child again, wrapped in a tartan blanket.

When I arrive home at Rutland Road, I feel that the effect of the drug is weakening, to the extent that I am at least aware that I have taken a drug. But the world is still opalescent, whirring within itself, shining. My father takes me up to my room and puts me to bed, not knowing what else to do. The stars on the paper on the ceiling reel.

After a while, I hear sounds coming from downstairs. To my amazement, it seems that Jean has brought her friends back from the tennis courts. My uncles and aunts begin to parade up to my room to look at me, and sigh. I am still barely cogent and do not really recognize them, although I am annoyed that they are there. At certain moments I feel that they too are gods and have come to judge me.

After a while, my mother appears in the room. She is pale and looks shaken. I have steadied enough by now to wonder idly what she will find to say. She looks down at me with pained, incredulous eyes and looks for some phrase that will express the complexity of her feelings. She opens her mouth to speak. The moment seems to stretch.

Oh, Timmy, she says. *Where did we go wrong?*

I am now sane enough to feel let down by the cliché and an ironic smile edges my lips. It seems to be me who shakes my head in despair in reflection of her. Even in this condition, I am a snob.

Much later, I wonder why it was that my father came alone to see me at the police station. I learn that when the police came to Duke's Meadows, Jean simply carried on playing tennis, while Jack set off urgently in the car. She played well, without any apparent disruption to her accustomed rhythm.

I think of the television that she switches off when pictures of famine appear. I think of Jean hiding in the cabin of the boat as we head for the weir. I think of Jean telling Irene that her brother, actually in gaol, was away on holiday. It is becoming clear what Jean's final line of defence against life was. I think I always knew it, really. But I did not then, of course, understand what was on the other side of that line.

The second happening is perhaps closer to a process in that it is a series of linked events. The first tile of this domino line – for I think of them arranged into linear steps of cause and effect – is set in place on my fourteenth birthday. For the first time, as a birthday treat, I have been to the West End, with my best friend at the time, a shy, gentle boy called Frank Brezine. The experience was bewildering, the sheer weight of people seeming to have increased my natural sense of invisibility. I do not tell my mother that I became hopelessly lost twice and frightened. But I am relieved to be home in a place where I am not so completely diluted. Jean behaves briskly in the kitchen. She is preparing tea, soft baps with liver sausage and tomato, lettuce with egg and salad cream. There is home-made Madeira cake for what Jean has now learned to call dessert instead of afters or pud.

There is the sound of the front door opening. It is too early for my father, so I know it must be one of my grandparents, Gran or Gramps. And it is indeed Billy, retired from baking now and with too much time on his hands. Still, it is unusual for him to come around by himself without Grace.

He walks into the kitchen, too fast, as if there is something that must urgently be done. What is left of his silver hair is uncombed. He seems terribly old to me, but he is only in his sixties, neat and apparently healthy. He is mouthing something that at first I cannot make out. It sounds like *Chisgorn*.

He is repeating this phrase wildly. I cannot make sense of it. He is shaking his head, as if something quite infuriating has happened. I can see that my mother is also confused, but senses that what he is saying is important, vital.

Chisgorn. Chisgorn.

My mother puts her arms around Billy, who has begun to shake. I stand up from my chair, as if to do something, although I cannot imagine what it should be. I have understood suddenly what it is Billy is saying.

She's gone. She's gone.

I realize that what he means is that Grace, my grandmother, has died. Something goes still within me, as if resting before some great activity. Neither my mother nor Billy is crying, but the way they hold each other appears to form a support arch, to prevent each slipping down. I feel the overwhelming need to do something, while realizing that there is nothing to do.

After a while they separate and Billy sits down next to me. My mother remains standing and starts to make tea, to soak and soften things. As Billy talks, he does not meet anyone's eye, as though he is ashamed of what has happened. He concentrates on the surface of the table, occasionally raising his eyes to dart a look at my mother, who is stiff with something now, grief or forbearance.

Went out, me and Alan. An hour or two. Needed some milk. She wasn't there. I called out, but — We had the milk. The Co-Op was closed so we — Anyway, it was raining. She wouldn't have — She was in the toilet. I knew right away. Had a turn. Alan went round to Dr Smith, but I knew. Oh, chisgorn. Face all purple. Heart attack, it was. Well, she was a big woman. Oh, God. What am I going to do?

My mother began to cry, and went on more or less continuously for three or four hours.

She was more controlled when Billy himself died, two years later. This time, it had been expected. From the moment Grace had been cremated, he had begun to erode. This disintegration found its expression in lung cancer, which began to consume him particle by particle. He now lived in the house with just Alan, who was well into middle age, more eccentric than ever and working as a park keeper, mocked and ridiculed by local schoolboys. Alan and Billy fought bitterly; Grace had been the buffer and with her gone they collided.

Billy was terrified of dying. I would take his dinners round to him sometimes and he would prop himself up on his pillow, muttering.

Timmy. Timmy, I'm so scared.

I would not answer at first. This was not how dying was meant to be. My mother always told me that as you grew older, you 'adjusted' to the idea of dying, you accepted it. But the fear that spread from Billy's bed was thick as dust. It made me uneasy. It was embarrassing.

Timmy, I'm —

You'll be OK, Grandpa. You'll be up in no time.

Nah. Nah. I'm dying, son. I'm going to die.

He would begin to cry. I was shocked.

You'll be up in no time.

Nah.

Billy finally died, in King Edward's Hospital, a few months later. My mother seemed to accept it. The death of Grace had prepared her and the grieving seemed brief, restrained. For me also, I had somehow become accustomed to the idea of this impossible absence, this ridiculous hole in life. When Grace died I was, more than anything, incredulous that such a thing was possible. But now I got it, now I understood. One day, sooner or later, people simply disappeared.

It became clear after the deaths of Billy and Grace that Alan, hitherto thought of as merely 'a little simple', had more complex problems. At the funerals of both his mother and his father, he gave the impression that he was attending a party rather than a wake. Chattering non-stop, and at ten or fifteen decibels above a normal level, he grinned and nodded as the cortège pulled up outside Rosecroft. In the slow haul of the cars towards the crematorium, the stream of chat – about his model boats, which he sailed on the Serpentine, his Airfix aircraft, his minor health problems – went on without pause. Even as the doors opened and each coffin began to slip into the flames, as his mother and father, his only protectors, disappeared for ever, Alan muttered and called out, a grin pasted on his face. At no time did he cry. No one had ever seen Alan cry.

Jean knew now that the responsibility for Alan remained with her. Norman, who had married and then been abandoned with his three daughters, did not have the time, or much inclination, to help. To leave Alan to his own devices was not an option. Jean's sense of duty to her family, being the greatest part of what she was, could not be avoided.

After Billy's funeral, Jean took Alan under her wing. He was an essentially good man, although eccentric and, in some ways, faintly autistic. Every night he would come around for dinner, despite the fact that he was vexatious company. Smoking non-stop, his voice would somehow get louder by degrees, running like a tape-loop of static, incessant and deeply banal. He would repeat himself constantly. When the TV was on and we were trying to watch *Morecambe and Wise* or *The Good Life* or *Harry Worth*, he would carry on his monologue, interrupting it only for laughter that was idiotic and cacophonous, blotting out everything else. The laughter was always in the wrong place. His voice was rough as ground pepper and cast a harsh light, like a probe into the hidden root of family.

I 'ad a job in Sowfall Pahk, right? They give me the push for skiving. Fell asleep in the bleedin' wheelbarrer, didn't I? Then it was the council. A right con. Doing the verges and that. Got off on the sick. I got piles, see? Then I got this, what is it? Ulcer. Half me gut hanging out. I just lay in the ahse not doing nothink. Well, that was that.

And so on.

Then Jean began to notice that Alan was becoming gradually more dishevelled and indifferent to himself. His complaining – about his health, his doctor, the dole office, the weather, anything at all – was becoming more relentless. After a while he stopped coming round to dinner.

Alan had gone to bed and would not get out. As if his body was grieving on his behalf, the skin opened and wept. He developed large, plate-sized sores all over his body and face. Soon he could not even be bothered to go upstairs to bed. He lay on filthy rags in the back room. The *chaise-longue* had gone now, but the record player was still there, and a Rayburn fire, and a bookshelf with unread copies of Zane Grey on it.

Jean began to take his dinner round to him, to clean and tidy the house, to sponge-bath and shave him. Nothing made any difference. In a strange echo of my grandfather's breakdown in 1939, my Uncle Alan had, through grief, withdrawn from the world.

The house, once neat and meticulously ordered, its step bleached white, began, despite Jean's efforts, to crumble under the force of entropy and indifference. The front garden became overgrown with weeds and inside there were grease marks on the disarranged furniture. Alan's abandoned train sets and Airfix models dominated the rooms, while he lay motionless, apart from a soft, endless picking at his skin that made the sores larger and deeper.

The sight of Alan tormented Jean. She had made a promise to her mother she would look after her simple brother whatever happened, but it was a promise she did not know how to fulfil. She considered bringing him into her own house, but feared it would damage her marriage. Instead she visited every day, bathing his sores in salt water and bringing hot food, which he would often leave untouched, declaring openly his wish to die.

I'll stick my head in the gas oven. I'll do meself in.

Meals on Wheels began to visit. For the first time, the social security blanket descended on the family. It was a kind of shame, but Jean could not look after Alan single-handed. Jack took him to the family doctor, Falconer Smith, in Allenby Road, and Alan was prescribed an assortment of sleeping pills, since he complained of insomnia. The pills, which he took overlarge doses of, seemed to crush him further. He took an overdose, a whole bottle of phenobarbitone, only to sleep for thirty-six hours and wake with a cracking headache. Now he would not even get out of his rancid pyjamas or shave.

One day Jean went round to take his dinner. Alan was outside the house, in his pyjama bottoms, his buttons undone, his cock and balls visible. He had dropped his plate from Meals on Wheels and was scraping the food off the pavement. His torso was bare, pitted with red welts. It was as if he were decomposing. Jean tried to lead him back inside, but a neighbour, a recently arrived Ugandan Asian, who worked for the health service as a nurse, intervened.

Don't take him back inside. They won't do anything if he's indoors. If you take responsibility, they will not. Leave him. Call an ambulance.

And so it was that Alan was admitted to St Bernard's Hospital. Jeff and I had sniggered, as children, as we passed it on the way to Aunty Olive's in Brentford.

That's where the loonies are.

We would whisper, half in mockery, half afraid, staring at the barred windows with a thrill. And now Alan had been admitted into one of the long wards, where men in dressing gowns sat for hours, staring into air smelling of paraldehyde and pissed-on sheets.

Each time Jean went to visit, she left in shame and despair, horrified at the parade of sadness that was arrayed inside the walls.

How can they live like that? People just standing around. Not doing anything. It's terrible. Terrible. Poor Alan. If only I could –

But there was nothing she could do. It was for the doctors to sort out, those shrunken, infallible gods.

★

Around this time, the time my uncle, with his bog-brush hair and busted-klaxon voice, was admitted to what I then still cheerfully referred to as the loony bin, two obliquely connected events took place. First, I went to see a particular movie at the Ealing ABC with Debbie. Her perfume was Rive Gauche. Her hair was cut in a soul-girl bob and she wore a velvet choker and hoop earrings. Second, two patients at a hospital in Stockholm committed suicide.

The film was sharp and affecting, one of the best of that decade – better even, I thought, than *Emmanuelle* or *The Exorcist*. Since I had pretty much given up reading books, the movies and TV were the main part of the flickering hypermarket where I picked up information about, well, more or less everything, I suppose. I didn't see them at the time as forming my beliefs, because I wasn't aware of *having* any beliefs. I didn't believe in them, you might say. I didn't understand then that you *have* to have them, one way or another. You don't have a choice. It's really just a question of acknowledgement. And films fed them, if anything did. Fed, frame after frame, those unstated, unacknowledged beliefs – 'overbeliefs' someone smarter than me once called them. What I thought about Vietnam was what I took away from *Apocalypse Now*. What I thought about social workers was what I picked up from *Cathy Come Home*. And what I thought about mental illness was lifted raw from *One Flew Over the Cuckoo's Nest*.

It was this film that I went to see in 1975 with Debbie. As I say, it was a good movie; at the time, I thought it a great one. I was moved, I think, to tears of pity and rage. I found the movie deeply cathartic. The picture it presented of a mental hospital imprinted itself indelibly on my mind, as much a matter of poetic fact as of fiction.

One Flew Over the Cuckoo's Nest tells the story of how a 'free spirit', R. P. McMurphy – played by Jack Nicholson – is crushed and destroyed by a hostile, almost psychotic medical establishment. He is drugged, shocked and finally lobotomized into submission and conformity. When I left the cinema, I had several impressions formed, or perhaps they were existing impressions reinforced. First, I thought that mental handicap and mental illness were much the same: types of craziness personified by staring eyes, stutters, jitters, mutism. Second, paradoxically, was the idea that mental illness was not anything real, but an individual weakness promoted to 'illness' by a whole profession of middle-class control freaks. Third was the idea that the medical treatment of mental illness, by drugs, electric shock or surgery, was worse than unhelpful – it was barbaric, cruel and dangerous.

I did have another, more direct source of information about the subject of depression and madness: Uncle Alan's hospital treatment. Unlike my mother, I did not visit every week; in fact, I remember going only once. It didn't seem too bad to me at the time. His room was light and airy, and his terrible, self-inflicted sores seemed to be recovering. He moaned and complained when I went to see him, but Alan always moaned, it was a sort of hobby. There were, as my mother had told me, abstracted-looking men shuffling around the corridors in soiled pyjamas, but I didn't pay it much mind. The mental agony my mother was going through seeing her brother in an institution was invisible to me. I was nineteen and as selfish as a newborn baby. Also she hid it, for if there was one thing Jean knew about, it was concealment.

Alan did appear to recover after three months, but then he relapsed and was taken back into hospital. Released again, he relapsed once more. Eventually, it was becoming clear that Alan was dependent on the hospital care and the drugs, mostly tranquillizers, that were being prescribed. Tranquillizers – Valium, Mogadon, Librium – were as much a 1970s fashion for doctors as loon pants were for me, and Alan had a medicine cabinet full of them. By the end of the decade one in ten men and one in five women had been prescribed them. In 1975, the year I went to see *Cuckoo's Nest*, there were 20 million prescriptions for Valium alone in America. There were epidemics of tranquillizer over-doses across Britain.

It was Jack who decided, after talking with doctors, that Alan had to be left, effectively, to go to the wall. Jean, always more delicate than my father, found this a terrible decision to take. The threats that Alan continually made to end his life fell upon her like blows, but what, Jack, always the realist, continually asked, could they do? The doctors, those gods, who had put Alan on tranquillizers in the first place, had got him addicted. Now they said he had to stop, and in the stopping he might kill himself.

Jean and Jack told Alan that he could no longer come round for dinner. Jean, struggling against her deepest instinct, did not go to help him, or clear up his house, or bathe his always reopening wounds. Effectively, he was ignored. Either he pulled himself together or he died. Jean sat at home, drinking tea, thinking of her brother a few hundred yards away, lying on blood-soaked sheets, wasting away, filthy.

You don't know how I suffer, she said to me once, but only when pushed, for my mother tried her best not to be a martyr, always strived to reject that most maternal basic power-play.

Almost miraculously, the cold-turkey approach worked. After attempting an overdose and practically starving, Alan, quite of his own volition, was forced into a decision. He took responsibility for himself. He flushed all his tablets down the lavatory. He began to recover, slowly at first, then more quickly. He started to sleep upstairs in the bedroom instead of on rags on the back-room floor. He put on weight. His sores started to clear up. After a while, he began to dress and shave, and go back to the Serpentine to sail his boats. He had been cured, cured of self-pity and dependence, and the curing had been his own doing.

I thought of Alan, I thought of R. P. McMurphy. It was clear to me that depression – if such a thing, separate from unhappiness, existed, which I heartily doubted – was simply an expression of weakness, or botched medicine. Alan had not been mature enough to deal with his grief and had looked for pity, from Jean, from the system, and for medicines to blot out his pain. The road of the doctors was the road to complete degradation and sapping dependence.

No, there was no depression; it was all *bollocks*. There were only forms and varieties of unhappiness, and the consequences of personal failure. Anything else was just excuses. Margaret

Thatcher had in this year, 1975, been made leader of the Conservative Party, and our class – the respectable, upwardly clambering subtopians – were always Thatcherite in this respect at least: do it yourself, because no one was going to do it for you.

Of course I did not know about the other thing that happened in 1975 in Stockholm, because it took place in academic circles which were as alien to me as Papuan tribal life. It was an experiment in neurology, and it followed, as I say, on the suicide of two patients.

A researcher called Marie Asberg decided to examine the chemical compositions of fluids from the brain cavities of the suicides, the cerebrospinal fluid. She discovered that this fluid had low levels of a substance called 5H1AA. Further investigation revealed that more than twice as many depressed patients with low 5H1AA levels had attempted or committed suicide than those with normal levels. Those with the lowest levels killed themselves by the most violent methods. Every study since has confirmed the results of this experiment.

This was the clearest evidence yet that there was something distinct from unhappiness called depressive illness, and that its roots were organic. It was a deeply unfashionable view in 1975, a decade still in thrall to the ideas of anti-psychiatry expressed in *Cuckoo's Nest*, at least among intellectuals (doctors, as the tranquillizer epidemic attested, were often of a different opinion).

The idea of depression as an illness had fallen out of favour with good reason. After the war the first real systematic study of 'mood disorders' took place. This was, as in the nineteenth century, overwhelmingly biased towards an organic, 'scientific' view of what more romantic individuals – most people, I suppose – like to think of as the human spirit.

With this in mind, electric shock treatments and lobotomies became the favoured treatment, particularly in America, where unhappiness was considered a kind of antisocial deviancy. In the 1940s, 20,000 people had their brains deliberately damaged in operations. In the mid-1950s, Professor Freeman at George Washington University developed the treatment of thrusting an ice pick through the frontal sinus at the root of the nose once the patient had been rendered unconscious by ECT. As news of these radical treatments leaked out, the idea of modifying personality by drugs, shock and surgery became tainted; the whole idea of an 'organic' personality began to fall out of favour.

Yet, in the same decade, Robert Heath at Tulane University discovered that if you implanted electrodes at the base of the forebrain, intense pleasure could be produced. Janice Egeland claimed to have discovered a depression 'gene' in her study of the Amish. Twin studies showed time and again that there was a concordance of depression in 65 per cent of cases with identical twins, even when separated at birth, compared with 14 per cent for non-identical twins. New antidepressant drugs like Iprioniazid, which, unlike tranquillizers, restored 'balance' rather than 'damping down' mood, were tested and found to work. Cross-cultural studies showed that depression appeared in every society.

All these studies seemed to show that there was something in the brain called a 'mood centre' and this 'mood centre', in certain kinds of depression, simply malfunctioned, like a heart with angina or a liver with cirrhosis. Certain kinds of unhappiness – in some versions, almost all forms of unhappiness – were simply a kind of illness, as often as not inherited.

The 1960s, with its emphasis on freedom, the individual, non-conformity and the 'spirit', found the model of the mind as a kind of soft machine, a bundle of chemicals and meat and electrical impulses, revolting and, perhaps worse, unpoetic. Hence films singing the praises of antidepressants and electric shock treatments were in short supply. Thinkers such as R. D. Laing, Thomas Szasz and Michel Foucault – none of whom, of course, I had even vaguely heard of in 1975 – helped create a new climate. In this world, madness – including depression – was simply an invention, got up by society or doctors or drug companies. An increasing interest in Freud, Jung and a variety of therapies – gestalt, rolfing, EST – underpinned this reaction against medical solutions to 'broken brains', to what was increasingly not even seen as mental illness so much as convenient myth.

And this, on the whole – since I was unquestionably a child of the 1970s – was my view of the whole thing, inasmuch as I thought about it at all. Had I known about Marie Asberg, my mind would hardly have been changed. In those days I still had the trick of believing in whatever I wanted to believe, and I didn't want to believe in depression, because it let the weak, the fuck-ups, the lazy and the stupid off the hook, because it turned people into what they increasingly seemed to want to be: victims. And we were the C2s. We were not victims, we were conquerors. We were the new society of choice, and will, and endless, guilt-free shopping.

Chapter Thirteen

'It is not knowledge men desire so much as certainty' – Bertrand Russell

My story, my story. It's getting muddled up once more. It doesn't add up, it doesn't cut a swathe that is clear. For if my mother and I were simply ill, am I not wasting everyone's time? England, history, family, love, regret, identity, meaning. Does their poetry fall apart under the prose of science? Is it as absurd as looking for the meaning of a headache in history, the meaning of cancer in culture?

I've never claimed to know, to be the voice of authority, as it were. I never claimed there was just one story. There are dozens, some of them this much true, some of them that much true. I've never been good at coming down on one side or the other. I'm a wobbler, you might say. Uncertainty, it's a function of my class. Go up a bit, they think they know what's what. Go down a bit, they don't have any doubt. But here, in this mind-suburb, this ribbon-built self, everything changes as you look at it. One moment tragedy, the next, simply biology. One moment choice, the next, accident.

Perhaps there's a middle course, though it is confusing to think so. Surely each explanation cancels the other. There are more clues to consider, anyway, more facts to select and examine. Perhaps they will add up. I doubt it somehow, but I cannot shake off this idea that, in a blink, I will achieve some revelation, arrive at some place, which will explain everything to me, where everything will slot into place. I will be in bed or on a bus or out for a walk and it will all make sense, suddenly. I will smile, and nod, and the problem of life will be solved. I will have arrived. I will know what is what, what it all *boils down to*.

The 1980s begin well, not just for me but for all the children of subtopia, the second or maybe third generations of the respectable working class who bled out of the inner cities after the war. They are now commonly identified as a political tribe: the C2s. Ambition courses down the arterial roads, buzzes along the tube lines, like a force describable in physics. The nanny state has given us homes, health, education, hope, prospects. Now it is time to ditch the pilot, to kick away the ladder.

We are tired of the dull, soft round of consensus and compromise. We are no more or less selfish than our parents; simply, in spite of our view of ourselves, more naive, or perhaps the word is stupid. We have become unhinged from common sense and think that if we have more money, we will automatically end up with more liberty. We do not understand consequences. We trust simultaneously in beliefs that must contradict each other, both freedom and security.

We look out eagerly from our terraces in Southall, Streatham, Dagenham and Walthamstow towards villas in Iver, Epsom, Chigwell and Cockfosters. Money seems to thicken and spread, another force of nature. Our houses gather value, the weight of our taxes drops, oil floods the economy. We thrash the Argie menace. Our self-confidence ascends slowly, invisibly, into a kind of hubris. There is after all, it seems, such a thing as a free lunch.

By now, galvanized by the spirit of the times, I am running my own off-the-shelf company out of an office on the murky side of Marylebone with my partner, Barry. We have bought the freehold on the building and fly estate agents tell us it is already worth double what we paid. We have abandoned tabloid journalism and started publishing glossy, trivial magazines about the pop stars that surface after the decay of punk: Adam Ant, Duran Duran, the Human League. To our surprise, the magazines sell prodigiously. Cheques of a ridiculous size keep arriving from the distributors in the office post. We laugh incredulously: *it is so fucking easy*.

I discover Armani and Brylcreem, Church's shoes, John Smedley shirts. I show off my Paul Smith linen suit to my father, who shakes his head in wonderment, and perhaps disgust.

How much?

Three.

Three what? Hundred?

Unhmm.

It's all creased.

It's meant to be like that.

I don't know. Really, I mean —

He shakes his head in genuine incredulity.

What a racket!

I laugh, and reprise my teenage mantra: *You just don't understand.* Yet at the same time I wonder if it is true that labels, the shapes of packages, the quality of typefaces, can make me real, as they somehow, obscurely, suggest. For I still cannot shake this sense of . . . what? Of unease. Of imminently falling. Of being held in place by thin and fraying ropes.

Oh, but we are living, though. We lunch, we dine: Ma Cuisine, Tante Claire, The English House, Joe Allen, L'Escargot, Julies, Mon Plaisir, Frederick's, Ken Lo's, La Pomme d'Amour. At Inigo Jones we giggle as we stump up more than a hundred and come out hungry. We eat at Pru Leith's, paying £5 for a few mush and pots and toms bought from the shop my father works in to garnish some piece of semiprecious fish. We both buy brand-new Jeeps and Barry follows his up with a Porsche. We travel, to Barbados, Costa Rica, Cancun, New York, LA. The world, the world is unreal, it really is. And what is most unreal of all is that I have fallen in love, really in love, for the first time in my life.

Her name is Kate and I meet her at a friend's out in Harrow. She has long chestnut hair, a leather jacket and motorcycle boots. Her eyes are hooded and lidless, like Charlotte Rampling's, and her lips are bee-stung and full. Between bad teeth, she clenches a cheroot. Her neck is graceful and long. She rides a 250cc bike, too fast, despite the fact that she suffers from petit mal and might fall into an epileptic fit at some fast turn on the clearway. She is brave. She is what my mother would call *a bit gawky* and she has slightly knock knees.

Kate is not like Debbie, Marion or any other girl I have been with, although I cannot at first put my finger on why. It is some time before I realize what makes her so particular, but then it dawns. *She knows who she is.* Despite her natural introversion, she has a bred, central confidence. It is not the brittle kind, the flipped mirror of denial. She knows where she begins and she knows where she ends. She cannot be bullied or intimidated, because it is her who does the defining, not me. Yet there is a sense of raw honesty about her that makes her vulnerable and therefore lovable. My overbearing, bombastic character runs into something as tough and soft as chamois. To me it is intoxicating, for I see that she is a woman instead of a girl, a person, not an adjunct, or decoration, to my life and my vanity.

And – perhaps more to the point, I don't know – she is blatantly middle class. Her father owns one of the biggest advertising agencies in the country. She has been brought up in Kensington and a large, beautiful farmhouse in East Sussex. She has a degree in literature and was once presented with a prize for poetry by Ted Hughes after winning a competition at university. Although I am reluctant to admit it, she is cleverer than me, or at least wiser. She has books, she can ride, she has been blooded on the hunt. Oh, Kate is progress, there is no doubt about it. Kate is more than a girlfriend. She is the expression of a sort of wish.

We start, as my father and mother still call it, *going steady*. I do not see stars or walk on air; like my father, I am a practical man. But in a way that I cannot articulate, I have found what I did not even know I needed, a soul firm enough to steady my faintly sketched self, to hold the gyroscope that is spinning always in a thin vacuum. The dislocated rage I have felt since I was a child fades in the face of her calmness, her simple, sure presence. Before, I now realize, women had only blurred me; Kate seems to focus me, sharpen my always misted, just-out-of-sight horizons.

For someone unrooted, someone like me, to know this is a

wonder, not only because, obviously, it is love, but because, even more important, it is *known*. For the first time since being a child, I have discovered a truth that is certain, incontrovertible, something simple and clear in an inner landscape of fading, shifting shapes and doubts. I love Kate and I am proud, confirmed at last, in the fact that she loves me. It is that simple a foundation, a crampon through shifting gravel into bedrock. It is a cliché, like love always is. I am so grateful. I hold her in my arms and thank the gods, the gods I have never believed in.

The 1980s wear on. I am in my mid-twenties now. The meaning of money is suffering a sort of psychological inflation in that the more I have of it, the less it seems to be of value. I have too much time on my hands, for my job, with all its income, is easy, no more than a couple of days' work a week. I am losing structure. Kate seems to be the only thing mooring me to the earth.

My relationship with my parents, in my teens abrasive and frayed, has turned entirely around. I no longer see them as shallow and dim, but as what they in fact are: decent, kind and ordinary people. Although my father remains miserly with praise, I believe that they love me without question or complaint. We have become good friends who see each other out of pleasure rather than duty.

Jean and Jack seem happy, although the force of change that is the 1980s does not seem to affect them much for the better materially. Southall is becoming uglier, more threadbare by the day, as the little front gardens are ripped out to be replaced by concrete car ports. Stone-cladding and double-glazing ruin the simple harmony of the streets; it all looks broken up and bitsy. Jean's house, which she loves, is still immaculate, but something is changing. There is dog shit on the pavements. The children seem louder, more threatening. There are even beggars in Greenford High Street, with rat's-tail hair and gypsy rags. It is a strange world in some ways, very different from the place she once so modestly dreamed of. She wishes sometimes she could pick up her house and put it somewhere else – in a pocket of the

England she seems to remember. She cleaves to, she longs for, what I have spent all my life trying to leave.

Jeff has settled in New Orleans now with his wife, Helma. They married in England in 1981. None of the family were present since Jeff did not wish them to attend. He said it was a marriage of convenience and therefore not proper – it was merely to secure a green card. Neverthless, he and Helma subsequently lived together as man and wife. Jean was hurt that she was not invited, but accepted Jeff's decision without complaint.

James is a teenager now, a Goth with purple hair and black fishnet tights, good but uninterested at school. He disdains the ILEA teachers who insist on being called *Dave* or *Sue* instead of Mr this or Mrs that. The world he is taught about has changed from the one Jeff and I were shown: now Sir Francis Drake is a slave trader and the British Empire an exercise in colonial asset-stripping. Greenford County Grammar is now Greenford High, a comprehensive, predominantly black and Asian. But, though not academic, James is – like Jeff was, like I was – a centre of attention. He is charming and funny, he is handsome, he is careless of custom and adventurous. Jean knows he will leave home soon. How will she take to it, having no child in the house? What is she without a family to look after?

But my new concordat with Jack and Jean does not extend to worrying about my mother's life and future. The problems that concern me, as ever, are my own. Which is how Jean and Jack want it, because they dislike the sort of parents who try to extract some emotional levy simply for having brought their children up. *You have to let them go, Jean.*

My sense of purpose continues to dissipate. I can earn the equivalent of my father's weekly salary at the greengrocer's in a day, without getting out of bed in the morning. And yet in a strange way, I am bad at being an Essex Man. I do not feel particularly acquisitive. I am finding out that another of my parents' trotted-out clichés – *money can't buy you happiness* – is turning out to be true. Questions chivvy me. Why get up? Why work to make more money, when the money you have does not satisfy you? What do I do next? In other words, I am still asking the question of my age, of my class. Am I happy? Am I happy enough? And the answer is the same as ever.

I am not quite sure why it is, in the end, that I apply to go to university. I am not academically minded and was a mediocre school pupil. I rarely read books and my attention span is short. Nor do I imagine that it will advance my career; in fact, I know it will lose me a considerable amount of money, since I will have to withdraw from my publishing company. But some dumb instinct tells me that this secret of life, the secret that some day will be revealed to me, lies not lodged in the world itself, but in the way I make sense of it all. My thoughts feel cheap, ephemeral, unsatisfying and I want them fleshed out. I want them laid complete, laid out in rows, neat and tangible, instead of fractured, always unfinished, written in invisible ink. I want them to be lovely and elegant and copperplate instead of brazen tabloid headlines.

And there is something else. Perhaps on some level I feel that there is something in Kate that disdains me. I feel sure that she loves me, but sometimes when we are out at my parents', when we are drinking with my loud friends in a loud bar, when I pronounce Goethe wrong, or Jean Rhys, or Beauchamp Place, I see something in her eyes that . . . Or perhaps I imagine it. I am, after all, a little paranoid, like all social climbers, like Philip Pirrip in *Great Expectations* or Leonard Bast in *Howards End*. I do not admit it to myself, anyway. But university it must be, if I am to be properly reinvented.

But which one? I know nothing about universities. I do not know what a fresher is, or a faculty, or an alumnus. I do not know if York is good and Heriot-Watt is bad, or if Bradford is good on political science while Newcastle is famed for literature. No one in any part of my family has the faintest idea. I assume that Oxford and Cambridge are pretty good, but you have to pass an entrance exam. I do not know what subject to study or how to find out.

In the end, for no other reason than I happen to meet someone who went there and enjoyed it, I decide to apply to the London School of Economics. Apparently it has a good reputation, and it is easy to get to by tube. I decide, on little more than a whim, to study social anthropology. I go for an interview and am grilled by two professors, who ask me a lot of questions that seem easy enough to answer. A few weeks later, I am offered a place and I accept.

It seems sometimes that nothing I ever go for am I refused, not in jobs, not in women, not in life. My family love me, I adore my girlfriend and I am rich. Life, for me, is apparently charmed. So why do I always feel . . . what is it, what is that feeling? It's so familiar, yet so elusive. I feel – I think this is correct – *ashamed*.

It is six months later, the September of 1983 and my first week at university. Kate has inherited some money. Like many women of her class and generation, she is superstitious, far more so than my mother and her down-to-earth friends at the Tupperware parties and golf fours. Thus it is that she believes in omens and signs, astrology and fate, things that I think of as daft. When a shaft of light falls on a small ad in the *Evening Standard* for a houseboat on the Thames, she simply goes out and buys it, cash, believing that destiny has revealed itself to her. It is twenty miles out of London. I visit at weekends, but I have made up my mind now that I want to live with her. I take it for granted that she will agree. We will live in Hampstead and use the boat as a weekend retreat.

The London School of Economics, I now learn, is quite a prestigious university. It is certainly almost entirely middle and upper middle class in make-up. I am astonished by the know-ledge, the self-confidence of the people who physically seem little more than children. They make speeches at the student union, they picket and march, they write letters to Parliament, they throw eggs at politicians. It is highly politicized, a training ground for civil servants and cabinet ministers. Politics is the social life; everything seems to revolve around issues, what is supported, what is opposed, what is to be currently debated. Everybody seems quite sure of what they think about everything. Are you left or are you right? is substituted for the question at my last school: are you Rangers or are you Chelsea? Why do they not feel, as I do, that knowledge recedes endlessly? Because, I suppose, they are cleverer than me.

I am instinctively and habitually left wing, but an orthodoxy has emerged with which I am uncomfortable. I am asked to participate in demonstrations and pickets about the sacking of *Times* printers at Wapping and it is clear that to do less is betrayal. Yet I have met Fleet Street printers and know most of them to be surly and grotesquely overpaid.

At the same time I am asked to take as axiomatic the proposition that I am racist, sexist and homophobic, because I am white, male and heterosexual. I am told, in other words, to hate myself. I am told that policemen are all fascists, that criminals are all victims, that the striking miners are all heroes. I want to believe it, all of it, really I do. I want to have a story for myself. I want to have a team.

Yet I find myself stuck with the wishy-washy suburban English scepticism of my father written through my bones: *There's good and bad in everyone, I suppose. Everyone's basically the same, wherever you go.* But doubt is not an acceptable point of view. In this world, it is a mark of moral weakness. My father's words echo again: *It's not what you say that counts, it's what you do.* Here it is the other way round.

I know I am required to have opinions, to have commitment, but I can find only deepening layers of doubt. I can see only a sort of tribal self-righteousness on the one hand, facing cynicism and cruelty on the other. In other words, I have no team. I realize, more than ever, that there is no place of belonging here, not for me at least.

Uncommitted and struck through with uncertainties, I begin to try to make myself invisible. My normal extroversion is intimidated and bruised into careful muteness, in case I make a fool of myself. I fear that I will be found out. I realize with a shock that my idea about university – people sitting and trying to make sense of things for their own sake – is wildly wrong and outdated. My old perception, the one from my school ten years ago, has turned out to still apply. The world is about making up a story and sticking to it. The university is about passing exams, and convention, and a certain kind of forgetfulness.

Quickly bored by anthropology, I have switched to politics and history. I start writing essays without the faintest idea of what I am doing. To my tutor's surprise, they emerge with the structure of lurid tabloid news stories (thirty-five-word intro, build it like a pyramid). Most of the essay questions seem to be about causality. There are clearly techniques for answering these questions, for passing the exam, but I do not understand that that is the point. I want to know the *answer*. I do not know yet that there are no answers, only stories. I get Cs and Ds.

I become obsessed by the idea of certainty, since it is clearly what I crave. Yet, as I read about fascism and communism, about the French Revolution and the Spanish Inquisition, it seems to me that certainty, and the need for identity which it serves, is a sort of virulent and dangerous disease. Yet it becomes equally clear that the need for it is the deepest impulse there is. And I am also beginning to understand why, as doubt about everything deepens and spreads within me. Was doubt also a disease that left you crippled, purposeless, free-floating? Yet it seems inescapable. Like a quark or a gluon, everything recedes the more it is examined.

It dawns on me that I have a whole language, a whole mode of communication to unpick. References, sources, quotes, evidence. Will it help the making of sense? Why can I never reach any conclusions, as you are clearly supposed to? All the different explanations and interpretations, I cannot escape the impression that each is exactly as convincing as another. My head seems, quite literally, to hurt. The ideas that confront me are completely bewildering, and there is more or less no teaching, only books, books, millions of incomprehensible books. The shy, day-dreaming child I was all those years before I cast him out into the darkness seems to me to be looming once more, threatening me with his freakish introspection: *Timothy lives in a little world of his own.* I am stupid, I think to myself every day. Stupid, stupid, stupid.

But my family, all of my family, are determined people. I do not give up, although I feel increasingly lost and disoriented. I thank my gods once more for Kate, to whom I can cleave in this incomprehensible universe of plummy accents and exam skills, and roseate country-house cheeks and endless, unanswerable questions, all demanding answers.

I am sitting in the front room of the houseboat in Chertsey. It is a beautiful setting; light ripples from the water on to the low ceiling. There is a gentle rocking from underneath and tree shadows feed through the windows on to the pale floor. I have asked Kate to live with me. Despite my infatuation, it has taken three years for me to make the offer because, like so many of my generation, I am concerned with maintaining what I think of as the Grail – 'freedom' – for as long as possible. She has said no, which is a surprise, because I have always thought she was the one who wanted to 'settle'. I put down the refusal as temporary, due to her obsession with her new boat. It seems to have become a sort of metaphor for her life: she is pulling it apart, scraping the hull, cutting out dead wood. It seems to occupy her endlessly. I have begun to see it is a rival, but I am still unshakeably certain about Kate's love for me. I do not realize the investment that I have made in this certainty.

It is Valentine's Day 1984. We have risen from bed, where we have not made love; sex seems to be slowly disappearing from our relationship, but I am blind to what this should tell me. I am drinking coffee. Kate is smoking a cigarette. I am happy, the last time I will be happy, even momentarily, for four or five years. The postman has come along the path and there is the sound of something falling on the mat. I hope that my card will arrive on time.

There is only one letter. Kate picks it up, tears it open and reads it, smilingly. It is not signed. I smirk and pretend it is not from me, and then I glance at where she has put it on the sideboard and I see, with a shock, that it really is not from me. Mine has not arrived.

I cannot keep up any sort of pretence in front of Kate for long. I tell her that the card is not mine, really not mine. And – just for an instant, just for a half-second – an expression ripples across her face. It is excitement. I see it clearly. She is hoping that the card is from a particular person who is unknown to me. Something in me kicks, feels sick.

But Kate loves me, is part of me. This I know. If I do not know this, I know nothing at all, nothing whatsoever. My story, my one and only story, will turn out to be fiction. So it has to be true. I shake my head, as if to dislodge some nasty speck of grime, and do not mention the matter again. I begin to tell myself, and I begin to believe, that the expression on her face was nothing more than the sense of flattery that anyone would feel on receiving such a card. It is forgotten. It must be forgotten.

A few weeks later, I go round to the boat and we go out for dinner. Kate is acting strangely. She sits at the table and hardly speaks for the whole evening. It is gradually becoming an unavoidable fact that something is wrong. I begin to quiz her, to press, to nag, to bother. She will not speak. She will not look at me.

For all my pretensions to honesty, I am an expert at denial. I do not ask Kate the obvious question, not because I am frightened of the answer, but because it *does not occur to me*. Or perhaps it is because I am so frightened of the answer that it does not occur to me. Instead, I accept her assertion that she needs some time alone, and leave the boat telling her to sort herself out, to find some words to speak. We will give it a rest for a month, then I will call her. In the meantime, we will not phone or talk. I am unhappy, but the action makes me feel strong, in control.

After a week or two, I do begin to have some doubts, but my confidence hardly falters. It is only when I finally ring Kate up again and she says, without committing herself, that she wants to come and see me and talk that I begin to feel nervous. Her voice is distant, changed. Perhaps it is the telephone line.

When she walks into my flat she seems cheerful, quite full of herself, but she still can't quite bring herself to say what it is she has come to say. I finally manage to find the question that has been eluding me so carefully for the last couple of months. I feel ridiculous as I speak the words, as if I am playing at being a grown up. *Is there someone else?* She nods. There is a man who lives on another boat, a few moorings along. They are sleeping together. They are in love.

Everything goes white. I stand up and begin pacing about the room. I pick up a table lamp and smash it against the wall. I kick the chair. I punch the door so hard it cracks. Some great reserve of anger and fear has welled up in me, so volcanic it threatens to tear me apart. I do not know what to do with it. Kate is frightened, although I know I will never strike her. Instead the rage begins to flow inward. I ask, I beg for an explanation, but she simply sits silently. I start to yell at her – to get out, and to never, ever contact me again. She leaves, whey-faced.

I sit down and cry, and shake. I feel something terrible is happening inside me, all at once. Something is freezing, something is shaking loose. Something is falling apart, something is tightening in order to hold it in place. I feel terrible. I feel lonelier than I have ever felt. I do not know what is to become of me, stripped as I am of my only true faith. And stripped, even more terrifyingly, of control. It is as if I am once again naked, and stamping my feet, and shouting, *No*.

Chapter Fourteen

We would rather be ruined than changed
We would rather die in our dread
Than climb the Cross of the moment
And see our illusions die.
   W. H. Auden, 'The Age of Anxiety'

'Little boys who are not good/might just as well be made of wood' – The
Blue Fairy, *Pinocchio*

Self-defence, I write in my diary with a steady, confident hand,
sometime early in the endless year of 1984, *is the prime instinct of the*
human mind. The fortification of ramparts, and bridges, and ditches, and
moats. Nothing else finally matters so long as the defences are kept up.

I do not really understand that I am talking about myself, as
my mind struggles to come to terms with a suddenly fluid and
unstable reality, where nothing holds good or true. Neither do I
understand that the very act of diary-writing, which I have only
recently begun, is a sort of self-defence, a grasping at control. The
diary continues: *But what happens if you fail? What is it, exactly, that*
you are defending? How can you defend what is in the first place
unknown?

I am going to keep those defences aloft, some obscure part of
me realizes, however much it costs me. I have to or – Or what?
Blankness. No story. A stare into what, like Medusa, cannot be
seen without paralysis.

I am gradually mimicking my Uncle Alan, scratching at scabs
until they bleed. But they are not physical, they are wounds
inside that I cannot leave alone, that I hector and pick at. I have
to find a solution, a healing. I struggle to find the will to let Kate
go, although I fear that my whole idea of self will go with her.

Despite my fierce instructions to stay out of contact, she sends
me a letter telling me she still loves me, but that she still 'needs

time'. This is all that is needed to keep me from doing what needs to be done — that is, for me to, psychologically, leave *her*. Presumably this is the intention of the letter. Kate is covering her bets.

To survive, I know now, I must decide to grieve, to let the past move through and beyond. In fact, I know it even then. Yet I am weak, I cannot do this with Kate. Fatally, I refuse to mourn her loss. Perhaps without that letter . . . But I am hooked now, trapped in my past, unable to resolve or to move on. In an attempt to deny the fluidity of the world, I have made it static, fixed, rigid. All that is important to me is Kate's return. It seems to be a matter of interior life and death.

I see Jack and Jean often and put on a brave face. They are both sad that we have split, for they are fond of Kate, but Jack naturally assumes that everything will sort itself out, one way or another. It is his most basic assumption about life. Jack goes every day for lunch at PizzaExpress in Notting Hill Gate, two doors along from the shop. The Galleon and the Varsi Grill have closed down. I join him from time to time on a Saturday, when I am passing the restaurant and see him, as always, with his face buried in a book. Nowadays his favourites are historical thrillers and, still, murder stories. Almost sixty now, he looks a decade younger, and is still handsome. He remains curious and engaged by what I am studying at the LSE. Over a single beer and his customary order of Eggs PizzaExpress, we discuss psychology, history, economics. He has picked up most of his knowledge from the potboilers he reads endlessly, but he is surprisingly clued up. James joins us sometimes, which foreshortens the discussions, for he feels that to disagree about something is the same as arguing, so he changes the subject the moment we get 'too serious'.

At home, Jean is more sensitive to what I am continuing to, rather badly, conceal. I understand that it should be concealed, for Jean is worried as it is about the family on the other side of the Atlantic. She and Jack have been on holiday to New Orleans to see Jeff and Helma and have had a miserable time. It is clear that their marriage is on the rocks.

I am a bad actor. Jean sees the rigidity in my face and the slow disappearance of my usual jokey, obstreperous self. She worries.

You've not been the same since you split up with Kate. A mother can tell these things.

I try to reassure her, again, that everything is OK.

Six months pass and the situation remains agonizingly unresolved. Kate still talks about coming back. I still hang on to my hopes, rerunning past and future scenarios through my head like an infuriating, pointless tape-loop. In the meantime, I suffer through each day at university, sitting alone in the library. There is a sense that I am drying out within myself, that a million tiny little taps and valves are being slowly turned off. Or perhaps it is a hardening, a cooling, as if a smooth, impervious stone is being formed at the very centre of my chest.

I have made few friends at the LSE, their tribe is so different from mine. But I have made one. She is a woman about my age, an Essex Girl from Chigwell. She is Jewish, trained as an actress at LAMDA, attractive and street-smart, who walks with short, stumpy, determined steps that remind me of – of me. In fact, nearly everything about her reminds me of me. Her parents are kind, loving and vaguely philistine, and live in a nice part of subtopia. She has the same passions, the same apparently limitless ambition, the same deep insecurities, the same compensating competitiveness, the same proud vulgarity and mouthiness. She seems instinctive, witty and honest, and yet is torn by one question: will the books she is reading do her harm? Like me, she both loves and hates the place she comes from. Like me, she both desires and fears the place she senses she is going to.

There is one film, she tells me, that she identifies with more than any other. It is Willy Russell's *Educating Rita*. This film, a sort of tragedy, is about Rita, a raw, charismatic Liverpudlian working-class girl, who goes to study literature and finds 'culture' while at the same time losing everything that makes her special: her spontaneity, her instinctive sense of rightness, her lack of pretension, her bullshit-detector. With each book that Becka reads, she is haunted by this fear of loss, and I know exactly what she means. As we force our minds into structured, careful, penned places, we seem to be losing something vital in ourselves. The conflict within us draws us together. I feel myself falling in love with her.

But I know that it is a pointless love. She is deeply involved with a man, an actor and model, who is pleasant, charming and handsome. She repeatedly tells me that she loves him, and on one occasion makes a point of inviting me over to dinner and sitting on his lap all the way through dessert. It is clear that she has a message for me that it is important I understand if our friendship is to continue.

I accept it. Anyway, I am still obsessed with Kate. Unlike my careful, private parents, I am happy to unload my angst on anyone who will listen and I am aware of myself turning into a bore. It seems that the stiffness of upper lips is something else Jack and Jean's generation were right about. My friends are patient and listen to my endless introspections, which help me not a whit. After a while, I even begin to bore myself. Nevertheless, I seem to be powerless to free myself. A decision has to be made. Kate refuses to make it and I don't know how to.

During the summer recess, I take a holiday in New Orleans, where I go to see my brother Jeff and his wife, Helma. Things, as Jack and Jean have found out, are not going well for them. I sense a tension so thick it is uncomfortable the moment I walk into the house. Jeff, like me, seems strung out on a tight inner cord. The rivalry between us, although it is submerged in adult politeness, is far from exhausted. It seems to me that he hardly stops trying to convince me – and therefore perhaps himself – of the rightness of his decision to marry and settle in New Orleans. He hardly stops proselytizing: the balconies, the food, the weather, the 'authentic culture'. Does he want my approval as badly as I want his? I can hardly imagine it to be so, for I feel myself to be irrelevant to Jeff, I know that I do not count.

Frustratingly for him, Helma and I get on almost too well. Although I try hard to avoid any sense of alliance with her, it seems that Jeff's insecurities run as deep as mine. He is constantly on the defensive, constantly in fear of losing control. Each day has to be planned to his schedule, each meal has to be eaten in the restaurant which he knows and approves of. His records are still in alphabetical order.

On one occasion we head off to the beach at Ponchartrain in Florida. We fool around with beach umbrellas, while Helma takes photos. In some ways, despite – or maybe because of – the tension so obvious within him, I am aware of caring more about him than I ever have before. His vulnerability makes him approachable. I feel a great sadness and empathy, but our habit of rivalry is so deep, I have no idea how to express it. I cannot escape the idea that we are locked into some entirely pointless and self-destructive game which we would both like to stop playing but cannot work out what game it is, or even that it is a game.

For some reason – some new harsh comment by Helma, some new atmosphere between them that pushes them apart – Jeff does something that utterly shocks me. Right there on the beach, he drops the umbrella, falls to his knees and covers his face with his hands. He looks up at me and says, *Tim, I'm so fucked up . . . so fucked up*, and begins to cry.

I have never seen my brother cry and I feel a great wrenching inside me. I want to fall to my knees and put my arms around him and hug him. I want to tell him what I have never been able to tell him, that I love him. But I am afraid. I am afraid he will shrug me off and turn his back, as it seems he has always done before.

Helma, also embarrassed and uncertain, says, *Let's go*, and takes my arm. I resist for a moment. Jeff is still crouching on the beach, head in hands. I feel sorrow and love, fighting with fear, and it is the fear that wins, as it has too often in my life. We walk away, along the beach.

When we return, Jeff is standing up and looking brisk and decisive. There is no sign whatsoever that anything untoward has happened. When he speaks, he is tight and matter-of-fact, determined to restore the ramparts: *Right. I know this restaurant.* And the matter is never spoken of again.

When I return to England, and university, everything remains unresolved. I have met Kate now on a few occasions. She has insisted passionately that she still loves me and will soon 'make a decision' once she 'sorts herself out'. My weakness occasionally wells up into a kind of tide of firmness, to end the whole thing once and for all. I even know it is what will get her back. But I also know that the very act of making the decision will cauterize my feeling for her. The paradox seems insoluble and I agonize over it endlessly. The very power of decision, of choice itself, seems to be sapping from me and this weakness makes me hate myself.

One afternoon, a few weeks after the term has commenced again, Becka comes up to me in the library and asks me to go outside. She seems agitated about something. I think as usual how attractive she is, but I have long ago put away any hope of it coming to anything. She takes me out on to the steps and glances around to make sure that no one is looking. Then she says some things I don't at first understand.

Look I've got something to tell you.

Hmmm.

It's just that . . . look it doesn't matter if . . .

I look at her, perplexed. I have never seen her like this. She seems to be holding something vital back.

Come on. Spit it out.

It's this. I'm in love. I've fallen in love.

I am surprised to feel a shock of disappointment. I wonder who it could be, and feel envy without even having a focus for it. I am also taken aback, because she seemed so close and committed to her boyfriend.

Well, that's great. Who with?

She looks at me strangely, as if I'm being idiotic. She is walking: stump, stump, stump.

With you. With you, of course. I'm in love with you.

My jaw, quite literally, falls open, and I stare at her in astonishment. She begins to gabble.

Of course, it doesn't matter if you don't feel the same, we can still be friends, but I couldn't keep it in, I had to say something. I mean, what do you . . . are you . . . ?

The puzzlement in me grows. The unspoken question within

me is this: why on earth would someone like Becka say she was in love with someone who was . . . what? Absent. For some reason, I am reminded that she is trained as an actress. Ridiculously, I think she is acting. I mutter that I love her too, and I know that I do, that I must do, because she is so like me. She seems transfixed with excitement; already she is making plans. She decides that she will telephone her boyfriend that evening to break off their relationship, but does not want to talk any more, because she feels it will be unfaithful to do anything until he knows.

We walk to Lincoln's Inn Fields and Becka, who thinks of herself as a woman of strong morals, nevertheless allows herself a kiss. As I hold her, she seems to become fluid, ecstatic in my arms. I feel her lips against mine. Yet the smooth stone in my chest does not shift, or soften, and it feels as cold as ever.

That night, Becka leaves her boyfriend, who is devastated and himself proceeds towards an eventual nervous breakdown. Shortly afterwards, and virtually without asking, she moves in with me. In a mirror image of my unquestioning vanity and certainty over Kate, she has no doubt whatsoever that I could be anything but grateful for her offer. She holds nothing back. An extraordinary passion is unleashed. She seems to want to consume me entirely, both physically and spiritually. She tells me quite clearly that she has found the person she wants to spend her entire life with. She stares at me as we walk along, as if enraptured by my very existence. I feel unable to live up to this idealization and it makes me feel uneasy, ridiculous. I retreat a little more. I am only vaguely conscious of my own fear.

My life is so good now. I imagine that people envy me Becka, my money, my youth, my success. But in a state of depression, the agony lies not in the poverty of your life but the inaccessibility of the goodness of your life. The most natural thing in the world – to have feelings – you have forgotten how to 'do'.

Predictably, when Kate finds out about Becka, she desperately and immediately wants me back. Determined to win that battle, I take her back and leave Becka. Somehow and for some reason 'winning' has become very important. But it becomes quickly clear that Kate remains unsure, that her hand has been forced.

And now I am unsure too. The deadness has spread to encompass my feelings towards Kate too and thickens inside still further and deeper. I feel that I am becoming some sort of robot. After a few weeks, I send Kate away and go back to Becka. She is overjoyed, and I wonder at her ability to feel emotions that for me seem more and more like memories, fantasies. Nevertheless, I know I must give this relationship a try, for it is the one I have always hoped for and dreamed of. I will work at it, although the faith in the future that is so naturally part of my parents' world continues to elude me.

I need that faith, for without it the tension between what life should be and what it feels like increases and tightens. What seems to go on inside me is bizarre. It is not that my feelings are absent – I feel my love for Becka, powerful and primal – but I cannot reach them. It is as if they exist behind a protective glass screen that cannot be breached. I pound on the glass, I hammer at it with my fists, but it will not give, not an inch.

It is not long after this episode that I truly, I think, begin to go mad.

Up until this point, the 1980s for Jean have been mainly definable simply as a time of ever-increasing leisure. James is nearly grown now, so there is less and less for her to usefully do. Jeff and I, of course, have long left home. With no career other than her job as a school dinner lady, she is becoming, in a sense, unnecessary. To fill this new gapping and loosening of her life, every weekend, and on a Wednesday evening in the summer, she and Jack go to Greenford Tennis Club. It has taken Jean a long time to pluck up the courage to join – she is terrified as always that her wig will be caught in a gust of wind and tumble into the exposing air. Afternoons in the week – for Jack is working only mornings now at the greengrocer's shop – they go to Perivale Park Golf Club. One or two evenings a week Jean learns 'art'. The remainder of the time is portioned out between gardening and housekeeping.

The idea of a tennis club, of a golf club, of an art class, seems to hint at social aspiration and clipped, tight outer suburbia. In fact Greenford Tennis Club is three worn-out courts with faded lines corralled between a square of terraces behind the Greenford Road, decorated with a crumbling Nissen hut, backed on to by gardens with sparse rockeries and creosoted sheds. They manage to survive by holding periodic bring-and-buy sales and themed social evenings. Perivale Park Golf Club is a nine-hole municipal course popular with plumbers' mates, gas fitters and truanting pupils from the local comprehensive. The art class takes place at Hanwell Community Centre, and sticks mainly to landscapes and still lifes of fruit and flowers copied from books and magazines. This subtopia is still in all essentials respectable working class; philistine, mildly prejudiced, decent, polite, self-sufficient, restrained, 'up' have-a-goers. Their lives revolve entirely around their families and their hobbies.

As I have said, my whole family is competitive, but no one more so than my mother and I. When she plays, despite now being in her mid-fifties, she skips about the court, her jaw thrust forward, her eyes darting. The remotest drop shot, she chases as if her life depends on it. She curses any unforced error: *Sugar!* or *Bum!* But she is always polite and well behaved, a good loser, as she has learned to get used to being. I am worse and disgrace myself by shouting forbidden words like *fuck* and *bollocks*. I will throw my racquet at the floor or whack balls into the air. We are never angry with others, only ourselves. We are both very determined people and imagine ourselves – wrongly, I suspect – to be in a condition of constantly falling short of our possibilities.

On one occasion she challenges me to a game of singles. I presume she just needs a knock-up, because I am twenty years younger than her, stronger, coached and more consistent. But she insists on playing a proper set, and it is clear immediately that she intends to win. From the moment the first ball is played, she does not smile. Her face is creased in concentration and she chases everything unremittingly. She still holds the racquet as if she is playing badminton, and because her natural tendency is always to hit down on the ball, as if executing an overhead smash, she is forced to crouch right down in order to hit her shot. She is incredibly tenacious and dogged. As if a challenger at

Wimbledon, she does not make eye contact when we change ends and marches across without a word.

Sometimes, with glorious hubris, after her serves she even rushes the net on her short, stumpy legs in an attempt to volley the return away. Since she is just over five feet tall, I lob her easily, but she tries again. Jean is not one to give up. In the end, I win 6–3, but it has not been as simple as I imagined. I am impressed, but not surprised, at the fight in her, knowing of old that iron streak in her pincushion-soft centre. She stalks off the court, red-faced, smiling only formally, with jaw still set as if something has been proved, which, of course, it has.

As with all such clubs, certain rivalries develop between particular players. There is one woman, Beryl Hall, who has been at the club longer than nearly everyone else. She has a skin that is leathery, almost always tanned, and a slightly buttoned-up manner that suggests a certain snobbery. Underneath she is nice, Jean asserts, but then she thinks everyone is nice underneath; yet there is a presumption about her that irritates. She is the kind of person who – on this level, at least – always tends to win, in the way that our family, for reasons unknown, always tend to come second. It annoys Jean. Jean is never a top-line player at the club, but year after year she gets close to winning the women's doubles, playing with her childhood friend Irene Downhill. Yet it is always Beryl, with her partner Marian Melhuish, who squeezes away with the title. And somehow, Beryl always seems to assume that this will always be the case, and, assuming it, makes it so.

One year around this time, Jean makes the final again with Irene, and, as usual, they are pitted against Beryl and Marian. As always it is close. The first set goes to Beryl and Marian, 8–6, the second to Jean and Irene, 6–4. Irene is wild and aggressive on court, veering between artistry and uncontrolledness. Jean is solid as a rock, chasing back to retrieve Irene's missed volleys, never making an unnecessary shot. On this occasion she is playing the game of her life. Marian and Beryl are the favourites, but this could go either way.

Suddenly Irene finds her top form. Everything she goes for

flies off her racquet like a bullet, an inch or two above the net and just inside the tramlines. Always temperamental, she is suddenly devastating. Jean raises her game a corresponding notch and Marian and Beryl find themselves being peremptorily crushed. Jean and Irene go 5–2 ahead. They have one game to win for Jean to take the title – any title – for the first time in her life. Her face is a mask of desperate concentration. She is oblivious to everything outside. Jack and Jamie and I are watching, cheering her on.

A wise tennis player, as he is a wise man, my father is especially tense because he knows that in situations like this, somehow, strangely, games become no longer a matter of luck or talent, but a matter of faith, a test of belief. If you are a certain kind of person, they are defining moments in their way: are you a winner or a loser? If you have always thought of yourself as a loser, do you have the strength of character to transform yourself? An inner dialogue takes place, an urging that transcends the relative trivia of the event. A question is asked. Am I really – really – any good? Do I have *what it takes*?

Jean and Irene go 40–15 up in the eighth game of the final set. It is effectively all over. Then Irene nets a simple shot, then another. It is deuce. The wind begins to change. Marian hits a clear winner, then Beryl lobs Jean on to the line: 5–3.

Now Irene's game, always mercurial, collapses. Just as every time she touched the ball before she triumphed, now she nets it or sends it flying out of court. Jean watches, grim-faced, faith drifting, as the points are thrown away like husks. She does not falter, but the game is moving away from her now. It is 5–4, then 5 all.

Now the thrust is with Marian and Beryl, the conviction that is their natural right returns to them. It all slips away: 6–5, 7–5. Game, set and match. Jean, on court, drops her head, then picks it up. She is stiff with disappointment. She shakes hands wordlessly with Irene, then Beryl and Marian, with a smile that uses the wrong muscles. Beryl looks at her, trying politely to conceal the fact that it was always a foregone conclusion.

Jean comes off the court, stumping, tightly packed. There is an aura about her that means no one tries to talk to her. A few people say 'bad luck', but she does not respond. Her knuckles are white around her tennis racquet. Irene is apologizing to her, but she does not respond.

My heart turns over for her. I know how much this has meant to her, this tiny tournament, in this eighth-rate club. I know she has received final, irrevocable confirmation that she will never, in this, her chosen arena, on her own terms, make the grade. As she approaches me, I reach out to give her a hug. Whenever in my life I have done this before, she has responded warmly, gratefully. But on this occasion she averts her eyes, shrugs me angrily off and mutters, through the tightest of lips, *Leave me alone!* and then makes her way briskly to the ladies' toilets, where she locks herself in a cubicle and cries as silently as she can.

Oh, she is so much like me, my mother, in some ways. She sometimes thinks, despite a spectrum of evidence to the contrary, that she is stupid and not worth very much. She reaches out for a sort of perfection and, always failing to achieve it, beats herself up. Thus winning – *doing* – takes on some existential importance.

It's only a game, says my father, often, infuriatingly. But it isn't, it isn't only a game, and he knows it. Everything's more than it is. Everything, however small, represents something larger.

Jean feels herself inadequate in other areas. At golf, she goes secretly to lessons in the hope of one day beating my father, a goal which she never achieves. Like all golfers, she finds the game is largely about a tolerance of fate, and suffering silently, an art she has perfected. When she has had a bad game, she walks around the tiny course in complete silence, lost in her own particular emotions, cursing herself and urging herself, *Come on, Jean!* but she never really improves beyond a certain level.

As always, it is not others she is competing against but herself. This is most apparent in her art classes, probably the least competitive pastime she indulges in. Yet it remains clear that she is determined to punish herself, complaining that her paintings are not up to scratch. Jack insists on having them framed and hung on the walls to reassure her that they have some value, but she finds them unsatisfying, short, as ever, of what she believes herself to be capable of.

Every Thursday now she goes to art lessons with Olive and another friend, Margaret, who works at the school with Jean. They go to Margaret's house or sometimes to the house of the art teacher, Ellen. Ellen has taken them on privately, for free, after the Community Centre class becomes oversubscribed. Ellen is a generation younger, middle class, well spoken, but she becomes firm friends with Olive and Jean, whom she considers both wise and kind. She sees that they are inarticulate, careful with words, but have a way of communicating their goodwill in between the silences in which they paint together.

Ellen suffers from depressions and undergoes long-term therapy, which she believes finally to be useless. During this time, Olive and Jean listen to her self-lacerations quietly, with sympathy and good advice. Neither ever complains of anything herself. Ellen grows to respect them for their solid kindness and common sense, their lack of self-absorption. She grows, in a way – and it is not too strong a word, for my mother, almost magically, often occasions this response in people – to love them.

The art classes are always much the same. There will be tea and some kind of cake, and music. If they are at Margaret's, this will most probably be Mario Lanza, or Paul Robeson singing 'Ol' Man River' and 'Mighty Like a Rose'. Perhaps Margaret will play *The World's Loveliest Music: The Classical Collection.* Jean's particular favourite is Deanna Durbin's 'Spring in my Heart', or 'It's Raining Sunbeams' or 'Home Sweet Home'. Most of the time as they paint they will sit in silence, but this is not to say they do not communicate. There are different kinds of silence and theirs is warm, open, connected. When Arthur, my father's brother and Olive's husband, dies of a heart attack in 1981, the group closes in and around Olive, supporting her, although the matter is hardly discussed. Jean makes up a room for her immediately at Rutland Road; she can stay as long as she likes.

Jean is not a good painter, although she has some technical skill. Ellen finds it hard to say exactly why. Perhaps because she is so exact, so controlled, Jean does not know how to express herself through her painting. Her ambition is to make an accurate copy, and her copies are good – dainty, compact, careful. But they are just imitations – imitations, like carriage clocks, of what themselves are imitations.

Neverthless, she labours endlessly to get the copy just right. She crouches over the painting, brow furrowed with concentration, trying to *get it down pat*. She reminds me of someone: a figure in a library, copying, this time, words from the pages of a book; trying to pin something down, to capture that thing precisely. Not knowing that such capture is never possible, she, I, we strain harder and harder, putting the flaws in the picture down to our own inadequacies. For surely, we reason, they cannot be actually *in the picture itself.*

Chapter Fifteen

In 1986, several events take place that shift the foundations of Jean's world. Or perhaps they merely cause her to reluctantly inspect them.

Terry O'Dwyer's shop, now the last greengrocer in Notting Hill Gate – the big supermarkets taking all the trade away now – is sold to a couple of young men on the make. They are upper class, Oxbridge-educated, smooth and tractable. They reassure Jack that the business is safe with them and that everything will continue as before. Jack, who is a trusting man, thinks that they are gentlemen and takes them at their word.

However, it is not very long before strange wrinkles begin to develop in the business. Bills that are due from market traders Jack has dealt with all his life are left unpaid for months. Humiliatingly, Jack has to plead at the market for extended credit, and finds himself continually embarrassed with people he has come to consider friends. He brings it up with the new owners, who smile and reassure him. It is merely modern business, they say, paying at the last moment. Jack shrugs. The world must move on, he supposes.

In order to ameliorate the ordeal of going to the market, he starts to pay the market traders with his own money, which he claws back out of takings later in the week. I try to warn him that this is a mistake, that the owners are clearly spivs, 1980s wide boys – I should know. But he doggedly refuses to believe ill of them and takes their reassurances at face value. However, he is clearly under stress. Jack hates uncertainty and feels very uneasy with people who are not straightforward. His overtolerance has been exploited more than once in the past.

The situation drags on and on. Jack decides to take a holiday and bring things to a head when he comes back. They go to Devon for a week. It is a good week. The sun shines non-stop.

On the Monday following, he drives up the Western Avenue and parks the van outside the shop. To his amazement, it is boarded up. He leaves the van and stands and stares at the wooden planks, as if his innocent gaze can make them disappear. Jack's life at the shop – all thirty-five years of it – is thus ended. The shop has closed. All his customers – the eccentric old ladies, the dukes and duchesses, the TV people, the thesps – people he has known for decades, nattered and swapped anecdotes with, one entire pattern of connections, have been summarily wiped out. Jack, having been used to extend the shop's credit as far as possible, is suddenly uneconomic, non-profit-making. He is crossed out as peremptorily as a figure on a balance sheet.

Jack drives home in a daze. He immediately tries to ring the owners of the shop, but there is no answer. They will not talk to him. One has gone abroad, the other is unavailable. He realizes that he has not even got a week's notice, or a penny in compensation. Nevertheless, he assumes that they will be in touch concerning his redundancy payment. He hears nothing.

When he finally tracks them down, he does not remonstrate, never believing that anger is a solution to anything. They negotiate; it is insisted that Jack is owed nothing. He goes to the local law centre and gradually, over a period of eighteen months, he extracts a total of £5,000, payable in three instalments. This is his pay-off for all the years of getting up at five in the morning, six days a week.

And as for the remainder of his life, he'll just have to readjust. My father is not bitter, although he is deeply disappointed, never having had a chance to say goodbye to all the friends who came in the shop for all those years. Nevertheless, he wastes little time on grieving. My father, as we know well now, is a practical man.

★

The other significant matters, for Jean, concern her sons. James turns eighteen in 1986 and I invite him to come to live with me in Notting Hill Gate. I drive over to Southall. James cannot wait to get away and I can understand why. The air of shabbiness and absence seems to thicken daily. Jack always makes a fist of it, making light of those who concrete over their gardens and let the pebble-dash crumble into patchwork, but Jean is sometimes nakedly upset. She had always loved the quiet pride in the privets and flowerbeds, the friendly competition between neighbours. Now that competition takes the form of the largeness of car or system of double-glazing. Not that Jack and Jean are immune to the appeal of double-glazing: the single aluminium windows that drove out the wood four-way-split panels, spread along Rutland Road like a virus, reached them two or three years previously. They had decided on Everest.

I arrive at the house and begin to pack up James's boxes of clothes and records. Jean helps briskly. It does not really occur to us that this is a significant event in her life. Her riposte when the subject comes up is always, *I'll be glad to see the back of him. Get a bit of peace and quiet.*

It does not take long to fill the car. Jean makes us a cup of tea. James betrays no particular excitement – like Jack, he understates his emotions. Then we head towards the door and get in the car. I switch on the engine. Standing on the doorstep is Jean, waving slowly behind the privet hedge.

I wave back, and notice, caught in the sunlight, that although her face and mouth are smiling, there are tears in her eyes and they are overflowing and dripping on to her cheek. It occurs to me, blankly, that I have hardly ever in my life seen my mother cry; over slushy movies, yes, but not over real life. Even now she shields her eyes, as if to hide the fact. I smile to myself over her sentimentality, give another wave and drive off. The fact that the house is empty of children for the first time in thirty years does not really make an impact; Jack and Jean are always, in their way, so independent, so concerned with living their own lives.

We drive off down the A40 towards Notting Hill. The luggage

overflows from the back and gets in the way of the gearstick. This bothers me all the way through the drive home.

In the same year there is some good news from America, where Jeff is still living in New Orleans, having finally divorced Helma eighteen months previously. Jean tries to brush this off as 'the modern way', but she is upset. For her generation, divorce still carries stigma, and for her generation of women, the success of the family is a sort of unwritten test of the qualities of the mother. Although she never readily admits it, she is as much ashamed as saddened by Jeff's divorce.

The good news is that Jeff is getting married again. He has met a woman from Honduras, Maria Zuniga, who has been settled in New Orleans for decades. She already has two children and Jeff is keen to adopt them as his own. When Jean speaks to him on the telephone, he seems happy and positive. There may even be a chance for the grandchildren that she is beginning to crave, now that James has left home.

She thinks of the wedding, and whether they will be able to afford to travel to New Orleans. But they will find the money somehow; to be at the wedding of one of her sons is an ambition. It will be a wonderful moment. The first marriage, she accepts, started as a marriage of convenience, although it hurt not to be asked to attend. But this time . . .

A few months later, she hears that Jeff has got married in a New Orleans register office, with a few friends in attendance. As with the first marriage, none of the family was invited.

Circumstances gather as clusters and pods. Consequences in themselves, they bloom and merge. I sit in the LSE's vast library, poring over books like a monk. I feel ridiculously old and hopelessly stupid. The words in the books stare back at me, refusing doggedly to yield up their meaning. Occasionally, understanding comes and then it is like turning a rusty flywheel.

I sit in the library, sit in the library. All the books drift into one another somehow, written, it seems, deliberately to confuse and obscure, to protect the mystique of academia. On one occasion, for some course or other, I stumble across a book which is an exception. It is a text about working-class culture, written in the 1950s. Although I have never heard of it, it is a classic: *The Uses of Literacy* by Richard Hoggart. I read one part of it again and again, amazed at its perception, and I know that the writer has lived a version of my life. It is clear that, despite his calm, academic prose, he is writing about himself. It tells me precisely what it is that I am, and its truth scares me.

> They wander in the immensely crowded, startling and often delusive world of ideas, like children in their first Fairground House of Thrills – reluctant to leave, anxious to see and understand and respond, badly wanting to have a really enjoyable time, but underneath, frightened.

I read on, absorbed.

> They have lost hold on one kind of life and failed to reach the one to which they aspire. Beneath their apparent cynicism and self-pity is a deep sense of being lost, without purpose and with the will sapped. They are inwardly depressed by their constant suspicion that everything and everyone has been found out.
>
> They are the poor little rich boys of a world over-supplied with popularized and disconnected information, and much less able to find meaningful groupings for its information.

For perhaps the first time at the university, I feel knowledge acting as a clarifying mirror instead of a distorting lens. The clincher, which I read in a breath, comes towards the end of the book:

> He is usually ill at ease with the middle classes because with one side of himself he does not want them to accept him; he mistrusts or even a little despises them. He is divided as in so many other ways. With one part of himself, he admires much he finds in them – a play of intelligence, a breadth of outlook, a kind of style. He would like to be a citizen of that well-polished, prosperous, book-lined and magazine-discussing world of the successful intelligent middle class which he glimpses through doorways . . . with another part of himself he develops an asperity towards that world;

he turns up his nose at its self-satisfaction, its earnest social concern, its intelligent coffee parties, its suave sons at Oxford . . . he is
rather over-ready to notice anything that can be regarded as pretentious or fanciful, anything which allows him to say that these
people do not know what life is really like.

I photocopy the passages and underline them and highlight
them. Still, I think to myself, it's taking it a bit far, really. The guy,
I decide, is obviously really fucked up. Me, on the other hand, I'm
normal. Unhappy, but normal. It is incredibly important to me
to think of myself as something called normal.

But am I? A craving for distraction is the first 'symptom' that
something may, in fact, be seriously wrong. I furiously seek out
anything that will keep my mind from turning inward on itself.
Music, company, the television. I am deeply uncomfortable
when alone, but presume that there is nothing peculiar about
this: it is the modern condition. If we could all sit quietly in a
room and relax, society would collapse; dissatisfaction and inner
stress were built into both human nature and the structure of the
twentieth century. The only thing that seems odd is that the
stress never lets up. I am never, ever properly relaxed or happy,
not even for a moment. My fists still seem perpetually clenched.

I become vaguely aware that some sharp break with my accustomed character is taking place. My extroversion and arrogance
collapse into shyness and a sort of nervous twitching. I am even
losing that most English of gifts, my sense of humour, my ability
to laugh at myself and just about everything else. The lodestar
within, which has always told me what is true and right and sensible and ugly or attractive, which I could believe and trust more
than all the reasoning in the world, has been eclipsed, so that
I cannot even remember a time when it shone. I have become
serious, endlessly reflective, tediously analytical, self-censoring,
cautious, mannered, pompous. I am becoming a caricature of a
middle-class fool and I do not know what to do about it.

My essays are getting far better marks now, as they become
more stodgy and constipated, but some perverse perfectionism
has overtaken me. Anything less than an A appears to be the most

abject of failures. It gradually dawns on me that the person Becka
has fallen in love with is gradually ceasing to exist and that only
by an enormous effort of will can the ghost be brought back to
life. Being with her exhausts me, as I am having to perform this
exhumation every time. Periodically I leave her, and she always
takes me back, as confused as I am as to why I have left her in the
first place. While I am with her, the sheer life and energy and
love of her terrify me. Without her, loneliness and panic cripple
me. I have lost interest in sex; in fact, I find it hard to be truly
interested in anything at all. There seems to be nowhere to turn.
With each separation and each reuniting the stresses seem to
worsen.

I cannot understand what is happening to me. I have felt this
way for so long now, it seems hard to imagine that I ever felt any
other way, that I was once a different person, with life and heart
and libido. To my dismay, I even begin to feel cold and distant
towards my family. I put it down to age and growing apart. But it
is odd, because we have been so close for so long now.

Other peculiar observations crowd in on me, to be brushed
away with increasingly desperate explanations. The fact that I
spend fifteen minutes staring at supermarket shelves, trying to
decide between one brand of washing powder and another, is
simply a rational consumer in action. On another occasion, I
turn the car around seven times on a short stretch of Westbourne
Park Road: I cannot decide whether to go to a particular lecture.
Eventually, I pull into the kerb and burst into tears.

A sense of disgrace deepens in me. Not only have I, in some
obscure fashion, betrayed my own class and roots, but the new
class among which I find myself judges me even more harshly.
Teenage Marxists frown at me: what are you doing for the
miners? for the ANC? for the homeless? My shameful answer,
too shameful to actually speak: I don't really give a shit. Also, my
guilt over the pain I am bringing to Becka piles up like so much
radioactive waste.

At some uncertain point I begin to pad out the long trial of
library work with idle fantasies about suicide. Would hanging be
best? No, if the drop was too high, your head came off. A tube

train would be quick and effective, but upsetting for the driver and inconvenient for passengers. A high building would unquestionably be the most reliable, though the few seconds before impact would be nerve-racking and there would be pain, if only for an instant. I had no serious intent. It seemed to me little more than inconsequential mental graffiti.

Something was certainly wrong, but what? I found it increasingly difficult to speak to people now, whereas previously I had always been social and outgoing. I had panic attacks which made me physically shake with fear, although I did not know what it was I was scared of. The thoughts of suicide multiplied. North Sea Gas? But was it poisonous? A razor? Too brutal. Before I walked out on Becka for the third – or was it fourth? – time, she, knowing the depth of my unhappiness, suggested I see a psychiatrist. I gave one of my increasingly rare laughs and dismissed the idea as absurd. Psychiatrists were for lunatics.

I leave the LSE in 1986 with a good degree in politics and history. I do not go to the presentation ceremony; despite the fact that this has been the hardest task of my life by far, I feel no particular sense of pride. Every Tom, Dick and Harry seems to have a degree nowadays and although my parents are proud, I know that in the larger sense my family are unimpressed. As always, being good at abstractions in my class is seen as faintly ridiculous and pointless, a sort of indulgent game. I am once again beginning to agree with them. The three years have been so deeply painful and lonely, and yet I am not sure that I have learned anything of any particular value. My career with the publishing company is finished. My relationship with Becka is still stumbling along, off and on, more characterized than ever now by disappointment and anger on her part and growing desperation on mine. I know that she is beginning to hate me; my only consolation is that it is better than indifference.

Also, I am unemployed and I begin to doubt that I will ever get another job. I know that Becka will be extremely successful – she has already been accepted on to a prized BBC trainees course – and I feel that she will, sooner or later, disdain my failure. I must keep up, I must push on, although I do not know where to. Ambition is, perhaps, my last remaining sentiment.

In the autumn of 1986, a new phase begins. Now the depression – which I do not characterize as depression, merely unhappiness – has turned some strange corner and become what I can only describe as manic.

Manic depression can be profoundly satisfying. In Martin Scorsese's *Taxi Driver*, there's a shot of the psychotic Travis Bickle staring fixedly at the spray of an effervescing Alka Seltzer. It is an accurate observation of a mind about to collapse. In a similar way, all sorts of trivia now become fascinating to me – the steam rising from a coffee cup, the play of light on the ceiling, the flight of an insect, a crisp packet bowling down the street in the wind. I am fascinated by the play of invisible forces – wind, gravity, growth, decay. I put out an orange and watch it slowly rot as the days pass. The fact that it is transforming, of its own volition, in front of my eyes amazes me. I become fascinated by time-lapse photography, which seems to reveal a hidden world and process: spurting, unstoppable nature. Hidden worlds obsess me – I get books on the micro-universe of atoms and creatures smaller than the eye can see, on space and the infinities of matter present beyond the horizon of sight. I feel I am approaching some fundamental truth, that I am entering a new, heightened reality.

All these phenomena I write up in furious detail in notebooks. I have always been a patchy diarist at best; now I write page upon page, every day, for hours and hours, full of tortuous philosophy. Over the following eighteen months, I write thousands of pages, sometimes for eight hours a day.

At this point, I suppose, I am building my final defence against breakdown. I am aware that I am trying to keep a hold of something, but I am not sure what. I know only that it is an enormous effort. My handwriting becomes very neat and precise and unlike the random scrawl of my previous self. My train of thought is systemic, laid out clean and pure, and has become me, what I am. My feelings have closed down entirely, so what is left is simply what is in my head, and it is imperative that that makes sense, because otherwise I think I will lose my continuity as a very person. If the stream of ordered thought in my head stops, then I will stop too.

The diary writings are not mad, or even rambling. They are just relentless and rather dull. Reading them now is like dipping into the collected works of a slightly drunk, reasonably clever but frighteningly single-minded saloon-bar philosopher. I am as high as a kite and, I believe, intoxicatingly rational. My thoughts seem to be structured almost mathematically, reading out premises and conclusions like a ticker tape. But actual thoughts of suicide have stopped. As far as I am concerned, I have recovered, although I vaguely sense that I am still acting and thinking abnormally.

In 1987, a year after leaving university, I achieve a remarkable career boost. I am offered the editorship of the (now defunct) London listings magazine, *City Limits*, in charge of some eighty staff. My inexperience does not seem to make much difference to the interviewing board: they are faced with someone in the grip of mania, crackling with nervous energy and apparently unassailable self-confidence. Articulacy has always been my strong point, and depression, at this level, is a quickening of the mind, an astonishing clarity. The panel are bewitched.

Amazingly, I am still with Becka at this point. She believes that now I have this job everything between us will be fine. She continues to try hard, but instead of our relationship improving, I leave her again, fighting down a rising sense of panic. She is completely frustrated and bewildered. I am bewildered myself. I simply know that I cannot carry on any more. Having to act, to pretend an entire life on two fronts, is just too demanding.

I realize very quickly that the job is not going to work out. *City Limits* is a bizarrely structured remnant of the 1970s, a socialist collective, containing many long-established competing factions. I do not have the emotional – or, in fact, the practical power – to hold eighty people together. I do not belong here, I am not a member of their tribe, although I have convinced them that I am. I do not have a tribe, or if I do, it is a shameful one: white, male, not 'properly' working class. Perhaps it is shameful, but it is mine. Why, then, can I not claim it?

I am a strange combination of left-wing and libertarian. I see myself as a sort of Fabian P. J. O'Rourke, rather than the conventional, ideological socialist I feel is expected. This means that I find the censorious environment incomprehensible and intolerable. Even the idea of being a liberal seems to be tantamount to moral ignominy. But in the face of eighty more or less like minds, I am not confident enough to state my case.

At an interview for a new designer, when I sit on a panel with a cleaner, a secretary and the news editor (we all have an equal vote), applicants are quizzed about their stance on the miners' strike, which has long-since finished. I realize finally that the only solution to *City Limits's* problems is to sack three-quarters of the staff and recapitalize the magazine, but I understand that I will be removed by the people I am trying to sack. That is the way the collective works. I know what I have to at least try to do, but I lack the requisite ruthlessness, management skills and rhinoceros skin. I have the fatal weakness of wanting to be liked, and this contradiction seems to set up a final, intolerable stress in me. It lobs a hand-grenade into the limbic system of my lower brain, which then short-circuits. I resign, four weeks after joining. The magazine will fold shortly afterwards. I sense that this will be the case and feel still more guilt that my habit of destructiveness towards people has extended to institutions.

The day after resigning, I have a panic attack far more extreme than anything I have experienced before. I am sitting in Holland Park Open Air Theatre, where a comedy event is being held. The stand-ups are good, but I am unable to raise a smile of any kind. My lips begin to move to the sound of my own thoughts. Something is wrong, something is wrong. And what happens now? What is it that must happen? What is it that is going to happen? I start to sweat when the breakdown that has been gathering within me for so long finally begins. I am suddenly steeped, soaked through to the spirit, in sticky black pitch. My power of speech begins to disappear, as does the ability to reason.

I take to lying in bed most of the time, consciousness hardly flickering. I know immediately how it will end. I don't in the least want to die. What I 'realize' is that it is inevitable, a destiny that needs to be fulfilled. Thoughts of suicide are no longer the mental doodlings of a bored undergraduate. I compare myself to Hamlet, the Prince of Denmark. Self-importance is one of the several profits of depression.

Hamlet was prisoner of a tragic destiny. Compelled from within, it did not matter how much he vacillated and demurred: 'There's a special providence in the fall of a sparrow. If it be now, 'tis not to come; if it be not to come, it will be now; if it be not now, yet it will come.' This is the speech of a man who has submitted to the demands of implacable fate.

The sense of guilt and failure that has for years bowed me down now takes on a religious flavour. I am ashamed of everything – my country, my class, my very self. Up until now, I have been a militant atheist, but I begin to believe that my soul is lost to the devil, that I am evil and must die. In short, I am going crazy, and like a crazy person, I do not know it.

My new ideas of religiosity and sin, beliefs that I thought I had cast off in my infant schooldays but now find were merely dormant, reach their fullest expression when I start wandering the streets, unshaved, sometimes with piss on the front of my trousers, merging in with the winos and beggars I have in the past awkwardly ignored, or, just as awkwardly, rewarded. My eyes are muddy. My mouth hangs open like a cretin. There is recognition in the faces of the winos, who offer me mouthfuls of warm cider. But I have tried drinking as an anaesthetic; it just makes me feel sick. Otherwise I am indistinguishable from the other human street-litter, except that my creased, dirty trousers are Paul Smith, the stained shirt is from Joseph. I am a designer scumbag.

On one occasion, walking blank and aimless as usual, I come to a church, near Goodge Street station. I decide to go in, feeling hopeless and foolish. It is open and there is a door marked for the priest. I knock on the door, because I will speak to anyone who will listen. There is nobody there.

I walk to the pews, fall on my knees and begin to pray, for the first time since school. I pray for my soul to be saved from the devil, to be forgiven for what now appear to me to be terrible sins. There is only silence and emptiness in the church. It is cold.

I clench my eyes tight and try to make a sound in my head that will be heard by someone. Who is the Holy Ghost? I pray above all that my parents, most particularly my mother, will be saved from the impact of the pain of what is happening to me, of the destructive force that I have become. After ten minutes or so, I get up and leave. I do not feel any different.

I begin practising suicide notes, often at great and tedious length. At this point, surprisingly, I have not lost my capacity to satirize my own situation. At the end of one particularly over-blown effort, I observe in a postscript that the Labour Party 1983 Manifesto was no longer the longest suicide note in history. On another, I observe that my life is 'like Mantovani rather than Otis [Redding]; a sticky, ersatz version of life at 15 removes from the real thing'.

It is not only me who seems to be falling apart but, eerily, the world outside. In August Michael Ryan goes insane and mas-sacres fourteen people in Hungerford. In October, incredible storms seem to tear England apart. I lie in bed, rigid, listening to the howling wind shake at my window like some strange sum-mons. A few days later, the stock market crashes on Black Monday. Then, within weeks, eleven people are blown up at En-niskillen and there is a tube fire at King's Cross that burns thirty people to death. It all seems to knit together in a great cross-stitch of decay and chaos that merges with the darkness inside my mind.

My prevarications come to an end in the early hours of one November morning. I put on a pair of jeans and a T-shirt. I play 'Brown-Eyed Girl' by Van Morrison softly, once. I leave a note for my family: *So low. Not low: non-existent, rambling, utterly mad, totally sane. I loved you all so deeply when I had a heart to love with, when I possessed a soul. Now all I care about is cigarettes.*

My time is up. I am to die against my will, but fate cannot be denied. I make my way up the fire escape, trying desperately to find courage. A neighbour looks out as I approach the roof. I smile and wave. He goes back to bed. Romanticizing my fate to the last, my thoughts still court cheap melodrama. *This is the last moon I will ever see. I am to die against my will. But fate cannot be denied*. I weep, for my family, for my stupid life and, most of all, for myself. From the roof, I stare down to the gardens far below, waiting for the moment when I will find the nerve.

Always casting about for certainty, I have at last found it. My belief about my need to commit suicide is the greatest certainty I have ever known. This is what I have always needed, and this is what my mind has duly come up with. I have done what the deepest part of my self has demanded, which is to build myself a system of belief, at any cost, a system of belief that will make sense to me. Suicide in this sense, like just about everything else in life, is a strange form of self-protection. I must die in order for my beliefs to survive, in order to prove to myself that I am free-willed, in control, in possession of a self, that I am good. It is clear and consistent and precise and, in its conclusion, quite mad.

I feel transparent, as if the wind is blowing through me. My own self-pity disgusts me more than I can bear. My head is sharp and clear. It seems that some immutable force is working within me. Above all, I feel that to launch myself into the air is the right and appropriate thing to do; something, obscurely, I can be proud of. I am convinced that all the streams and tides of my personal history, all my choices and non-choices, have inevitably led to this moment of truth. I feel soaked in a mysterious sense of destiny, which bids me jump.

I don't think of anybody else; or rather, I don't hurt for anybody else. It is a shame that my family will have to suffer through my death, but anyone who can feel so little for themselves that they want to die is hardly capable of feeling for others. Which, of course, is why life becomes absolutely without reward.

Although I feel compelled to die, so great is my fear of the plummet that I feel, once again, helpless. I fear the devil, I fear pain, I fear oblivion. I balance on the edge of the roof, thinking *Just let yourself slip*. Now, no . . . now! I wobble and stay upright. The wind hits again. Now! I hold back again.

What is pushing me forward? I cannot say. Try to remember some moment in your life, some decision you had to make which you felt involved only one choice because failing to take it would be a complete denial of yourself and your personal destiny. At those moments, there is some reverberation within you, some deep certainty which asks you to trust it. Such a certainty is upon me, as real as the bricks which stand solidly in the way of my will.

Now! I lurch forward again. Music blares from the flat beneath me. I am getting cold and begin to realize the true depth of my failure. I am too weak, too indecisive, even to kill myself successfully. After twenty minutes on the roof of the building, staring at the indifferent moon, I flunk the one choice in my life which I feel would have been brave and worthwhile. I climb down the fire escape and go back to bed.

Chapter Sixteen

It is several weeks before Jean receives a phone call from me to say that I have been standing on the roof with the intention of throwing myself off. In the interim, I have tried to rally myself, but repeatedly fallen back to a place where I wish, truly, to die.

Jean's first reaction is what her first reaction to family crises always is. What can I *do*? There has to be a way to help. My mother's greatest definition of herself is as a doer. To not be able to do is to feel helpless and weak, and out of control. It is one of the worst feelings imaginable for someone like her. So, the first thing Jean and Jack do when I arrive from Notting Hill after a shaky drive down the A40 is to sit down and talk to me about what action is to be taken. By now, I am over the worst of the panic attack and begin to imagine, as I sometimes do, that the crisis in my mind is exhausted now. However, I remain bleak and fatalistic and clearly unhappy.

My parents, up until now, have been about the only people close to me who have not known of the severity of the problems I have been experiencing. I have protected them thus far, hoping to find a solution through my friends. They – my friends – are for the most part kind and understanding, although one or two of them assiduously avoid me, as if fearful of despair or, more plausibly, boredom. None of them, however, has suggested that I am ill in any way, or might need to see a doctor. The idea of tablets and treatments remains beyond the pale; they too have seen *One Flew Over the Cuckoo's Nest*. One of my wisest and closest friends, Bev, has recently suffered the suicide of her mother and tells me that before she killed herself, she underwent drug treatments and ECT that she felt to be worse even than the depression and quite useless.

Likewise, my parents are extremely reluctant to accept that I am suffering from an illness that might be ameliorated by drugs. Drugs – although, oddly, I am happy to take them recreationally – are against our whole experience and philosophy; our experience of Alan, our belief in self-reliance within the family. We think that talking and kindness and tolerance are the answer for just about everything, and so Jean and Jack talk and are kind and tolerant towards me, offering to take me in and look after me until I 'feel better'.

I turn down their offer and return home. Over the next few weeks it becomes clear, however, that the solutions our family have always relied on in crises are useless in my case. Although I have a brief time of feeling better, I soon relapse. I begin to hang around on the platforms of tube stations, trying to let myself slip in front of trains but losing my courage as ever. I return to the roof of the flats, again staring beneath, praying for the strength to do what I most desire. In an attempt to combat my cowardice, I drive out to the country with a length of rubber hosing and a pair of handcuffs. The idea is that I will run the pipe from the exhaust to the window, switch on the motor, then handcuff myself to the wheel. Then, I reason, all I have to do to die is let go of the key. The scheme does not work, because I am too afraid to set it in motion. Whatever else it may be, suicide is not the coward's way out. Death is a tremendously frightening prospect, however much you may desire it.

Most of the time I conceal these attempts from Jack and Jean, but on one or two occasions I tell my mother what is happening. Her voice goes small. She sounds flat rather than terrified. My apartment is beginning to disgust even me and she begins to come round to clean it up. At least it is *doing* something. Her helplessness begins to weigh on her like an always heavier yoke.

My parents ask me to come home again, as much in order to keep an eye on me as anything. I do so, indifferent. My power of speech has more or less dried up by now and I lie in my child-hood bunk bed, curled up in a foetal position. My mother comes in to bring me food, which I listlessly eat. I am putting on weight, becoming bloated. I am unshaven, and utterly listless. My sense that I have returned to a sort of awful inverted childhood is overpowering.

In the few hours of the day when I can be bothered to get up, I wander around the streets of Southall. I spend much time in Jubilee Gardens, where once I stood in the middle of the field shouting, *Buggerfuckcunt*, and muttering, with all the spirit that was in me then. *Some day*.

Now I am back where I started, fifteen years later. I wander to the library which adjoins the park and feebly pick at the books. A quotation seems to slide around my head from somewhere: *He who increaseth knowledge, increaseth sorrow*.

Without feeling any interest, I nevertheless find a copy of the Bible and look for the exact quote. Eventually, I find it. It reads: *And I gave my heart to know wisdom, and to know madness and folly: I perceived that this also is vexation of spirit, For in much wisdom is much grief: and he that increaseth knowledge increaseth sorrow*. I stare at the page. The words stare back at me. I cannot make sense of them. I can barely even read a newspaper now, so parched and throttled are my thought processes.

Jack and Jean have reluctantly come to the conclusion that I may be ill and need to be in hospital. They begin ringing around private clinics, which charge thousands of pounds a month for treatment. Their only source of income is Jean's salary from the dinner lady's job and a small wage from Jack's new job with Age Concern. They decide that they will remortgage the house in order to pay for treatment and worry about it later. After twenty-five years of hard work, the house is fully paid off now and worth about £60,000. It will be a shame to have the worry of a mort-gage again, but still –

They need not worry, for I have already refused to accept any kind of treatment. I am suffering occasional religious delusions now and have decided that I am damned to hell, deserving of every ounce of my suffering. Anyway, if I am simply ill, then my mind is not my own, I do not possess a real, choosing, consequential self. My thoughts are not autonomous, they are a bunch of chemicals, and this is a conclusion intolerable to me.

I do not shave any more and sleep as much as I can. Jean comes and sits on my bed, often not saying anything, simply sighing and staring at the space above my unmoving head. Jean is caring for me the best she can, but it is clearly hurting her.

I stare at Jean, as if through too-thick spectacles. She reminds me of someone else now, though I can't think whom. Then I see it. It is Mary Tyler Moore, late, as in *Ordinary People*, rather than early, as in the *Mary Tyler Moore Show*. She has that same stretched, too-fixed-place air, that sense that she has become tight, as if her life no longer fits. I liked that film, *Ordinary People*, I vaguely remember. There is a moment at the end, when Donald Sutherland turns to Mary Tyler Moore and says something that has always stuck in my mind for some reason: *You are determined but you are not strong.* You are determined, but you are not strong. I wonder if there is a Latin translation of this. It will make an ideal motto one day for our family, or at least for Jean and me.

Jean still makes a fist sometimes of being cheerful and optimistic. At other times, though, the pretence is clearly too much. She stares down at me and says, *It's like a living death.*

I nod in agreement, then attempt myself, hopelessly, to be cheerful: *It will probably be all right again.*

The echoing nod of Jean's head is unconvinced and unconvincing. She sighs once more and shifts her gaze to somewhere above my head, as if staring at some point very far away. *You were always so full of . . . wonder, as a child. Such an imagination. Now it's all turned into a nightmare.* Her eyes refocus on me. *You know, the trouble is, I'm becoming very depressed. You're making me depressed, too.*

Doubtless, this is true. The room is dark. I close my eyes and try once more to fall asleep.

A few weeks later, Jack and Jean finally achieve what they might consider to be a form of progress. They convince me to go and see my doctor, Dr Soboniescu, in Notting Hill Gate. I consider it to be a waste of time, but I go anyway. The moment I enter the door, I burst into tears and do not stop sobbing throughout the interview. Calmly, Dr Soboniescu makes an appointment for me to visit the Acute Mental Health Unit at St Charles's Hospital in North Kensington.

The Acute Mental Health Unit. How these words shame me, for I am now a designated other, a crazy person. Even as I trudge towards the hospital, I feel disgusted by the idea that I am entering the Cuckoo's Nest. I nearly turn round and go back, but some residual sense of duty to my parents, or perhaps unacknowledged hope, insists that I continue. I reach the waiting area, and it seems that some other sinking of my already drowned self-image is taking place. Appalling wretches smoking sad, rolled-up cigarettes wander around in dressing gowns. There are young men with tattoos on their knuckles. One girl is walking around on crutches and smiling sweetly. I wonder why she isn't in another part of the hospital. Then I overhear a snatch of a conversation she is having with another patient.

No, well. They don't want to let me out just yet.

Why not?

They're worried I might, you know . . . She nods at the smashed legs. *Do it again.*

She gives a lovely smile and a wave, and moves towards the doors of the closed ward that adjoins the waiting area. My sense of wretchedness increases.

I am called into a small interview room, where a young woman is sitting with a clipboard. She introduces herself as a trainee and begins to ask questions in order to make a diagnosis. I have puffed myself up, clenched myself. I am determined to prove to this woman that I am not a cretin. I am also irritated that I merit only a trainee.

So — Mr Lott, isn't it? Timothy. May I call you Timothy?

I'd rather stick with the formalities.

As you wish. Now, I'm going to ask you some questions and I want you to answer as best you can.

All right. Can I ask you a question first?

If you like.

242

Are you a Freudian or an organicist?

I think it would be best if you just answer the questions. Now, how has your sleep been?

OK. *I sleep too much, if anything.*

Do you have trouble concentrating?

Yes, I suppose so. *Sometimes I can hardly think at all.*

Do you find it easy to make decisions?

I'm not really sure.

Try and think.

That was a joke.

I see.

No. *No, I don't find it easy to make decisions. What's the point of all this?*

I have fixed her with an unrelenting stare now and when she speaks again, she will not meet my eye.

It's me who's doing the interviewing.

Ach, so it is ve who ask ze kvestions.

Do you feel guilty?

Do you?

Do you think you have done wrong?

Define your terms.

Do you feel you have sinned?

'Use every man after his desert, and who should 'scape whipping?'

Do you feel that you have sinned?

Sinned? Not in a religious sense. I feel that I have failed.

Are you interested in sex?

Is that a proposition?

And so on. The woman is only slightly flustered and in the end manages to extract the relevant information. I cannot make decisions, I cannot concentrate, I feel emotionally cold and distanced from everything. I have lost interest in sex. I fantasize about suicide. I am tormented by feelings of guilt and worthlessness. Most of these feelings I have been having for years, although they have worsened recently. She dismisses me from the room and I feel that I have put in a decent enough performance; that she will not put me in the wrong category.

The consultant psychiatrist arrives and enters for a conference with the young woman. On impulse, I put my ear to the door and listen. I can pick up only snatches, but they please me.

He's extremely intelligent. He made me nervous.

The intelligent ones are the worst. You have to be firm.

He doesn't seem remotely crazy.

I feel vindicated. My sense that my reasoning is solid is re-assured. The door opens and the consultant beckons me in. He is a man in late middle age with a brittle and impatient air. He bids me sit down, then tells me that I have been suffering from a severe but treatable illness for the last four years. Those four years, he is sorry to say, have been unnecessarily wasted. The pathology, he says, makes it quite clear that I am experiencing something quite distinct from 'unhappiness' or simple despair. The illness can be cured quite quickly with drugs. Some therapy will also help.

I snort and shrug my shoulders in a way that I have developed over time when I wish to express contempt. The idea of taking pills remains repulsive to me; the idea that my filigree thoughts and beliefs can be reduced to a simple malfunction of neuro-transmitters. He tries to explain to me about serotonin, reuptake inhibitors, synaptic gaps, but I do not wish to listen. I simply do not believe in depression as a medical condition. Certainly, someone as self-reliant as myself could never suffer from it. Depression, in my philosophy, is a word to excuse self-pity and weakness.

I refuse the pills. Perhaps I have nothing to lose, but to take them is to concede some principle I cannot quite articulate, something about ownership of my self. And I know they are only the thin end of the wedge. They still do ECT and, for all I know, lobotomy. They can still hospitalize mental patients against their will. Tablets were simply step number one. They opened the awful Pandora's Box of the psychiatrists.

The psychiatrist seems to become quite agitated. This may be for the benefit of the student who is still sitting by his side. I sense he needs to put me in my place.

Look. Do as you damn well like. If you want to go on suffering like this, it's your decision. You will come out of it eventually anyway – if you

*don't kill yourself first. But if you want to save yourself a lot of pain,
these tablets will help you. They are not addictive, they have no serious
side-effects. They work. It's up to you. In the long term, you should also
seek counselling. I will make an appointment for you at our King's Road
centre.*

He hands me a prescription and begins to prepare for his next
appointment. The student gives a faint smirk. I pick up the prescription, slightly cowed by the psychiatrist's performance, put it
in my pocket and leave. I have no intention of taking them. To
do so is, I think in some strange way, cheating, second rate. To
take them is to *lose*, although I am not quite sure what the game
is, or how it can be that I have not already lost. However, I meet
the doctor half-way and go to visit the psychotherapist he has
suggested. I have as little faith in therapy as I do in tablets, but I
find it less threatening somehow. It seems less entirely dismissive
of my personality.

The Chelsea centre is by the river. Before going into the
appointment, I take the towpath down to the edge of the
Thames and try to find the will to throw myself in. It looks very
cold and I am not sure that it will work. The series of suicide
non-attempts is by now farcical. I am a para-parasuicide. Gathering my coat about me, I walk up from the river and towards what
is called the World's End Centre. Had I any sense of humour left,
the name might have raised a smile. But now it just seems
another harbinger.

When I am led into the psychotherapist's office, I think I have
been the victim of an elaborate joke. The man sitting in front of
me is clearly a Freudian, at least in terms of fashion. He has the
little pointy beard, the high forehead, the grave, professorial air.
But in a nod to the contemporary, he wears a baggy sweater and
loose-fit jeans. He puffs on a pipe whose smell revolts me. He
strikes me as insufferably smug and I am more than ever re-
assured that psychotherapy is bunk. I chain-smoke, and wait for
him to tell me the secret of my life.

He asks me a few questions about my childhood and family relationships, and seems doubtful when I suggest that both were
and are very good, and that it is hard to remember much fault

with either my mother or my father. Although I knew them not to be perfect, I am unaware of having been abandoned, underloved, overloved, untouched or abused. It is clear that he believes me to be in denial.

He asks me if I take drugs and I mention that I took LSD as a teenager. In one of the only moments of our consultations that I find diverting, he tells me that it is far from rare for depressed patients to have taken LSD, once itself prescribed for depression. And it is true, now I think of it, that life has perhaps always been a disappointment, a diluted thing, since the intensity of that experience.

After I have told him some more basic facts, he lapses into silence. I guess that this is a therapeutic technique to make me talk about what concerns me, but I can think of nothing whatsoever to say. The result is that we sit in absolute silence for thirty minutes, at the end of which the therapist picks up his diary and says, *When can you make it again?*

I attend on two more occasions, but find myself spending the majority of the time in embarrassed silence, punctuated occasionally by unprovoked tears. When asked to remember dreams, all I can recall is one in which I go up too fast in a crowded lift, so fast I crash through the ceiling and into the sky. I imagine that he is disappointed in me, that despite his professional distance, he dislikes me. In the end we both give up.

My mother and father, despairing now, urge me once more to take the tablets, which I have reluctantly cashed in the prescription for. They sit in my bathroom cabinet. Out of absolute indifference as much as anything else, and the insistence of my parents, I begin to take them. Two Mianserin and six Trimiprimine every day. I have absolutely no faith that they will work; I just want to be able to tell Jean and Jack that I tried.

I have absolutely no faith, in fact, in anything. In a muddy way, I see that depression manifests itself as a crisis of faith. Not religious faith, but the almost born instinct that things are fluid, that they unfold and change, that new kinds of moment are eventually possible, that the future will arrive. I am in a time-locked place, where the moment I am in will stretch on, agonizingly, for ever. There is no possibility of redemption or hope. It is a final giving up on everything. It is death.

Idly I calculate when the absolute failure of my life will be proved, when it will be realized that my crisis is spiritual and Shakespearian rather than some tawdry off-the-shelf illness. Since the tablets supposedly take about three weeks to work, that day, I estimate, will be 28 December 1987.

In the meantime, I am still spending a great deal of time with my parents. My mother seems entirely normal, except for some hollowness in and about the eyes which is noted only later, through memory. She does not cry or seem unduly irritable. Never an obviously neurotic woman, lacking in phobias, addictions or obsessions of any kind, she goes about her business as ever: tennis, golf, yoga, art, housekeeping, gardening.

Still, she is behaving strangely in some ways, I think, worrying about odd, trivial details. The telephone she has just had installed trills electronically in the modern fashion, rather than ringing a bell. When it sounds on one occasion, she stares at it fiercely as if she has been slapped. *I hate that phone*, she says, through clenched teeth. It seems an odd thing for Jean to be worked up about – Jean, the soul of patience.

On another occasion she lays her paintings out for me to take a Polaroid of. They aren't at all bad and she has always, despite her habitual self-doubt, shown a certain pride in them. Now she stares at them balefully. *They're no good*, she mutters, smiling ironically as if discovering something she should have known all along.

Unshaven, I sit up and try to jolly her. I really do think they are OK. *No, Mum. Really, they're very good. They're lovely.*

She shakes her head firmly. *No. They're no good.*

She looks unutterably sad. I close my eyes, blank as air.

A week or so later, after a painful and strained family Christmas during which I sit in a corner, not speaking, I have gone back to my flat. I watch the seasonal broadcasts about Christmas for starving children in war-torn countries. It occurs to me that I am wearing a £400 jacket and sipping at a £10-bottle of wine. My sense of guilt and worthlessness is once more heightened.

The next day is 28 December and I awake, unusually, first thing in the morning. I am alone. I have an odd perception. There is a pigeon cooing on the balcony outside my bedroom window. It is pleasant and soothing. I haven't noticed birdsong for a long time. I imagine, pleasantly, that it sounds like a woman climaxing.

I shave and wash, and make myself some coffee, in which I take simple enjoyment. I feel strange, in that I feel normal, average. It occurs to me that I have not felt like this – neither stiff with tension, nor collapsing into chaos – for several years. As if by magic, all my thoughts about sin and redemption, God and the devil, have disappeared. It occurs to me that the desire to kill myself is utterly ridiculous. Why would I want to kill myself anyway? I know, quite clearly and calmly now, like a camera suddenly finding focus, that I really have been ill, and equally that I have begun to recover.

I pick up a newspaper and read it from cover to cover. Yesterday, I think, I could hardly read a headline. There are pictures of starving children; they do not bother me. Is it OK not to feel guilty about this now? Does it show proper adjustment? I smile with a sort of dazed incredulity and reach for the telephone. Above all, I want to tell Jean. I want to tell her that everything, after all, is going to be all right.

In fact, it is my father who picks up the phone. He is placid as usual, but seems extremely pleased. He says he knows that Jean will be thrilled. In fact, I do not see my mother again until our birthday celebration a few weeks later (all of us, apart from Jeff, have our birthdays in January). We all meet to have dinner at a PizzaExpress restaurant in Soho. When we swap gifts, it turns out that James, Mum and I have all bought Dad wristwatches. We laugh out loud. It turns out that Jack already has three unused watches in his drawer anyway.

I explain to my mother, as I have to my father, how I have been ill and have recovered. She seems pleased and quite normal in every respect. It is a nice evening, and at last there is a sense in the family that things are getting better. Not only have I recovered but Jeff's new marriage appears to be happy and the divorce from Helma forgotten. Jack is adjusting well to his redundancy and has finally received a pay-off from his former employers.

However, in the weeks and months after my recovery, my sudden discovery of 'illness' is treated with some scepticism. Neither my parents nor my friends feel comfortable with the idea that the mind can be healed by medication. To come from somewhere so wretched and low must surely involve a greater struggle than the swallowing of tablets, as if for a headache; years of therapy, perhaps, some . . . penance. And there is a part of me that even now doesn't quite accept the psychiatrist's simple assertion that I have been unwell. Although in some ways it is obviously true, it also obviously falls short of an explanation. And it is true that I am not suddenly transformed into someone jolly, optimistic and life-enhancing. I remain rather gloomy and reserved, and pessimistic about the future. I feel weak and milky in the head. I still spend too much time in bed. Yet I know it to be incontrovertibly true that something inside me has changed, has regained a long-lost equilibrium. Instead of barren, I feel fallow. I presume that Jean will begin to believe it over time, when I get stronger.

Continuing to take the tablets, I do set about my life with a new sense of purpose. An old acquaintance has come to me with a project for a new magazine, and I set about it with application and some flair. When working on the project, my mind clears completely, and seems incisive and fast. I begin to go out to dinner parties – oh, I can pass easily as middle class nowadays – where I laugh properly for the first time in years. The muscles that allow me to smile feel out of condition. It is at first an effort, but the sense of humour that was once sharp enough to be saleable to newspapers is beginning to return. I can laugh at the world and myself.

Faith, like some tiny plant macadammed over, begins to push back towards the air. Revelations seem to press forth. I see that what you feel leads to how you think; that it drafts out your conclusions in advance. I see – feel – that life is not a thing, but an unstoppable process. I see that conscience is different from guilt. I see that the future must always arrive and that it is never wholly predictable. Thus my habitual pessimism is no truer than optimism, only more uncomfortable, self-important and, finally, life-denying. It occurs to me that you do not have to be Mickey Mouse or Cliff Richard to be positive about life. You do not have to be an idiot, or self-deluding, to be happy. And so this is the choice I make, the choice to be happy. Maybe I have the right after all.

The stone in my chest has dissolved. Unaccustomed feelings begin to flex. There is warmth there, a certain half-forgotten responsiveness. It is true all the same that a death has taken place. The angles and planes of the person I once was – intensely wilful, relentlessly ambitious, over-intense, self-punishing and cocksure – have either softened, cracked or gone for ever. I feel a sense of deep fatalism about nearly everything, but it is not an unhealthy fatalism; more an acceptance that there are powers larger than my will that have to be accommodated.

I continue to see my mother and father regularly. My father seems more cheerful, convinced that I have passed the moment of crisis. My mother remains doubtful. I try to tell her that I am better, but on one occasion she looks right at me and says, *No. No, you're not.*

But I have few doubts. My powers of concentration have returned. My self-confidence is flowing once more, like oxygenated blood. I have even tried to win back Becka, telling her briskly that it can work out now, because I have simply been ill and that this illness has been at the root of all our problems. I neglect to mention the possibility that she might have been in love with my symptoms, just as, in a way, I was.

She is deeply sceptical, and it does occur to me once again that this packaging of my experience into something called 'depression' is very convenient, lets me off the hook. Instead of weakness, emotional cowardice and casual cruelty, I can simply blame a sort of brainstorm. Becka turns me down and I can't really blame her. Perhaps I am being over-forgiving of myself, but I don't care. I understand now that to be over-forgiving of yourself is far less destructive than to be over-punishing. That self-hatred is the root of nearly all evil. Nor does it take long for this freshly minted hypothesis to be confirmed.

The first part of 1988 makes for an average English winter: cold, lead skies, dull sheets of rain. I view each with equanimity. Now it is no longer tundra inside, everything seems to speak of possibilities, even frost and wind. I have the sense that the grimness and waste of the last four years, an unnecessary ruination as it turns out, must be redeemed. I have lost a coveted job, I have lost Becka, I am unemployed, I am single, I have mislaid my self-respect. Yet I have decided that life now should be lived to the full, that depression, whatever it is, whatever its cause, should take nothing more away from me.

If Jean seems fragile during the first months of the New Year, nobody in the family or among her friends really notices. She remains apparently full of energy and plans for the future.

There is, with hindsight, the odd clue. On one occasion Jean phones up Olive and asks what she is doing, and Olive, who has nothing in her diary, invites her over to the house in Acacia Avenue. But by the time she arrives, Olive has remembered that she has been invited to a coffee morning that day, so she apologizes and says she cannot spend time with Jean after all. To her surprise, Jean looks crushed and desolate. Her head drops. Olive immediately rings the organizers of the coffee morning and secures Jean an invite, but she does not think of it again.

Bertha Staple, who has lived next to Jack and Jean since 1958, has become something of a mother-substitute for Jean since the death of Grace. In her eighties now, exactly as old as the century, she is still healthy and has a sharp mind. Jean often drops in for a chat – it has always been open house between them – but most particularly once a week, when Jean cuts, perms and blue-rinses Mrs Staple's hair, a service for which payment is always offered and always refused. Around the middle of January, Mrs Staple gets a funny idea that Jean is 'not herself'. She can't put her finger on it, but there is a fragility there, a fear of being alone.

And Jean has begun to complain, always with a defensive, apologetic smile, that she is no good at gardening, that she is no good at tennis, that she is no good at painting, that she cannot enjoy these things. She is given to sighs and stares out the window, but only momentarily. Then she snaps back into persona: chirpy, purposeful, doing. Her clothes and turn-out, as ever, are immaculate. Mrs Staple begins to think her fears are all in her own imagination.

On a Monday at the end of February, Jean, as is her custom, lets herself into Mrs Staple's house to 'do' her hair. They sit together at the back of the lounge, Jean preparing her scissors and rollers. She touches Mrs Staple's neck, and her hands are freezing. Jean appears to be shivering, even though it is warm in the room. Mrs Staple sees that she is hugging herself.

Mrs Staple – Stapes, as Jean always calls her – beckons Jean to sit down.

Jean. I don't like to see you like this. What's the matter?

Jean does not answer directly, but puts her head on Stapes's knee, and says, *It's nice to have a friend like you.* Then she pulls her chair up and they hold hands. Jean's hands are icy.

Stapes repeats, *What's the matter with you?* and when Jean says, *Oh, I don't know – nothing that a cuddle wouldn't solve,* they hug. Stapes is now holding back tears, for she senses the depth of Jean's distress, but she does not cry, for fear that she will 'start Jean off' and that the toxin of embarrassment will ensue. She instead rubs the back of Jean's hands and says, *Can't you tell me about it?*

There is a long pause, as if Jean is weighing the pros and cons of something very important. Then she says, quite brightly, *Well, I'd better be going.*

And at this, despite Stapes's protestations, she gets up and leaves.

The next day, Jean is parking her car in Rutland Road and decides to turn it around, so that it will be facing the right way for the next time she goes out. She is not concentrating; she pulls forward without checking her mirror and another car smashes into the side of her blue Jetta, badly damaging the panelwork. She admits blame, and is shaken and upset. This is the second accident in recent months.

On the Thursday morning of the same week, a neighbour sees a car coming down from the Top Shops. The car is veering madly from side to side, hitting each kerb in turn. The neighbour thinks the person inside must be drunk or mad. She thinks there is going to be a crash, but somehow the car makes it to the bottom of the hill without doing any damage. The neighbour can now see through the windscreen. The driver is Jean.

An hour or two later, Mrs Staple's daughter, Eileen, who always visits her mother on a Thursday, hears a knock on the door of No. 33. It is Jean, who normally gives her a lift up the hill to do her mother's shopping. She apologizes and says she cannot use the car because there is something wrong with it, and that she is going to do her own shopping in Greenford, some three miles away, by bus.

Later that afternoon, Eileen sees Jack working on the car. He says he can find nothing wrong with it. Eileen walks up towards the shops. She sees Jean coming down Somerset Hill, pulling a great shopping trolley full of groceries. She has walked all the way to the supermarket in Greenford and is now on the way back.

How are you? Jean says.

Going up the wall, what with a new grandchild and my poor old mum. I shall end up in the loony bin, Eileen replies.

At least you've got something to occupy your time all the while.

Well, you've still got your garden.

Oh, I've even lost interest in that.

That same evening, Jean goes around to Margaret's for her art class. Ellen, the art teacher, is there, but Olive is absent. Jean is working on a painting copied from a calendar. It is washed of colour, with low-lying hills and faint, perpendicular trees. There are greens, browns, yellows, and the sky is very pale. The trees are reflected in the water of a narrow river which stretches to a bridge. It does not seem to continue, oddly, after the bridge. The river is very still. There are no people, no wind in the trees. Fat yellow clouds are pinned to the horizon. But mostly it is sky, grass and water. Ellen thinks it is extraordinarily still and hollow as a painting, yet compact, neat and dainty, as Jean herself is.

Jean seems the same as ever, in perfectly good spirits, although Ellen thinks she sees some wistfulness in her eyes. Jean talks of her disappointment at not having grandchildren. But Ellen has no particular reason to shift her accustomed view of Jean as a happy and positive, fulfilled person.

The painting is unfinished. Jean says that she will leave it there and finish it next time. This is the first occasion she has not taken a painting home with her, but no one thinks anything more of it.

The following morning, Jean goes round to see her brother Alan, with plans to take him to a model railway exhibition which is on at Greenford Town Hall. The house in Rosecroft Avenue, although still a mess, is bearably tidy now, and Alan is quite himself, talking nineteen to the dozen, enthusing about his model boats and planes, his collection of big band records.

On this occasion, unusually, Jean brings around a gift for Alan. It is a watercolour she has painted herself. She has never given him a painting before. Being still in his mind a kind of child, he has not lost his sense of childlike excitement and is thrilled and loudly grateful. However, he cannot make it to the model train exhibition, as he is sailing his model boats that day, so he says goodbye to Jean at the door. He is still holding the painting. It is a portrait of model boats on the Serpentine in Hyde Park, where Alan sails his own miniature yachts and schooners, tiny, working imitations that he has made himself. The most recent model he has christened *Lady Jean*.

Jean kisses Alan's unshaven, old man's cheek and says, *Cheerio then*, for this is the last time they will meet and Jean knows it.

The next day, the Saturday before the Monday of Jean's suicide, Jean and Jack play golf, and then in the evening meet up with Helen and John at their house in Weybridge. Helen cooks a chilli con carne, and they all sit and plan a golf holiday together. Jean goes through the advertisements in *Golf World* excitedly. She is chatty and seems to be looking forward to it.

Later on, as usual, they play cards, nomination whist and Black Queen. Jean is not doing well and begins to look down-hearted. She says, *Look. I can't even play cards any more.*

And Helen says, *Oh, Jean. It's only a game.*

Jean nods, smiles and makes a random discard. At the end of the round, she has made the lowest score.

Chapter Seventeen

What does it mean to a family when the mother takes her own life? Was it really a sacrifice, as Jean imagined? Or was it vengeance of some sort? Or was she just mad? Perhaps it means whatever you decide it means, and nothing else. Of course, the stories must attempt the best connection with reality. But so many explanations fit the facts, so many meanings are sustainable. You make a choice, in the end. Each version has its profits and penalties.

My story is this: that while Jean, in that darkest moment, took much away, she has yet given us gifts. To understand these gifts, we must finish the story, or at least trace it forward. For we are good at telling stories now, we survivors, Jack and my brothers and myself. We each have different stories, but they all work in their own way, and keep us afloat and capable of happiness.

Jean's suicide was hardest of all, as you might expect, for my father. He truly did love Jean, and for a different man her death in such a manner would have been a hammer blow from which there could have been no recovery. But in his quiet, unexcitable, dull, English way, my father loves life, although he would never say so. His games of tennis and bridge, his dinner-dances, his park bowls. His straightforward library books in which good still always triumphs, his tea in a mug, his Cheddar cheese and crusty bread, his children, his small house in its terrace of six. And he has faith, although he would not call it faith – he would just call it common sense – that things move forward and life goes on, that things change, and that change cannot, finally, be resisted.

So Jack, after an initial period of intense mourning, in which he cried at night, and alone in the day, and yet felt ashamed that he did not cry more, works out a strategy – a narrative, if you like – for survival. He decides that without question he has had a good life, far better than most, and that if this is the only disaster that befalls him, it will still have been a good life. He continues – although it seems meaningless at first – his daily round of hobbies and sports, and book-reading. He refuses counselling; it is not for our kind of people, he decides.

He cannot help but feel guilty, wondering why he did not see what must have been in some way clear. He turns the past over and over in his mind, looking for clues that he might have taken more notice of, or signs or subtle cries for help. But all he can remember is Jean's eyes, which, now that he thinks of it, were, in the last month or so, hollowed out and empty. He cannot stop seeing her eyes, which, he understands now, were terrified.

He fears that the family will break up, and that without Jean he will lose his sons. Already, his network of friendships is falling apart under the blow. The old gang – Bert and Barbara, Helen and John, Irene and Bob, and Olive, now without Arthur – are stricken by Jean's suicide and cannot make sense of it. They have a wake, before the funeral, to remember Jean. Not a single one can recall a clue that might have told them what was in her mind. Her death affects them all and things are no longer the same between them. They gradually see each other less and less often. Helen and John eventually divorce, for John, always a reticent man yet very fond of Jean, retreats into himself in a kind of shock and is never really the same again. The death, as an event, ripples outward, touching families and clusters of families. For if Jean – happy, sociable, perky Jean – is not safe from despair, then who can be?

Birthdays and anniversaries are the worst for Jack. Following the lead of our practical father, James, Jeff and I try to put Jean's death behind us, although always the most communicative of the brothers, I will more frequently try to talk about it. Yet the simple mention of Jean's name, for years afterwards, immediately makes James start to cry and so not much discussion is possible, not without opening wounds. We try, in our pragmatic English way, simply to forget.

And it works, in a way, although not on anniversaries and birthdays, when Jack feels his loss most sharply, and we, being in some ways insensitive though loving sons, do not make a point of remembering these dates. So it is on the first anniversary of Jean's death that my father sits at home with no one to share the grief with him, as James and I have wilfully forgotten the exact date. Yet there is a knock on the door and a distant neighbour to whom Jack has hardly ever spoken appears. She hands him a bottle of wine and says, *I thought you might need this, tonight.* She asks how he is, smiles sweetly and walks out into the night. For she has made a note of this date and cared enough about a stranger to remember through a whole year, and it reminds Jack of what he has always, in his heart, believed, which is that people, though often stupid and often blind, in the end wish to be good.

Having this belief, Jack finds it possible to carry on. He still thinks of Jean much of the time, and grieves at all the empty air in the house and at the part of him that died when his wife died, but he has had the courage to *let* that part die and so he can live once more, changed but still alive.

Guilt continues to nag at him, but he is convinced there is no way in which he could have known and nothing he could have done. Also, he chooses to believe that my mother was ill, as the coroner has said, and that therefore her death was not really a choice, a rejection of him, but an act of chemical dysfunction. And on the days when he does see it as a choice, he sees it as a noble one that reinforces his idea of his wife as a heroic woman who was responsible, in the end, for her own destiny. So Jean's death, although without doubt a terrible thing, is processed and made manageable. Life inescapably continues and Jack tries to go with it.

After a few years, Jack meets another woman through his bowls club. She is some years older than him and, to his own amazement as much as anything else, they form a passionate relationship. She is wealthy, educated at the Lycée in Cairo, a high Tory and dripping with jewels. The rest of us do not understand the relationship, but it is enough that Jack is, if not happy, then clearly well on the way to a sort of new life.

The relationship runs for a couple of years and then Jack, now in his late sixties, leaves her and takes up with another woman, this time in her early forties, and a professional, a solicitor. He finds the relationship delightful and stimulating. They live together, eventually, and are happy. When I see her, and I see the kind of fulfilling relationship my father, always cleverer than my mother, now has, I cannot help but think once more of my mother's note: *You have so much to give such a bright mind and I am holding you back* . . . and think, though it is heresy, perhaps, perhaps . . .

No, I cannot bring myself to write it, for it might suggest that any part of any one of us might have embraced my mother's death, and that is not true. I simply wish to assert, what is plainly the case, that bad things can have good consequences. Nothing is of itself entirely terrible.

As for my younger brother, he also takes my mother's death hard, but carves out a story he can live with. As I say, when we meet – as we, as a family, continue to do once a week – it is he who finds it the most difficult to talk about what is so clearly not being talked about. When we first have our family dinner together after Jean's death, we just go about the meal in the way we might have done had she been there, but unlike Jean's careful, tasty, inventive meals, we make a mess of the whole thing and sit down to eat it, then simply all burst into tears at this attempt, and this failure, to reassert normality. But still, we do not really talk about it. We finish the meal. James and I go home.

James does not obviously change, but he is given to fits of irrational rage about nothing in particular. I try to tell him that it is OK for him to be angry at Jean for leaving him and he seems relieved. But like my father, he has a personality that is rooted and sure. He is good at denial, or, if you prefer, he has a certain focus; his workmates at the hairdresser's nickname him, affectionately, 'The Ostrich' for his ability to filter out unwelcome information.

Nevertheless, like Jack, James feels guilty. He thinks of the educated, well-heeled girlfriends that he would not bring back to the house out of shame at its ordinariness and fears that Jean might have thought he was ashamed of her. He thinks of the times he mocked Southall in front of Jean. These things he lives with, and his life does not collapse. Instead of our family flying apart, it becomes closer than ever. We are, and remain, friends. There are no recriminations between us.

James makes a success of his life, building up his own business as a hairdresser in his own shop in Soho. He watches football, he takes Ecstasy, he drinks lager, goes clubbing and sleeps with lots of pretty girls. He misses Jean, but eventually she fades. All of us fade, all of us must. James is happy.

Of Jeff it is harder to speak, because after the funeral he returns to New Orleans. The resentment between us at first does not appear to have gone away. I write an elegy for Jean to be read at the funeral and show it to my father. He is moved to tears and grateful. I then show it to Jeff for his approval and I am stunned when he angrily rejects it. I am immensely hurt and do not understand that the reason he is angry is that I am even now claiming ownership of what is also rightfully his. That it is not what I have written, but the fact that it is me who is writing it, that it is me who is claiming ownership of the meaning of Jean's death. We have a screaming row, almost physical, as my father pulls us apart as he once did in our childhood. The funeral cortège pulls up outside. We are duly ashamed. Life, it seems at such times, is only playing at grown-ups after all.

By the time we reach the crematorium we are reconciled. There are more than a hundred people at the funeral, including my Uncle Alan, who puts his head on Norman's shoulder and cries for the first time in his life that anyone has seen. The elegy is read. After it is all over, Jeff, with great dignity, apologizes and we embrace. I did not then understand that I also owed him an apology.

It appears that – perhaps and at last – my mother's death does unblock something in our relationship. When we meet in the years after, on occasional visits to each other's countries, the old rivalries seem to have faded. Maybe we no longer have anything to prove to each other, or perhaps the person who we really have to prove it to is not around, even in our imaginations, to judge any more. Jeff does not seem to feel any guilt about Jean's death and this sometimes irritates me, that he so easily assumes that there is no fault on his part, that he could even have had the slightest portion of responsibility. Yet I come to truly like him, and I hope he comes to like me.

We are still very different people. He thinks I am pretentious, I think he over-simplifies, and we remember very different lives. He claims that he never had any resentment towards me in the slightest and that his childhood was absolutely happy. As I say, each of us has his story. But now we tolerate each other, and get on with the business of being brothers. For the first time, some-how, this closeness has become possible, even to the extent that at one point Jeff tries to move back to London, lock, stock and barrel, after twenty years abroad. In the end, and at the last moment, he cannot find the money or the will. He stays in New Orleans with his wife and the two children Jean will now never see. He, too, is happy.

For me, Jean's death once again proved something that I have difficulty in accepting: that life is deeply unpredictable and random, and immune to most attempts at control. Of course Jean's suicide itself is ample proof of that, for nothing could have been as truly unexpected as that strange act, however much hind-sight seeks to make sense of it, but it does not stop there. I ex-pected, through all my life, that the death of one or other of my parents would crush me, so close did I always imagine us to be. For it to happen in such a way, and at a time when I had recently been acutely depressed, I could only anticipate that I would fall, very quickly, to pieces. In fact, nothing of the sort happens. I grieve, I weep, but all the time I simply continue to feel stronger and stronger. Having suffered years of depression – which is a blocking of emotion – even the feeling of pain and loss is wel-come in that it affirms that I am, finally, human.

There is no solution to unhappiness of course. My mother's death makes me very unhappy indeed, as is natural and proper. But it does not make me depressed, for it moves through and beyond me, changes me and then leaves, to recur in ever less frequent – though never shallow – waves. It is real grief, with a beginning and a kind of end, with a source and a resolution. It is the opposite of depression, which is a desperate attempt to avoid change.

And now I am changing. Whether it is as a result of my mother's death or my own breakdown, I do not know. I have lost the childish conviction that the world is subject to my desires, and I know I must give it its due. In other words, I begin to understand what my father has always understood: that life has a shape that we must know through a sort of secular faith and must then try to trace.

And so I wait, hopefully, instead of smashing myself – as I once did – against sheer cliffs of circumstance. I try to have a little bit of faith. I risk a little bit of hope, even. And sure enough, six months after my mother's death, I am selected from several thousand applicants for a job as a researcher with a television company. Within two months of taking it on, I am made a producer and am running my own morning arts news programme for Channel Four.

Television, though, is not for me. My experiences have pulled me apart from my old, thrusting self and I cannot help but find the whole thing ludicrous, with its power plays and secret politics. I resign and become a journalist, this time for quality newspapers. Still this is not enough and my ache to become a writer, always latent, pushes me out of journalism and into my room, where I start to write a novel.

My depression has not entirely gone away and I remain subject to days when everything seems hopeless and sad, and when I hate my life and am filled with regret. I have stopped taking the antidepressants, but on one occasion, having read a story about Prozac in the newspapers, get the doctor to write me a prescription when I am feeling particularly down. It works; the depression dissipates like a cloud. Yet I still remain unconvinced that it is all in my body. There is something in the way I choose to see things.

I fall in love again and marry a woman from a background similar to mine, an escapee from an ordinary, suburban background. She is a polytechnic lecturer, quiet, attractive, Italian. Neither of us wants children, yet she falls pregnant twice, by accident or carelessness or unacknowledged choice, and we find ourselves with two daughters. This most ordinary of developments, stumbled into accidentally, like most things in my life, which I would have once disdained as dreary, turns out to be the best thing that has ever happened. Now I hardly get depressed at all; in fact, I feel almost daily, plain joy, routine exuberance.

However, my writing career is not going well and my novel is universally rejected. I become despondent and pessimistic once more, for if I am not a writer, then I have no function beyond being a father and that does not feel like enough. This, Prozac cannot cure. I cast about for a subject, yet I cannot think what story I could write, for my life is so ordinary and unglamorous and stupid. And then it occurs to me what my mother's final, and greatest, gift to me truly was.

And so this has been the story of 'what happened' and how our lives unfolded. But it does not answer Jack's question, *Why, Jeannie, why?* It does not tell you why I went mad, or if I am guilty, or if my book is not really an autobiography and a biography, but in fact a confession, an attempt at expiation. For consider the blow I dealt her, unloading, wilfully, my own sadness on to her. Think of her final plea, unheard by me, *I don't think I can last that long.* Judge me, if you wish. But let me first finish my story.

To begin to answer the question 'whose fault?' – and you can only *begin* to answer anything – you have to understand depression. You have to understand that particular variety of despair.

The image that haunts me most of Jean's last days is that of her hurtling down Somerset Hill in her old blue Jetta, crashing insanely from kerb to kerb. What is going through her mind, in this one and only moment that her almost supernatural self-control deserts her and all the chaos and fear that are lurching under her tidiness and perfect poise swing into public view? If only she had crashed, then –

If only, one of the great clichés of the suicide survivor, or the survivor of almost any disaster, along with *Why?* and *Why me?* If only I had done x, if only y had done z. Yet life is sometimes random and frequently unfair, as my father has always instinctively known, however much we wish to apportion order and, therefore, blame. Presuppose a just universe – and how many of us wish it, for it gives us the hope of controlling our destinies – then if something goes wrong, it follows that you must have *done* something wrong to deserve it. Then you have to find out what it is and do penance. Wasn't this the trap that both of us fell into, when we became suicidal? We had beliefs – in my case secret, hidden even from myself – in a kind of immutable order that held us accountable. But let go of that childish belief, accept randomness and uncertainty, tolerate chaos, and the whole thing slides into place. That place is shapeless, that place is always moving and out of focus, but it is the reality of things.

To put it briefly, I cannot ever know if I am guilty, but if I am, I no longer have difficulty forgiving myself. I have decided that I would rather not be such a supernaturally good person – as my mother fantasized herself, finally, to be – that it involves me killing myself, or living a life of despair, in order to prove it.

I know now, without any doubt at all, that depression is an illness and that my mother and I both suffered it. But I also know that the explanation does not stop there, that depression is a very particular type of illness, in that it seems to hinge on your interpretation of the world, the story you tell yourself.

How can this be true of an illness? Ask yourself why is it that my Uncle Arthur dies of a heart attack in 1981? The conditions are quite simple, uncontroversial, you might say. He has a weakness in his heart, as a result of a childhood illness, in this case rheumatic fever. His personality tends towards the overconscientious, hence he worries and frets about doing well enough at his job as manager at Dolcis. In his own way, like Jean and I, he is a perfectionist, never quite satisfied with himself. This anxiety and susceptibility to stress – his doctor tells him quite clearly, after he suffers his first heart attack in 1979 – may one day be translated into the physical realm and kill him. He advises Arthur to take retirement.

Arthur, however, is driven by his generation's bred sense of loyalty to the employer and his own high standards. He carries on working, and working hard. He cannot stop worrying about what he considers to be his responsibilities. One day, at a highly charged executive meeting, he slumps forward on the table, dead. Nobody questions the fact that a combination of childhood damage and psychological stress has led to a catastrophic illness. It seems like common sense.

However, while heart disease is without stigma, unladen with values, mental disease is contorted under the weight of both. So the idea that I may suffer from a physical, possibly inherited vulnerability in the chemistry of my brain, combining with a certain psychological disposition which, under stress, leads to a 'brain attack', is . . . sticky, in the way a coronary is not. The brain is the part of the body that thinks, and thinking is the activity that most completely expresses identity, defines me as a personality. The idea that mood, values, belief, thought itself can simply be the coral outcrop of a physical organ is disturbing for most people.

If what Jean and I went through is indeed an illness, then it is one that in some ways is worse than any other. For the terrible thing about depression is that you don't quite believe that anything is malfunctioning. And unlike, say, schizophrenia, it may be that no one else will notice either. It is not like cancer or AIDS, when you can be brave, or cowardly, but at least you will have a condition with which you can have a relationship, a coming to terms. Depression is the only potentially fatal illness that, right up until death, you may not know you have.

Even if you recover, you cannot say for sure that you have been physically ill; there are plenty of people, both professional and lay, who will insist that you were not, that it is all down to you. And if you are a depressive, a part of you will be only too ready to agree, since that is what depression is about – not, as some would have it, a shrugging off of responsibility but the reverse: a sort of addiction to responsibility, or, to be precise, blame. If, on the other hand, you are 'lucky' and are recognized as being – how I still hate the phrase – *mentally ill*, you are as liable to face fear and pity as the sympathy and understanding that a less threatening illness might elicit.

This paradox between mind and body – between illness and attitude – is not as insoluble as I once thought. If it is easy to believe that my Uncle Arthur's heart attack was partly the result of a certain kind of relationship to the world, if you believe that some cancers stem from a kind of impacted anger – and both views are backed by good medical evidence – then it is no great trick to think that a physical depression can be caused by culture, by a way of seeing and imagining the world, and yet end up as a physical illness.

Of course, there are many kinds of depression, just as there are many kinds of pain. Some are largely physical, some mainly psychological. It's also worth remembering that not all suicides, by any means, are depressives. But where depression exists, it always has what you might call an existential ingredient. The provoking question is, if anxiety can lead to coronary thrombosis and anger can lead to cancer, what kind of thinking leads to depression?

Depression is about anger, it is about anxiety, it is about character and heredity. But it is also about something that is in its way quite unique. It is the illness of *identity*, it is the illness of those who do not know where they fit, who lose faith in the myths they have so painstakingly created for themselves. Thus, in this current confused, self-hating England, it is spreading like a virulent, dimly understood virus. And it is a plague – especially if you add in all its various forms of expression, like alcoholism, anorexia, bulimia, drug addiction, compulsive behaviour of one kind or another. They're all the same thing: attempts to avoid disappearance, or nothingness, or chaos.

Once I realize this, the reason for undertaking this book, which, I can now admit, has sometimes seemed obscure while writing, begins to become clear to me. For in finding a solution to identity, you begin to find a solution to depression.

Depression is not grief. It is an attempted defence against the terror of losing your invented sense of self: who you believe yourself to be and the way in which you think the world operates. It is fear of annihilation, of doubt, of insignificance. It is a reaction to a very particular kind of stress, the kind that brings into question the world that you, being human, have to imagine and reimagine, maintain and defend every moment of every day, in order to keep chaos at bay. When that stress is acute enough, depression follows on, sometimes so deeply that it is not only refracted in the brain – like all mental activity – but sticks there, a bad habit, or a fishbone lodged in the throat.

When my mother decided to kill herself, she was both crazy and entirely sane, both severely ill and well. She hanged herself because her story, her idea of herself as a successful wife and mother – the only real test of worth that she knew – was no longer sustainable in her shocked mind. She had no function, now that James had left home. She had not succeeded in protecting me from whatever it was that left me wanting my own death – that was left to medicine. Her oldest son had divorced, then remarried without extending her an invitation to the ceremony. The story of her life no longer stood up, but she was not prepared to let it collapse. She was more frightened of that than of the noose.

Larger forces were at play. As Southall rotted, another scrap of identity went, the idea, so large for her generation, of pride in being English. At the same time, the illness that is depression cut her off from her own feelings, separated her from Jack.

Under the terrible magnifying glass that depression, once set in train, becomes, all these things expanded into catastrophes that were *her fault*, since in her view of the world they had to be *somebody's* fault. It wasn't in her philosophy to blame accident or anyone else. Thus it was that she no longer deserved to live. She knew that to carry on living meant the person she had always imagined herself to be could no longer be sustained. She believed, having lost that person, she would became instead a burden, a nuisance, and without pride. She killed herself to save herself, to avoid change, to duck meaninglessness. And, since depression feels like a collapse of faith, she could see no hope of things getting better.

As for me, I wanted to die for much the same reason as my mother: because it was the only way my interior life would go on making sense; because killing myself was the only way I could preserve my identity – that is to say, my story. Oh, we want to *pin things down* so much, get them just so. We are so afraid of the alternative. We do not believe that the water will buoy us up, so we thrash around, and drown.

Like Jean, like all of us, I was a prisoner of my own logic. Having at one point in my life refused, or been unable, to mourn a particular loss, I had come to feel emotionally dead and in mental torment, and there could be only one story that would explain that to me (and a story had to be told, you can't stop yourself). I believed, like many good liberals, indifferent Christians and prime-time Americans, that our inner selves were the sum total of all our choices. Since I was in a kind of mental hell, it had to follow that I was wicked and damned. Nothing else made sense, and to make sense of things is a need, it seems, greater than life itself. If you want to get historical about it, you can talk about nationalism, Nazism, holocausts, ethnic cleansing; they are all merely ways of holding fast to your story, of avoiding the awesome responsibility that accepting uncertainty and insignificance entails.

In the end, for me, the fear of death overcame the need to have a meaning or to assert an order – a cowardice for which I am eternally grateful. Jean had more courage and, in a sense, more dignity. She had the guts to kill herself and I admire her for it, although, of course, she was quite crazy at the time, with a brain misfiring like a cross-wired laptop. Pressing the keystrokes *love*, the screen read *die*. Pressing the keystrokes *survive*, the screen read *die*. The damn thing, her mind-machine, was shot.

Is there an antidote to depression, this modern plague? Drugs work, up to a point. From time to time, I still suffer mild, brief depressions, when under stress. Then I will sometimes take Prozac, and it seems to work quickly and well, restoring whatever chemical imbalance that hypothetical flaw in my brain inclines me to. But I need it rarely, hardly ever, because I have written a different story for myself now, with a different premise in mind, with a different question underpinning it.

Once I would just ask myself, as my certainties collapsed one by one: *What is true? What is the case? What is the good thing to do?* And with my terrible fear of the real answers snapping at my heels — *there's no way of being sure* and *there's no one to judge* — I would try, with greater and greater urgency, to get things nailed down. That rigidity, that hunger for certainty, led me into a very mad kind of logic. The same was true of my mother.

Do you imagine that you're immune? I hope you are, truly. Perhaps I really am just a crazy person, a glitch, *other*. Jean too. And Alan, my uncle, and Art, my grandfather. And Norman with his drinking, and Eileen who froze inside and Marion with her bulimia and Bev's mother, who took an overdose. I know of so many more.

Doubtless your feet are more firmly planted. Doubtless your deepest assumptions about the world are clear to you and are incontrovertibly the case. Or perhaps, being English, you will say that you are familiar with doubt, and can accommodate it.

However, what you think you know and what you secretly believe may be very different things. Such was certainly true of me, who always styled himself a sceptic. That secret knowledge, which binds you and supports you, may be as invisible as bone and as painful to reveal. That knowledge — that story — may fit reality or may depart from it wildly; but that is hardly the point. All that matters is whether the story holds up and performs its function: to make you feel that you are a good person, and of significance, and that the world is a just and rational place and that you are therefore safe.

Maybe it will hold up, now and in the future. But maybe one day, however well it has worked in the past, suddenly, it won't — and even the best-tailored stories have their loose seams. Some wrongly shaped or too large fact will present itself. Some nasty — or perhaps even pleasant — surprise. And what then?

Do you think you can do without something firm to trust in?

Do you think it bearable that things are not solid?

Finally, do you believe things can always be framed, contained, brought into focus? It is comforting to think so, almost inevit-able. It is a habit I still find irresistible.

For I have finished my book now and, although I do not see it as therapy, I have used it to work through some conclusions that I consider to be firm, to be final. The central one, I suppose, is that my mother was struck, out of the blue, if you like, by depres-sion. That she was a fundamentally happy and contented woman who was subject at one single point in her life to such stresses of a type and power that neither her body nor her mind could cope with. It is a point of view with which everyone who knew Jean seems to concur. Her life was a good life. Her mind was always healthy.

The book is with my publisher and I am content and pleased to have finished it at last. There is a bit of minor editing to do, and some research facts to be confirmed, but I have confidence in it as a document and a record. I am slowly, inevitably falling into the myth that I have secured the True Story of my mother. That I am a Historian. It is over; I have a story now, written down, fixed in time and space, something to hold to that is mine.

The manuscript sits next to my box of family photographs, which are jumbled out of chronological order now, a mess of sepias and lurid colours, and rounded corners, and dead people, and forgotten vistas. They are arranged, you might say, in a more lifelike fashion. A picture of me as a child falls out and I think, as I stare at that small, dreaming stranger, that we are also our own ancestors. The manuscript, the photographs, they are the same really. Perhaps this is why people take photographs. Perhaps this is why people write books. They are attempts to fix in place what is unfixable, what is always moving, twisting and changing as we watch, finally uncomprehending.

There are two more objects on the desk, both of which my father gave me a day or two ago, both of which I have been press-ing for for a long time, but both of which hardly seem to matter any more. One is a video of my mother and father, nine months before Jean's death, at Helen and John's daughter's wedding. Coincidentally it is my parents' thirty-fifth, and final, wedding anniversary. My father has declared it extremely boring, so I have put off watching it. I am tired, tired of the whole thing really.

The other object is a manila envelope. I have only glanced at it, and the documents inside seem unenlightening. It is my mother's medical records, which I have been asking for for nearly a year. They have at last been released, but, having considered the book to be finished, I have not given them too much attention. They refer almost entirely to her hair and there is nothing from the last week of her life. My mother, it turns out, specifically instructed the doctor, shortly before her suicide, never to release certain of the records in the event of her death. What can this mean? It is mysterious, but it is insoluble and hardly matters any more. I am content to let it rest. I remove the photocopies from the envelope again and take a final look, just in case I have missed anything. I notice, immediately, and for the first time, that the pages are photocopied not just on one side, as I had previously assumed, but on both sides. There are six or seven notes I have not seen. I glance at them. They are faint and hard to read. Again, they seem to concern nothing more revealing than the endless battle with Jean's alopecia. I put them to one side for the moment.

I take the video out of the box and begin watching. As my father has declared, it is very boring indeed. The visual quality is atrocious and the sound jumbled into murmurs and squawks. The occasional exclamation – *ooh, very nice, what a carry on, I can't take you anywhere, oh, dearie me* – is all I can make out. Jean is badly blurred and slips in and out of the frame. She is tanned and wearing what at first appears to be a white matching skirt and blouse, but it is overlit. In fact, like most of the women, she is wearing a floral print combination. Her hips are wider than I remember, but otherwise she looks well, almost glamorous. There are sun-streaks designed into her wig.

The video is set mainly at the reception after the wedding at a modern red-brick hall in Chertsey. There is a set meal, followed by dancing to a live band and, later, a disco. Jean kisses the bride at the line-up. Jack is behind her in a white shirt and black bow tie. Neither appears in the footage of the meal, but when the dancing begins Jack and Jean are there. For the early part, where big-band standards are being played, both are adept and confident. Then the disco begins – 'Love Train' and 'Boogie Wonderland' and 'Tie a Yellow Ribbon' and 'Brown Girl in the Ring' – and, like all the others of their generation, they jig and gyrate hopefully, but look foolish and a bit lost. The dancing has no rules now or guidelines even, and they are confused by the freeness of the form. Jean twists and turns, spins and bobs, always smiling. She takes tiny steps and her arms are too stiff. But nobody cares or judges. Everyone is enjoying themselves thoroughly.

Sometimes the camera pans in on Jean and her lips move. She is almost always out of focus, but then everyone seems to be. Bert and Barbara are there, and Olive, and Irene and Bob – the whole gang. The tape is two and a half hours long.

I cry only once, when the tape is nearly over. It is, as I say, my parents' thirty-fifth wedding anniversary and someone has told the DJ to play 'The Anniversary Waltz'. It is a slow and in some odd way melancholy song. They hold each other close and move in time to the music, as they have on this day, year after year after year. Jean mouths the words, but if she is singing I cannot hear her.

The reception finishes with group dancing – the conga, the hokey cokey, then novelty records, the 'Birdie Song' and 'Agadoo'. All the time, Jean can be seen dancing and clapping and mouthing the words, and smiling. She seems to be genuinely having a good time and, to my slight shame, I realize the emotion I am overwhelmingly now experiencing is one not of sadness but of faint embarrassment.

I genuinely cannot see my mother, I realize as I watch the screen fade into snow and static, as a tragic woman. I am sure the story I have told myself must be correct – that in the long run she was an ordinary, straightforward and basically happy woman.

I return to my desk and open the manila envelope to check once more the medical records. As it initially seemed, everything focuses on her hair. In October 1950 the first mention is made of alopecia areata, with two bald patches appearing at her left

271

temple and behind her left ear. She is prescribed something sinister-sounding called Thorium X paint for her head, and various ointments and pomades. In 1952 the paint is applied again, but it is clearly not successful because in June 1953 a dermatologist writes to the GP: *These marginal alopecias do not generally go well . . . there is a likelihood it will go on indefinitely.* The doctor then prescribes a course of ultraviolet light. The light treatments seem, briefly, to work, for in November 1954 the consultant dermatologist writes: *The patches have cleared up satisfactorily . . . however, I agree that she now has a further patch.* Various ointments are prescribed.

The next note comes in July 1956, six months after my birth. This is the first of the notes that I missed originally because it was copied on the back of another page. It is very, very faint and difficult to read, but I can make out this sentence: *It would appear that her present relapse has been going on since the birth of her first child.* Potassium bromide and various ointments are prescribed.

There is another note in August 1957 saying that she still has a bad case of alopecia, and ultraviolet light is once again prescribed. Then there is a gap up until February 1959, when a note reports that her hair has satisfactorily regrown and her 'Ledercort' has been reduced to 2mg. Clearly, there are some records missing, as there has been no previous reference to Ledercort, which is, my medical dictionary tells me, a 'corticosteroid, anti-inflammatory drug, also used for replacing body hormones in rare disorders. It was much misused and overused in the 1950s. Side effects can include mood changes, mental disturbances and depression.'

The next entry also suggests a gap has been left. Again, from the dermatologist at King Edward Memorial Hospital, the note, dated 29 April 1959, informs the GP: *I have increased her Ledercort of 4mg b.d. and put her back on phenobarbitone gr ¼ b.d.*

I am conscious of some faint tremor inside me. This is the first time phenobarbitone has been mentioned, but the note says, 'I have . . . put her back on phenobarbitone', so she has been on it before. I reach for my medical dictionary and begin reading. It tells me what I have already guessed, that phenobarbitone is a tranquillizer, powerful enough to be used mostly in cases of epilepsy.

The next note, like the previous three, I have not seen before. It is dated 27 May 1959 and reads: *This patient's alopecia areata has not improved since I last saw her a month ago. As you know, she has been on Ledercort for the last six months, and I have now reduced the dose. She should continue with Phenobarbitone gr ¼ b.d. indefinitely.*

I think it is quite possible that there are many emotional factors playing a part in continuing this reaction, but I was unable to confirm this during outpatients. I have arranged for her to see the Lady Almoner to see whether or not she can find out more about this patient.

I look up 'almoner' in my dictionary. It is an old word for a social worker. I look at the word 'indefinitely', and think it surely cannot mean what it appears to suggest.

There are only a few notes left now. The next one is dated 23 July 1959. It reads: *This patient's alopecia areata is now very much better. I have now stopped the phenobarbitone and prescribed Largactil 25mg b.d. I suggest she remains on Largactil for three months.*

I look up Largactil. It is another name for chlorpromazine. It is a 'phenothiazine for treating schizophrenia and other mental illnesses, especially paranoid symptoms'.

There are only two more notes. The first, dated 14 June 1961, reads: *I saw this patient today. She has not lost any further hair since I last saw her two months ago. I have now stopped her Triamcinolone and prescribed Largactil 25mg b.d., which she should remain on indefinitely for the time being. I am seeing her again in three months.*

Triamcinolone is another corticosteroid. The second, and final note, reads: *I have seen this patient again with severe alopecia areata of the scalp. No evidence of the hair regrowing can be seen. I have now arranged for her to be fitted with a wig. Internally, I have prescribed phenobarbitone gr ¼ b.d., which she should remain on indefinitely.*

I am with my oldest daughter, Ruby-Jean, in the front room of the house I share with my wife, Sarina, in North Kensington. Ruby-Jean's effect on me has been that I am flooded with feeling now, with tenderness, concern and blind love. The me that was for so long frozen and dead is only a faint memory. I am happy, although I am still unsure of what my story might be, and still itch to work it out. Every time I think I am coming close, it seems to change and warp out of recognition.

Ruby has been painting, but now she is watching a cartoon. Absently, I pick up her paintbrush and dip it in a cup of water. Spread in front of me is a child's palette and a sheet of cartridge paper.

On the coffee table in front of me is a copy of a magazine that has been pushed through the door, mainly full of estate agents' ads. It is decorated with lush English landscapes of the type my mother liked to paint. One of the photographs in an advertisement is of Constable's *The Haywain*. I stare at it, then dip my brush in the water and idly begin to paint, despite the fact I have always been hopeless at art.

I make an attempt at a tree – it is incredibly difficult. It looks like a smudge, a smear. The grass is all globby, it is pea soup out of a can. I begin to try to imagine what the original scene that Constable painted from must have been like. Then I see that it wasn't 'like' anything. The clouds were never in this place, the grass never in this light, the bird never in that position. It was just a general idea. It was something that Constable made up. And if he had tried to paint what was *really* there, if he had been absolutely determined, well, it just can't be done. He'd have gone mad. Because there isn't anything there, really, if you get close enough. Or, to look at it another way, there are a million things there, all depending on what you select. There are atoms of air, there are worms on the ground, there are birds flying in and out of the frame. The whole thing is flux, is process. The whole thing is a big guess, a bloody great lie. Pan in and it's an electric void. Pan out, it's a dot of green on a vast blue planet. Pan out again, it's an invisible planet in a cold stellar waste.

It is a good painting, I suppose, though not to my taste. It does the job it sets out to do. It puts the world in a frame; it reassures, it seals it off from the chaos of endless air outside. I start again, this time using green for the sky. It is neither better nor worse than my previous efforts, only bad in a different sort of way. I really am pretty awful at this.

I try it again, and again, and again. I do not improve. One of my mother's landscapes hangs on the wall – a mountain snow-scape. It is over-exact, dull, but there is some kind of technical skill, born, perhaps, more of determination than talent. But mine is just a farrago, a mess. It seems to become worse rather than better. I cannot get the hang of it, so I stop and put the paint-brush down. I get frustrated, even slightly angry. I try again, the brushstrokes heavier, more pronounced. Now it looks like someone has been sick on the paper.

I come to a solution at last, a way of escaping this dilemma, and dilemmas like this. It is so obvious really, I wonder why I didn't think of it before. I simply put down the paintbrush, screw up the picture and throw it away. Then I walk away and sit down next to Ruby in front of the television.

The cartoon is one of my favourites, *The Ren and Stimpy Show*. It makes me smile, as always. I turn it up. My daughter turns to me and says something ridiculous and cute. I laugh out loud. She dances to a stupid song that Ren and Stimpy sing, and giggles. I hold her hands and dance too, round and round and round. Un-bidden, my eyes brim with tears. I love her so much. The televi-sion blares.

She stops and sees the paints and the paper I have discarded in the bin. She picks up the paintbrush and offers it to me.

Daddy paint?

I shake my head, but she will not give up. She just repeats, again and again and again . . .

Come on, Daddy. Paint a picture. Pleeeeeeeze.

PENGUIN MODERN CLASSICS

CIDER WITH ROSIE
LAURIE LEE

'I had ridden wrapped up in a Union Jack to protect me from the sun, and when I rolled out of it, and stood piping loud among the buzzing jungle of that summer bank, I feel, I was born.'

Cider with Rosie, Laurie Lee's bestselling autobiography, immortalized an era and a place. In it he recalls the glories of a country boyhood in the beautiful Slad valley in Gloucestershire. His was a slow, mellow England, one 'of silence ... of white roads, rutted by hooves and cartwheels, innocent of oil and petrol'. It is an unforgettable elegy to a world that has all but vanished.

'It distils and preserves the essence of a bygone rural age and the heady spirit of childhood which haunted it' *The Times*

With an Introduction by Susan Hill

PENGUIN MODERN CLASSICS

DOWN AND OUT IN PARIS AND LONDON
GEORGE ORWELL

'The white-hot reaction of a sensitive, observant, compassionate young man to poverty' Dervla Murphy

George Orwell's vivid memoir of his time living among the desperately poor and destitute is a moving tour of the underworld of society.

Written when Orwell was a struggling writer in his twenties, it documents his 'first contact with poverty': sleeping in bug-infested hostels and doss-houses of last resort, working as a dishwasher in Paris, surviving on scraps and cigarette butts, living alongside tramps, a star-gazing pavement artist and a starving Russian ex-army captain. Exposing a shocking, previously hidden world to readers, Orwell gave a human face to the statistics of poverty for the first time. In doing so, he found his voice as a writer.

'Orwell was the great moral force of his age' *Spectator*

PENGUIN MODERN CLASSICS

GOODBYE TO ALL THAT
ROBERT GRAVES

'His wonderful autobiography' Jeremy Paxman, *Daily Mail*

In 1929 Robert Graves went to live abroad permanently, vowing 'never to make England my home again'. This is his superb account of his life up until that 'bitter leave-taking': from his childhood and desperately unhappy school days at Charterhouse, to his time serving as a young officer in the First World War that was to haunt him throughout his life. It also contains memorable encounters with fellow writers and poets, including Siegfried Sassoon and Thomas Hardy, and covers his increasingly unhappy marriage to Nancy Nicholson. *Goodbye to All That*, with its vivid, harrowing descriptions of the Western Front, is a classic war document, and also has immense value as one of the most candid self-portraits of an artist ever written.

PENGUIN MODERN CLASSICS

THE RAGGED TROUSERED PHILANTHROPISTS
ROBERT TRESSELL

'A torch to pass from generation to generation' Tony Benn

At the building firm Rushton & Co. the bosses and shareholders get richer and richer, while the workmen and their families struggle against poverty, hunger and debt – yet think they can do little to change their lives. Political firebrand Frank Owen, however, is different. He refuses to believe that his masters are his betters and encourages his fellow workers to fight for a new, just society – although convincing them is harder than he thinks …

The first authentic portrayal of working-class lives at the start of the twentieth century, *The Ragged Trousered Philanthropists* has inspired generations of political activists and remains a moving paean to human dignity.

With a new Introduction by Tristram Hunt

PENGUIN MODERN CLASSICS

THE GOD BOY
IAN CROSS

'I'm a God boy, Sister,' I said. 'You don't have to worry about me, I'm a God boy.'

Jimmy Sullivan believed he was protected by God until his parents' unhappy marriage finally broke down, with tragic consequences. Now a disturbed thirteen-year-old at a Catholic boarding school, Jimmy rages at God for failing him as he tells of his own violent and obsessive reaction to the turbulent events of two years before. Through his uncomprehending and often humorous voice of tough indifference, a very adult drama of marital strife, drunkenness and illicit abortion emerges. Ian Cross vividly evokes life in a provincial New Zealand town in the 1950s, in his tale of the crippling of a bright and hopeful young mind.

'Moving, exciting, amusing – superlatively readable' E. H. McCormick

With an Introduction by Roger Robinson

PENGUIN MODERN CLASSICS

STORM OF STEEL
ERNST JÜNGER

'Jünger's sense of the small change of war is invaluable ... Unquestionably one of the most striking accounts of the First World War'
Richard Holmes, *Evening Standard*

A memoir of astonishing power, savagery and ashen lyricism, *Storm of Steel* depicts Ernst Jünger's experience of combat in the German front line – leading raiding parties, defending trenches against murderous British incursions, and simply enduring as shells tore his comrades apart. One of the greatest books to emerge from the catastrophe of the First World War, it illuminates like no other book not only the horrors but also the fascination of a war that made men keep fighting on for four long years.

'Sublime ... Precise, economical, taut, interspersed with earthy humour and reflections, often uncanny, that linger in the memory'
Daniel Johnson, *Daily Telegraph*

'A fascinating counterpart to Graves and Sassoon ... Ernst Jünger is unarguably an original' Tibor Fischer, *Sunday Telegraph*

'Outstanding ... a blueprint for surviving, at least in a spiritual sense, the madness of war in a mechanized age ... Hofmann's interpretation is superb'
Paul Watkins, *The Times*

A new Translation by Michael Hofmann

PENGUIN MODERN CLASSICS

MEMOIRS OF HADRIAN
MARGUERITE YOURCENAR

Yourcenar conjures worlds. She can make us *share* passion – for beauty, bodies, ideas, even power – and consider it closely at the same time. She is that most extraordinary thing: a sensual thinker' *Independent on Sunday*

In her magnificent novel, Marguerite Yourcenar recreates the life and death of one of the great rulers of the ancient world. The Emperor Hadrian, aware his demise is imminent, writes a long valedictory letter to Marcus Aurelius, his successor. The Emperor meditates on his past, describing his accession, military triumphs, love of poetry and music, and the philosophy that informed his powerful and far-flung rule. A work of superbly detailed research and sustained empathy, *Memoirs of Hadrian* captures the living spirit of the Emperor and of Ancient Rome.

Translated from the French by Grace Frick in collaboration with the author

With an Introduction by Paul Bailey

PENGUIN MODERN CLASSICS

THE GARDEN OF THE FINZI-CONTINIS
GIORGIO BASSANI

A new translation by Jamie McKendrick

'One of the great novelists of the last century' *Guardian*

Aristocratic, rich and seemingly aloof, the Finzi-Contini family fascinate the narrator of this tale, a young Jew in the Italian city of Ferrara. But it is not until he is a student in 1938, when anti-Semitic legislation is enforced on the eve of the Second World War, that he is invited into their luxurious estate.

As their gardens become a haven for persecuted Jews, the narrator becomes entwined in the lives of the family, and particularly close to Micòl, their daughter. Many years after the war has ended, he reflects on his memories of the Finzi-Continis, his experiences of love and loss and the fate of the family and community in the horrors of war.

PENGUIN MODERN CLASSICS

ONE FLEW OVER THE CUCKOO'S NEST
KEN KESEY

With Illustrations and a Preface by Ken Kesey

Introduction by Robert Faggen

'A roar of protest against middlebrow society's Rules and the Rulers who enforce them' *Time*

Tyrannical Nurse Ratched rules her ward in an Oregon State mental hospital with a strict and unbending routine, unopposed by her patients, who remain cowed by mind numbing medication and the threat of electric shock therapy. But her regime is disrupted by the arrival of McMurphy – the swaggering, fun-loving trickster with a devilish grin who resolves to oppose her rules on behalf of his fellow inmates. His struggle is seen through the eyes of Chief Bromden, a seemingly mute half-Indian patient who understands McMurphy's heroic attempt to do battle with the powers that keep them imprisoned.

Ken Kesey's extraordinary first novel is an exuberant, ribald and devastatingly honest portrayal of the boundaries between sanity and madness.

'If you haven't already read this book, do so. If you have, read it again' *Scotsman*

PENGUIN MODERN CLASSICS

CIVILIZATION AND ITS DISCONTENTS
SIGMUND FREUD

Civilization and its Discontents/'Civilized' Sexual Morality and Modern Nervous Illness

Translated by David McLintock

With an Introduction by Leo Bersani

'Narratives that have the colour and force of fiction' John Updike

In his final years, Freud devoted most of his energies to a series of highly ambitious works on the broadest issues of religion and society.

As early as 1908, he produced a powerful paper on the repressive hypocrisy of 'civilized sexual morality', and its role in 'modern nervous illness'. Deepening this analysis in *Civilization and its Discontents*, he argues that 'civilized' values – and the impossible ideals of Christianity – inevitably distort our natural aggression and impose a terrible burden of guilt. It is also here that Freud developed his last great theoretical innovation: the strange and haunting notion of an innate death drive, locked in a constant struggle with the forces of Eros.

General Editor: Adam Phillips

PENGUIN MODERN CLASSICS

THE LONELY LONDONERS
SAM SELVON

'Unforgettable ... a vernacular comedy of pathos' *Guardian*

At Waterloo Station, hopeful new arrivals from the West Indies step off the boat train, ready to start afresh in 1950s London. There, homesick Moses Aloetta, who has already lived in the city for years, meets Henry 'Sir Galahad' Oliver and shows him the ropes. In this strange, cold and foggy city where the natives can be less than friendly at the sight of a black face, has Galahad met his Waterloo?

But the irrepressible newcomer cannot be cast down. He and all the other lonely new Londoners – from shiftless Cap to Tolroy, whose family has descended on him from Jamaica – must try to create a new life for themselves. As pessimistic 'old veteran' Moses watches their attempts, they gradually learn to survive and come to love the heady excitements of London.

With a new Introduction by Susheila Nasta

Contemporary ... Provocative ... Outrageous ...
Prophetic ... Groundbreaking ... Funny ... Disturbing ...
Different ... Moving ... Revolutionary ... Inspiring ...
Subversive ... Life-changing ...

What makes a modern classic?

At Penguin Classics our mission has always been to make the best
books ever written available to everyone. And that also means
constantly redefining and refreshing exactly what makes a 'classic'.
That's where Modern Classics come in. Since 1961 they have been an
organic, ever-growing and ever-evolving list of books from the last
hundred (or so) years that we believe will continue to be read over and
over again.

They could be books that have inspired political dissent, such as
Animal Farm. Some, like *Lolita* or *A Clockwork Orange*, may have
caused shock and outrage. Many have led to great films, from *In Cold
Blood* to *One Flew Over the Cuckoo's Nest*. They have broken down
barriers – whether social, sexual, or, in the case of *Ulysses*, the
boundaries of language itself. And they might – like *Goldfinger* or
Scoop – just be pure classic escapism. Whatever the reason, Penguin
Modern Classics continue to inspire, entertain and enlighten millions
of readers everywhere.

'No publisher has had more influence on reading habits than Penguin'
Independent

'Penguins provided a crash course in world literature'
Guardian

The best books ever written

PENGUIN (Ⓟ) CLASSICS

SINCE 1946

Find out more at www.penguinclassics.com